HEINEMANN HISTORY

THE CHANGI
FACE OF
BRITAIN

PAUL SHUTER
JOHN CHILD

HEINEMANN
EDUCATIONAL

Heinemann Educational,
a division of Heinemann Educational Books Ltd,
Halley Court, Jordan Hill, Oxford OX2 8EJ

OXFORD LONDON EDINBURGH
MELBOURNE SYDNEY AUCKLAND
IBADAN NAIROBI GABORONE HARARE
KINGSTON PORTSMOUTH NH (USA)
SINGAPORE MADRID

First published 1989

British Library Cataloguing in Publication Data

Child, John, 1951-
The changing face of Britain
1. Great Britain. Social life. History
I. Title II. Shuter, Paul
941

ISBN 0-435-31034-8

Designed and produced by
The Pen and Ink Book Company Ltd, Huntingdon

Printed and bound in Spain by Mateu Cromo

Acknowledgements

The authors and publisher would like to thank the following for permission to reproduce photographs on the pages indicated:

Age Exchange Theatre Trust: p. 172; Amalgamated Union of Engineering workers: p. 160; Austin Rover: p. 80 (lower right); Bedfordshire County Council: p. 25; Bettman Archive: p. 151; Borough of Darlington Museum: p. 90 (top right); Bridgeman Art Library: p. 153; British Airways: p. 104 (lower right); British Coal: pp. 66 (top right) and 77 (lower right); British Gas: p. 78 (top); by permission of The British Library: pp. 98 (lower right) and 106; British Motor Industry Heritage Trust: p. 80 (lower left); British Museum: pp. 30, 53 (top right), 56 and 90 (lower right); British Waterways Board: p. 88; British Waterways Picture Library: p. 103 (top left); Camera Press: p. 166 (top right); B. Codrington: p. 146; *Daily Mirror*: p. 107 (top left); Derbyshire Archaeological Society: p. 51; Durham County Council: p. 49 (lower); Elmbridge Borough Council: p. 174 (top right); E.T. Archive: p. 32; Mary Evans Picture Library: pp. 36, 126, 141 (top left), 142, 145, 150 (top right), 170, 171, 185, 186, 188 (top right) and 189; Express Newspapers: p. 158; John Freeman: pp. 54, 60 (lower left), 60 (top right), 71 (top) and 127; Sally and Richard Greenhill: pp. 174 (lower right), 180 and 181; Guildhall Library: p. 139; Helmshore Textile Museum: p. 57; HMSO: p. 175 (top right); HM The Queen: p. 140; The Hulton Picture Company: pp. 41, 42, 44, 74, 84, 92, 98 (top right), 100 (top right and lower right), 101, 128, 135, 154, 155, 156, 164 (lower right) and 188 (lower); Illustrated London News: p. 71 (lower); Imperial War Museum: pp. 43 and 116; Institute of Agricultural History and Museum of English Rural Life: pp. 23 and 27 (top right); The Ironbridge Gorge Museum Trust: pp. 58, 59 and 67 (left); Lancashire Record Office: p. 96; Local History Museum, Manchester: p. 61 (top right); Macclesfield Museum: p. 53 (lower left); Manchester Local Library: p. 168; The Mansell Collection: pp. 29, 33, 36 (lower), 48 (lower), 52, 67 (right), 68, 82, 86, 93 (top left), 109, 129, 132 (lower right), 182 and 186; The Museum of London: p. 110; National Railway Museum: pp. 91 (top right), 93 (top right), 93 (lower right) and 103 (lower right); North Kesteven District Council: p. 49 (top); Popperfoto: pp. 66 (top left), 72, 104 (top right) and 162; Punch Publications: pp. 35, 118, 125, 130, 141 (lower left), 152, 157, 163, 164 (lower left) and 179; Rex Features: pp. 166 (lower right) and 107 (lower left); M.J. Shackleton: p. 102; Science Museum: pp. 90 (top left) and 91 (lower right); The Tate Gallery: p. 176; Topham Picture Library: pp. 69, 77 (top left), 98 (middle), 100 (middle), 105 and 133; Trade Union Congress: p. 136; The Trustees of the Wedgwood Museum: p. 63; Walker Art Gallery: p. 48 (top); Woburn Abbey: p. 27 (lower left).

We have been unable to contact the copyright holders of the photographs which appear on pages 14, 27 (top left and top right) and 148 (lower right) and would be grateful for any information that would enable us to do so.

One of the themes that runs through this book is continuity. We would like to dedicate it to our children.

For David, Marie, and Joe.

Details of Written Sources

In some sources the wording or sentence structure has been simplified to make sure that the source is accessible.

J. Addy, *The Agricultural Revolution*, Longman 1964: 3.3B; A. R. Ashwell, *Life of the Right Reverend Samuel Wilberforce*, 1880: 11.4C; J. M. Auel, *The Clan of the Cave Bear*, Hodder and Stoughton 1980: 1.3A; J. F. Aylett, *In Search of History: 1714–1900*, Edward Arnold 1985: 4.4D; P. S. Bagwell, *The Transport Revolution from 1770*, Batsford 1974: 5.1A; T. Barker (ed), *The Long March of Everyman*, André Deutsch 1975: 4.4A, 4.12B; L. M. Beier, *Sufferers and Healers*, Routledge and Kegan Paul 1987: 4.3A; B. Catchpole, *A Map History of the English People Since 1700*, HEB 1975: 4.3A; T. Coleman, *The Railway Navvies*, Penguin 1968: 5.5A; F. Engels, *The Condition of the Working Classes in England* Panther 1969: 4.4G; M. Falkus, *Britain Transformed: An Economic and Social History 1700–1914*, Causeway Press 1987: 4.2A, 4.2G, 4.11A, 5.1F; R. Hall (ed.), *Dear Dr Stopes*, Penguin 1981: 10.4F; W. W. Johnson and G. Wykes, *A Short Economic and Social History of Twentieth Century Britain*, George Allen and Unwin 1967: 3.12A; R. B. Jones, *Economic and Social History of England 1770–1977*, Longman 1979: 4.12A; P. Laslett, *The World We Have Lost*, Methuen 1971: 2.1B; J. Marchand (ed.), *A Frenchman in England*, (trans. S. C. Roberts), Cambridge 1933: 2.2F; H. Martin, *Britain Since 1700: The Rise of Industry*, Macmillan Education 1988: 4.9B; H. Martin, *Britain Since 1800: Towards the Welfare State*, Macmillan Education 1988: 4.13B, 7.1B; T. May, *An Economic and Social History of Britain 1760–1970*, Longman 1987: 8.2D; B. R. Mitchell and P. Deane, *Abstract of Annual Historical Statistics*, Cambridge University Press 1962: 3.6A, 3.7A, 3.7E, 3.11A; C. Morris, *William Cobbett's Illustrated Rural Rides 1821–32*, Webb and Bower 1984: 3.8A; George Orwell, *The Road to Wigan Pier*, Gollancz 1937: 4.14A; R. Porter and E. Royle (eds.), *Documents of the Early Industrial Revolution*, UCLES 1983: 4.9C, 5.1E; M. P. Reeves, *Round About a Pound a Week*, G. Bell and Sons 1913 (reprinted Virago 1979): 1.2A; P. Rogers (ed.), Daniel Defoe, *A Tour through the Whole Island of Great Britain*, Penguin 1971: 2.1C, 2.2A, 2.2D, 2.2E; E. Seddon, *Modern Economic History*, Macdonald and Evans 1966: 3.6B; P. Schweitzer, L. Hilton and J. Moss (eds.), *What Did you Do in the War, Mum?*, Age Exchange Theatre Company 1985: 10.3A; J. Scott, *Energy Through Time*, Oxford University Press 1986: 4.1A, 4.1B; S. Sillars, *Women in World War I*, Macmillan 1987: 10.4A, B and H; J. Steven Watson, *The Reign of George III*, Oxford University Press 1960: 3.5D; E. T. Svendenstierna, *Svendenstierna's Tour Great Britain 1802–3*, (trans. E. L. Dellow), David and Charles 1973: 4.2F; R. L. Tames (ed.), *Documents of the Industrial Revolution 1750–1850*, Hutchinson Educational 1971: 4.3B, 4.4C, 5.5G, 7.1A; E. P. Thompson, *The Making of the English Working Class*, Pelican 1968: 4.11B, 4.11D, 7.2A; G. M. Trevelyan, *English Social History*, Longman 1944: 3.5A; J. Wilkes, *United Kingdom*, Cambridge University Press 1984: 4.6C

CONTENTS

PART ONE HISTORICAL CONCEPTS

1.1	Causation	CAUSATION	6
1.2	Evidence	EVIDENCE	8
1.3	Empathy	EMPATHY	10
1.4	Change	CHANGE	12

PART TWO PRE-INDUSTRIAL BRITAIN

2.1	Britain in the Early Eighteenth Century		14
2.2	Agriculture, Industry and Communications		16

PART THREE AGRICULTURE

3.1	Agriculture in 1700		18
3.2	The Open Field System under Pressure		20
3.3	Enclosure		22
3.4	Social and Economic Effects of Agrarian Change		24
3.5	The Agricultural Revolution and the Role of the Individual		26
3.6	Agriculture during the Wars against France 1793–1815		28
3.7	The Corn Laws	EVIDENCE	30
3.8	From Depression to Recovery, 1815–45		32
3.9	Repeal of the Corn Laws	CAUSATION	34
3.10	High Farming		36
3.11	Depression: 1870–1900		38
3.12	Agriculture during the Twentieth Century		40
3.13	Agriculture and Society		45

PART FOUR INDUSTRY

4.1	Power		46
4.2	The Spread of the Steam Engine	CHANGE	48
4.3	Capital, Investors and Entrepreneurs		50
4.4	The Domestic System	EVIDENCE	52
4.5	Inventions in the Textile Industry		54
4.6	The Factory System	CAUSATION	56
4.7	The Darbys of Coalbrookdale		58
4.8	Developments in the Iron and Steel Industries		60
4.9	Wedgwood and Pottery	CAUSATION	62
4.10	Coal Mining		64
4.11	Industrialization	EVIDENCE	68
4.12	The Workshop of the World		70
4.13	The Triumph and Decline of the 'Old' Industries		72
4.14	Coal Mining since 1850		76
4.15	New Industries		78

PART FIVE COMMUNICATIONS

5.1	Roads, Turnpikes and Coaches		82
5.2	Navigable Rivers and Early Canals		86
5.3	The Canal System	CHANGE	88
5.4	The First Railway?	CHANGE	90
5.5	Building Railways and Train Travel	EVIDENCE	92
5.6	Development of Railways		94
5.7	The Effect of the Railways		96
5.8	From Sail to Steam		98
5.9	Trams, Buses, Cars and Lorries	CHANGE	100
5.10	The Decline of the 'Old' Transport System		102
5.11	Air travel		104
5.12	Other Methods of Communication		106

PART SIX POPULATION

6.1	Population Growth, 1700–1880		108
6.2	Why did the Population Increase?		110
6.3	The Effects of Population Growth 1700–1880		112
6.4	Population Changes since 1880		114
6.5	The Fall in the Birth and Death Rate since 1880		116
6.6	Emigration and Immigration since 1800	EMPATHY	118

PART SEVEN IDEAS

7.1	*Laissez-faire*		120
7.2	Class		121
7.3	Capitalism		122
7.4	Socialism		123

PART EIGHT EARLY PROBLEMS OF INDUSTRIALIZATION

8.1	Living Conditions		124
8.2	Working Conditions – the Factories		126
8.3	Working Conditions – the Mines	EMPATHY	128
8.4	Working-Class Reactions		130
8.5	The Luddites and the Swing Riots		132
8.6	Working-Class Self-Help		134
8.7	Chartism		138
8.8	The End of Chartism	CAUSATION	140

PART NINE COMING TO TERMS WITH INDUSTRIALIZATION

9.1 The Old Poor Law 142
9.2 The New Poor Law EMPATHY 144
9.3 Factory Reform 146
9.4 Public Health Improvements: Medical Progress 148
9.5 Public Health Reform 152
9.6 Social Reform, 1900–39 154
9.7 Social Reform Since 1945 158
9.8 Trade Unions, 1850–1918 160
9.9 The General Strike of 1926 164
9.10 Trade Unions since 1926 166

PART TEN WOMEN

10.1 Introduction 168
10.2 Suffragists and Suffragettes 170
10.3 One Woman's War EMPATHY 172
10.4 Women in the Twentieth Century 174

PART ELEVEN EDUCATION AND RELIGIOUS ISSUES

11.1 Schools before 1830 176
11.2 The growth of Elementary Education 178
11.3 The growth of Secondary Education 180
11.4 Religious Issues 182

PART TWELVE LAW AND ORDER

12.1 Law and Order Problems 186
12.2 Law and Order Reforms 188

Index 190

1.1 CAUSATION

One day a boy came home from school. He tried to creep up to his bedroom without his father noticing that he had come in, but this didn't work. His father noticed him and called him into the kitchen. 'John,' his father said, 'I can see why you are creeping upstairs like that. What has happened to your trousers?'

John's father had seen that his trousers were covered in mud. There was a pause, and then John explained what had happened. In the three boxes below you can see three possible answers John might have given. Read them carefully and then consider the questions which follow. One further thing is that John is an unusual boy in that he always tells the truth!

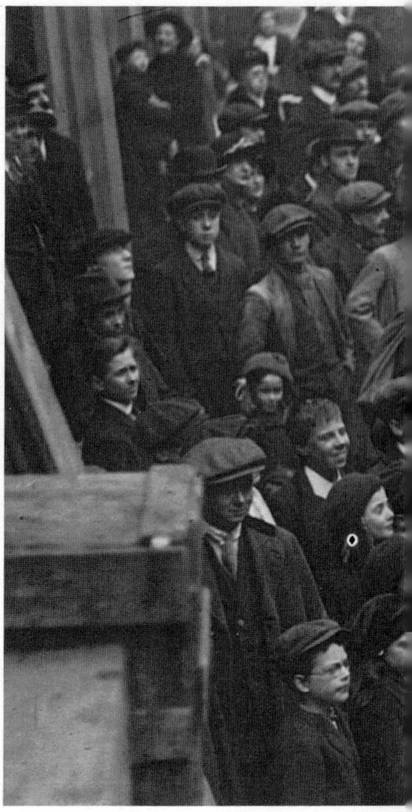

London, 1916.

Explanation one

'Mud, as I am sure you know, Dad, is a rather sticky mixture of water and dirt. My trousers are made from fairly coarse cloth which is a very good base for mud to stick on. Also, I am considerably taller than I am wide, which means that under certain conditions I am unstable and likely to fall. What happened is that I was crossing some mud, which is rather slippery, and thus I was more likely to fall. I fell, and the adhesive qualities of the mud meant that some of it stuck to my trousers.'

Explanation two

'I was going through a field and I slipped and fell into a puddle.'

Explanation three

'I had to stay late at school because I had not done my homework. Because I was late, I thought I would take the short cut over the field. There were some big kids on the field who said they were going to beat me up unless I gave them all my money. I started to run away, and some of them chased after me. They were still chasing after me when I tried to jump over a muddy patch but I slipped and fell right in it. They all just laughed at me.'

Adapted from J.H. Hexter 'The History Primer', 1971.

EXERCISE

1. Can all three of these explanations cover the same incident and still be true?
2. If you were the boy's father, which explanation would you think was the best?
3. Which of these explanations do you think is the most scientific?
4. All three explanations cover something which happened in the past. Which do you think is the best piece of history?

QUESTIONS

1 What event does this photograph show?

2 What do you think caused the event?

3 a What are the advantages of photographs as explanations of the causes of events?

b What are the disadvantages of photographs as explanations of the causes of events?

CONCLUSION

Some of the following sentences about how historians think about **causes** are sensible, and others are not. Make up a paragraph about causation by copying the sentences you think are sensible into your excercise book. Keep the sentences you use in the order they are here.

When historians try to explain the causes of events they have a very difficult job.

When historians use the word 'cause' they do not mean quite the same thing as scientists.

The best explanation of causes in history is the most simple. You only ever need one cause to explain one event.

Historians usually find that the best explanations of causes have more than one cause in them.

Because the actions of people usually have some part in a historian's explanation of causes, good explanations will have motives in them. (Motives are people's reasons for doing things.)

People are the only things that matter in explaining the causes of events.

People don't matter at all when you try to explain the causes of events; only the conditions at the time matter.

Historians find that the best explanations show how people's motives and actions are affected by the conditions at the time.

1.2 EVIDENCE

Historians have to work out what they think happened in the past from their **sources** – things which have survived from the past. These sources, however, are not always easy to use. Before the historian can use them as **evidence** to answer a particular question about the past, sources must be tested. Usually historians want to know three things. First the source's **provenance** – how and why it was created, and how it has come down to us. Second its **reliability** – whether the source, or some part of it, is accurate or not. Third its **utility** – how useful it will be. The answers to these questions are usually linked, as you will see from the sources here which are about working-class people in the early part of this century.

SOURCE B

SOURCE A

Mr Y is a builder's handyman, whose wages average 25 shillings a week. He allows, as a rule, 22 shillings and 6 pence to his wife, out of which she gives him back 3 shillings for his dinners when at work. There are six children under thirteen. The rent for the two rooms is 6 shillings and 6 pence, and burial insurance is 1 shilling.
Sunday – Breakfast: 1 loaf, jam and tea. A bloater for him. Dinner: Half shoulder of mutton, greens, potatoes, and suet pudding for all. Tea: Bread, butter, and tea.
Monday – Breakfast: Bread, dripping and tea. Cold meat from Sunday for him. Dinner for mother and children: cold meat and potatoes over from Sunday. Tea: bread, jam, and tea.
Tuesday – Breakfast: Bread, dripping and tea for all. Dinner for mother and children: Hashed meat (over from Monday) and potatoes. Tea: Bread, radishes, and tea.
Wednesday – Breakfast: Bread, dripping and tea. Dinner for mother and children: Dumplings in yesterday's gravy. Tea: Bread, jam, and tea for all.
Thursday – Breakfast: Bread, dripping and tea. Dinner for mother and children: Rice and treacle. Tea: Bread, jam, and tea.
Friday – Breakfast: Bread, jam, and tea. Dinner for mother and children: Barley broth and potatoes. Tea: Bread, dripping, and tea.
Saturday – Breakfast: Bread, dripping, and tea. Dinner for mother and children: ¾ lb sausages and potatoes. Tea: Bread, jam, and tea.

This is one of Mrs Y's weekly budgets:

	s	d
Rent	6	6
Insurance	1	0
Gas	0	6
½ cwt coal	0	8½
Wood	0	2
Soap, soda, blue, starch	0	5
Boracic powder	0	1
Baby's soap	0	2
	9	6½
Husband's dinners	3	0
14 loaves	3	4½
1 lb dripping	0	6
12 ozs. butter	0	9
8 ozs. tea	0	8
Meat	2	3
6 lbs potatoes	0	3
Vegetables	0	6
½ quartern flour	0	3
Bloaters	0	3
Suet	0	2
3 lbs. sugar	0	6
	12	11½

Maud Pember Reeves, 'Round About a Pound a Week', 1913.

A working-class family in London, photographed just before the First World War.

ACTIVITY 1

Read Source A. This source might suggest working-class families were very poor in the early years of this century. However, historians could not just accept this straight away.

Provenance and reliability

1 Is there anything mentioned in the source which makes you think it cannot be true, or that it is likely to be true?

2 You have been told little about the source's provenance. Below are two possible provenances for it. In each case say whether this makes you think the source might be reliable or not.

- **a** This was part of a report by government health inspectors.
- **b** This was part of a book produced by a group of middle-class women campaigning to improve the conditions of poorer working-class families in London.

Utility

A historian might still decide a source could be useful even if it was not reliable. For instance you might have decided in **2b** that the report might be exaggerated. However this might still be useful evidence about what middle-class women thought was shocking poverty.

3 For each of the suggested provenances in question **2**:

- **a** write an example of how a historian might find Source A useful.
- **b** write an example of how a historian might *not* find Source A useful.

ACTIVITY 2

Photographs are difficult sources for historians to use.

1 Is the family in Source B the same as the family in Source A? Give reasons for your answer.

2 Does this photograph prove that many families in London were desperately poor? Give reasons for your answer.

3 How can you be sure:

- **a** this photograph was taken in London?
- **b** this is a photograph of normal people in their home and not actors posing so that the photographer could make a point?

CONCLUSION

Copy the following sentences into your notebooks, using the material on this page to write a sentence or two of your own to explain each one.

1 It is important for historians to know the provenance of their sources.

2 There are many reasons why all or part of a source might not be reliable.

3 Historians can only decide about the reliability of a source when they know what they want to find out.

4 Historians may sometimes find sources useful even if they don't think they are reliable.

1.3 EMPATHY

SOURCE A

'Grod had nurtured the burning ember anxiously while they travelled. Maintenance of the fire could only be entrusted to a male of high status. If the coal died out it would be a sure sign that their protective spirits had deserted them. While Grod carefully placed the burning charcoal on a bed of dry tinder and blew it into flame, the women turned to other tasks. With techniques passed down for generations they quickly skinned the game. A few moments after the fire was blazing well, meat skewered with sharp green sticks set over forked branches was roasting.

With the same sharp stone knives they used to skin and cut the meat, the women scraped and sliced roots and tubers. Tightly woven waterproof baskets and wooden bowls were filled with water, and then hot stones were added. When cooled the stones were put back into the fire and new ones were put in the water until it boiled.'

Jean M. Auel, 'The Clan of the Cave Bear', 1980.

SOURCE B

Fred Flintstone, from the television cartoon about a Stone Age family.

ACTIVITY 1

Make a list of at least ten differences between Sources A and B.
Make a table like the one below. For each of the qualities listed, give both Source A and Source B a score out of 10 where 10/10 would be the best score possible and 1/10 the worst.

	Source A	*Source B*
How realistic is the source?		
How funny is the source?		
Does the source tell you about people's ideas?		
Are the people made out to be like us?		
Is the source likely to be based on a study of evidence?		
Is the source really history?		

In the activity you have just completed you have been looking at two different versions of what the past might have been like. Both of these are fiction, and history is very different from fiction. In *The Flintstones*, part of the joke is that the people in the television cartoon have the same possessions as people in the United States today. They also seem to have the same **ideas** and **attitudes**.

If we are to write good history, then we have to make sure that we understand not only what people in the past **did** but also what they **thought** about things. History is about not only **what** happened but also **why** it happened. To understand this properly we have to remember the ideas that people had at the time, because this helps us understand why they did things. Historians sometimes call this **empathy**, trying to look at events in the past from the point of view of the people who were there at the time.

SOURCE C

A crowd in Berlin, 3 August 1914.

CONCLUSION

1 Source C shows young men waving their hats and cheering. To understand why they are doing this, you need more information. Listed below is some information that might help. Copy into your book the sentences which seem to help. Keep them as a separate list.
   - Germany declared war on Russia on 1 August 1914 and on France on 3 August 1914.
   - Straw boaters were amongst the most fashionable hats for young men in 1914.
   - Most people in 1914 thought war was glorious.
   - Young men in particular thought war would give them a chance to show their patriotism and their bravery.
   - Between 1860 and 1870 Germany had been united by a series of short wars in which the Danes, the Austrians and then the French were convincingly beaten.

2 Underline in your book those sentences which help you understand the photograph *and which tell you about how people thought and felt.*

3 Do you think a historian needs to try to use empathy when explaining events in the past?

4 Do you think there is a difference between empathy and imagination? Explain your answer.

1.4 CHANGE

CHANGE

So much of history is concerned with change that historians sometimes try to study change itself, as well as what is changing. They distinguish between a **change**, where something new happens, and a **development**, where something that existed before has been modified. They are careful to notice that change and development are not necessarily the same as **progress** (where things get better) and may sometimes be **regress** (where things get worse). They also look for the examples of **continuity**, the things which don't change over long periods of time. They are also concerned with the **rate of change**, noticing that in some periods changes happen very fast, and in others very slowly. Finally they are interested in the factors which influence change, things like religion, war, government policy, chance, brilliant individuals, the level of education, technology and jealousy etc.

The first activity looks at **smallpox**, a killer disease which the World Health Organization said had been stamped out in 1980. In 1798 Edward Jenner, a country doctor from Berkeley, Gloucestershire, suggested a way of stopping people from catching the disease. He noticed that milkmaids, who usually caught cowpox (a much milder illness) from cows didn't get smallpox. He tried deliberately infecting a child with cowpox, and then later deliberately infecting the same child with smallpox. The child didn't catch smallpox because the cowpox had given him an immunity. Jenner called the process **vaccination** and published his results, claiming that this treatment could end smallpox.

SOURCE A

'Smallpox killed some people every year in seventeenth-century London. However, it was worse in some years than others. In 1659 smallpox killed 1,523 people, while in 1660 it killed 354.'

Lucinda MacCray Beier, 'Sufferers and Healers', 1987.

SOURCE B

Cartoon by Gilray published by the Anti-Vaccine Society, 1802.

SOURCE C

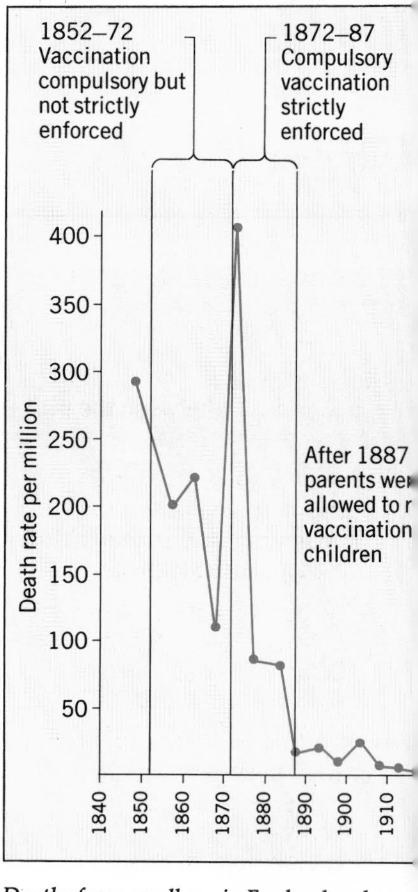

Deaths from smallpox in England and Wales, 1848–1920.

ACTIVITY 1

1. What examples of continuity are there in the story of smallpox?
2. Was Jenner's treatment a *change* or a *development*?
3. What does Source B suggest about the reaction to Jenner's idea?
4. Would you describe the pace of change in stamping out smallpox as fast or slow? Explain your answer.
5. In 1750 smallpox was one of the most common and most deadly diseases in Britain. Today it doesn't exist. What factors do these sources suggest helped bring about this change? Give reasons for your answer.

ACTIVITY 2

Study Sources D and E.

1. What examples of change can you see between the two photographs?
2. What examples of continuity can you see between the two photographs?
3. Which do you think has been the more significant, the change or the continuity? Give reasons for your answer.
4. Do you think the differences between Source E and Source D should be described as *progress* and *regress*? Give reasons for your answer.
5. What factors do you think influenced the changes between the two photographs? Explain your answer.

SOURCE D

'Tally Ho', a house near Swindon, c1880.

SOURCE E

'Tally Ho', 1989.

2.1 BRITAIN IN THE EARLY EIGHTEENTH CENTURY

In the years since 1750 Britain has changed more, and more quickly, than ever before. In this book you will see the way people's working lives changed, and the way the rest of their lives changed as a result. It is a very difficult story to understand in detail. For instance, in 1750 most people lived in the **countryside**, but now most people live in **towns** and **cities**. In order to explain this you need to know that **farming** got more efficient, so that those working on the land could produce enough to feed those people who didn't produce their own food. You also need to know that **transport** got better, so that the towns could be supplied with much more food. **Technology** also got better, so that food could be kept fresh much longer. **Industry** changed, so that there were many more jobs in towns, and so on.

In order to write the book we have divided society up by **themes**. We look first at **agriculture**, then at **industry**, **communications**, **population** and finally at the **social changes** that went along with these economic ones. You must remember that people didn't live their lives in little boxes called 'industry' or 'law and order'. All these different themes played a part in everyone's life.

SOURCE A

Robert Morvison, born 1775, photographed 1857, when 82. This one man's lifetime included many of the changes described in the rest of this book.

Before the industrial and agricultural revolutions

At the start of the eighteenth century Britain was a largely agricultural society which was changing slowly. Many of the things we are going on to look at, changes in farming and industry, new ideas and ways of life, had already started – but usually in only a small way, affecting very few people. All this was to change.

Pre-industrial Britain was a society divided up into many different **classes**, and people were very conscious of these distinctions. The best estimate we have of the size of the population at the end of the seventeenth century was made by Gregory King, a statistician, who made his estimate by class (Source B).

It is not easy to find **evidence** which describes what life was like in the past. Most historical sources were not written to be sources, but written for some purpose at the time. People didn't often describe the

SOURCE B

Number of families	*Ranks, degrees, titles and qualifications*	*Heads per family*	*Number of persons*	*Yearly income per family* £	s
160	Temporal Lords	40	6,400	3,200	
26	Spiritual Lords	20	520	1,300	
800	Baronets	16	12,800	800	
600	Knights	13	7,800	650	
3,000	Esquires	10	30,000	450	
12,000	Gentlemen	8	96,000	280	
5,000	Persons in greater Offices and Places	8	40,000	240	
5,000	Persons in lesser Offices and Places	6	30,000	120	
2,000	Eminent Merchants and Traders by Sea	8	16,000	400	
8,000	Lesser Merchants and Traders by Sea	6	48,000	198	
10,000	Persons in the Law	7	70,000	154	
2,000	Eminent Clergymen	6	12,000	72	
8,000	Lesser Clergymen	5	40,000	50	
40,000	Freeholders of the better sort	7	280,000	91	
120,000	Freeholders of the lesser sort	5½	660,000	55	
150,000	Farmers	5	750,000	42	10
15,000	Persons in Liberal Arts and Sciences	5	75,000	60	
50,000	Shopkeepers and Tradesmen	4½	225,000	45	
60,000	Artisans and Handicrafts	4	240,000	38	
5,000	Naval Officers	4	20,000	80	
4,000	Military Officers	4	16,000	60	
50,000	Common Seamen	3	150,000	20	
364,000	Labouring People and Out-Servants	3½	1,275,000	15	
400,000	Cottagers and Paupers	3¼	1,300,000	6	10
35,000	Common Soldiers	2	70,000	14	
	Vagrants; such as Gypsies, Thieves, Beggars, etc.		30,000		
1,349,586	Totals	4 1/13	5,500,520	32	5

Gregory King's estimate of the population of England, 1699.

everyday things, because they knew them so well. The most useful sources are often the writings of **travellers**, who describe a country or an area for people who have never seen it. **Statistics**, such as those produced by Gregory King, are not always completely accurate. The government collects information about the country now, and needs it to be accurate. In the early eighteenth century the government didn't even know how many people lived in the country. Most statistics were collected by ordinary people, because they were interested, or because they hoped to use them to write books which would make them money.

One of the most useful sources about Britain before 1750 is **Daniel Defoe's** book, *A Tour through the Whole Island of Great Britain*. Defoe wrote this travel book, describing the country, in order to make money. Source C is part of Defoe's description of Leeds, which was clearly an important town in the cloth industry before our story begins. If you read Defoe's account carefully you will see lots of ways in which things were different then. The **clothiers** (business people who made and sold cloth) usually had very small businesses, with one or two pieces of cloth to sell. How many more differences can you find?

SOURCE C

'From hence to Leeds, and every way to the right hand and the left the country appears busy, diligent and even in a hurry of work. Leeds is a large, wealthy and populous town. It has a stately and prodigiously strong stone bridge, so large and so wide that formerly the cloth market was kept in neither part of the town, but on the very bridge itself.

'The increase of the manufacturers and of the trade soon made the market too great to be confined to the bridge, and it is now kept in the High Street. The street is a large, broad, fair and well-built street.

'Early in the morning, there are trestles placed in two rows in the street; then there are boards laid across these trestles, so that the boards lie like long counters on either side, from one end of the street to the other. The clothiers come early in the morning with their cloth; and as few clothiers bring more than one piece, the market being so frequent, they go into the public houses with it, and there set it down.

'At seven o'clock in the morning, the clothiers being supposed to be all come by that time, even in winter, the market bell rings. In a few minutes, without hurry or noise, the whole market is filled. All the boards upon the trestles are covered with cloth, and behind every cloth the clothier standing to sell it.

'As soon as the bell has stopped ringing, the merchants and factors, and buyers of all sorts, come down and walk up the rows and down as their occasions direct. Some of them have their foreign orders, with patterns on them, and with those they match colours, holding them to the cloths as they think they agree to. When they decide they reach over to the clothier and whisper, and in the fewest words imaginable one asks, the other bids, and 'tis agree, or not agree, in a moment.

'In little more than an hour all the business is done. In less than half an hour you will see the cloths begin to move off, the clothier taking it up on his shoulder to carry it to the merchant's house. By half an hour after eight o'clock the market bell rings again. Immediately the buyers disappear, the cloth is all sold, or if here and there a piece happens not to be bought, 'tis carried back into the public house. In a quarter of an hour there is not a piece of cloth to be seen in the market. Thus, you see, ten or twenty thousand pounds' worth of cloth, and sometimes much more, bought and sold in little more than an hour.

'By nine o'clock the boards are taken down, the trestles removed, and the street cleared; and this is done twice a week. By this quick return the clothiers are constantly supplied with money, and their workmen are duly paid.'

Daniel Defoe, 'A Tour through the Whole Island of Great Britain', 1724.

2.2 AGRICULTURE, INDUSTRY AND COMMUNICATIONS

Industry and agriculture

If we were describing Britain today we would not link **industry** and **agriculture** together. Before the Industrial Revolution it would not make sense to divide them. Some historians describe society at the time as being a **family economy**. By this they mean that both agriculture and industry was often organized on a family basis. One family might both farm and be involved in one of the stages of production in an industry. They would divide their time between working on the land and working at home, doing something like spinning wool or weaving cloth.

Women played a vital part in this economy, working within the family unit. They worked with their parents before marriage, and made a new unit with their husbands after marriage. They also married quite late – 25 was the average age in the early eighteenth century. **Child labour** was common, with young children joining in the simple tasks of the family work from the age of 4 or 5.

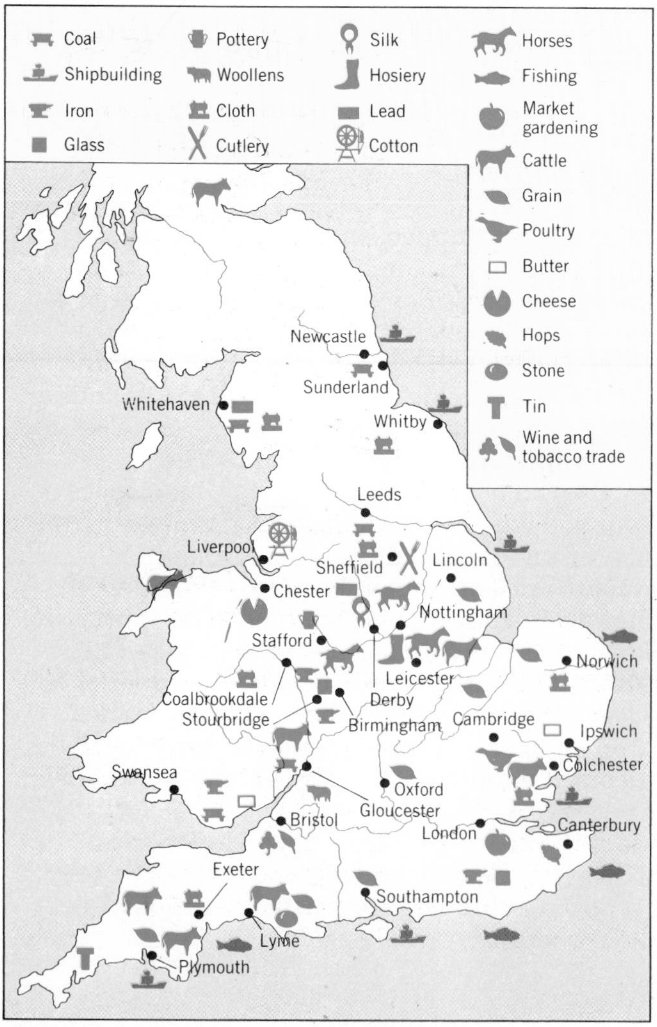

Map 1: Main areas of industrial and agricultural activity in the early eighteenth century.

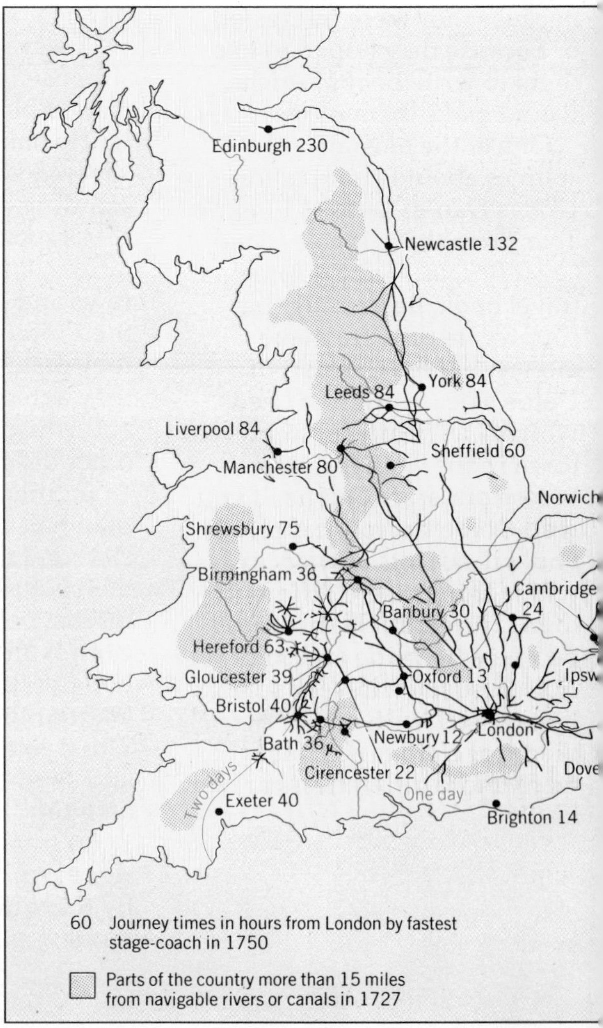

Map 2: Turnpike roads and navigable rivers, about 1750.

It is sometimes suggested that Britain before the Industrial Revolution was rather like a Third World country today, with most people living on the land and working in family groups. There were important differences, though:

- Britain was one of the richest countries in the world at the time.
- London was a vast market.
- The rest of the country was specializing to produce different things in different regions.

Communications

Transport was a problem in Britain before the Industrial Revolution. The **roads** were mainly very poor quality, without a proper surface. The rich used post-chaises, carriages for which fresh horses could be hired every few miles, or went on horseback. There were also stage-coaches, which ran between London and most main towns, and kept to some sort of timetable. Goods were taken by wagon or strings of pack animals (mules, donkeys or horses). Animals, from cattle to geese, were simply driven to market along the roads, often a hundred miles or more to London.

Because the roads were so bad, **water transport** was used where possible. Many goods were taken by sea, for instance coal from Newcastle to London. In the summer people often travelled this way. Rivers were used as well as the sea. Where the original river was not suitable for boats, because it was too shallow, too windy or perhaps obstructed by bridges and water-mills, it could be improved. This was expensive, but often worth the cost.

An industrial country, such as Britain was to become, needs transport which is fast, reliable and cheap. In the early eighteenth century, transport was slow, unreliable and often expensive.

SOURCE A

'It is impossible to give any idea of the number of travellers who are always to be met on the English roads. In Bury alone, which is on the London–Norwich road, there are 125 horses available in the town for the service of post-chaises. Over and above this large number of horses you may reckon on at least 50 hacks let out as saddle horses. Saddle horses cost three shillings when you hire them to go on a journey of two or three days. When you hire a post-chaise to visit someone five, six or even ten miles away, you pay something between five and eight shillings.'

François de la Rochefoucauld, a French traveller, writing in 1784.

SOURCE B

'Maidstone. This is a very considerable town, and the River Medway is navigable to it by large hoys of 50 or 60 tuns burthen. Round this town are the largest cherry orchards that are in any part of England, and which supply the whole city of London. (They) come up, hoy-loads at a time, to a wharf called the Three Cranes in London.'

Defoe, 'A Tour through the Whole Island of Great Britain', 1724.

SOURCE C

'Guildford. The river is called the Wey and, which joins the Thames at Oatlands, is made navigable to this town, which adds greatly to its trade. This navigation is also a mighty support to the great cornmarket at Farnham.'

Defoe, 'A Tour . . .', 1724.

SOURCE D

'Because of the cloth trade some years ago an Act of Parliament was obtained for making the rivers Aire and Calder navigable. This communication by water was opened from Leeds and Wakefield to Hull and the sea. By which means all woollen manufactures which are exported are carried by water to Hull, and shipped for Holland, Bremen, Hamburg and the Baltic.'

Defoe, 'A Tour . . .', 1724.

3.1 AGRICULTURE IN 1700

Agriculture was Britain's most important industry in the eighteenth century. Over half of the population owed their living to farming, either directly as **farmers** or **labourers** or indirectly as **craftsmen** such as coopers, millers, blacksmiths or wheelwrights.

Landowners

Between 80 and 90 per cent of the land was owned by the **aristocracy** and the **gentry**, who were only a small section of the population. They farmed a little of their land themselves and rented the rest out. Some of the aristocracy, like the Duke of Newcastle, might own thousands of acres scattered over many counties. Members of the gentry, like Sir Robert Walpole, might own a few hundred acres in one county, in his case Norfolk. (An acre is roughly half the size of a football or hockey pitch).

Some farms were owned by small landowners, or **yeomen farmers**, who owned anything from 5 to 100 acres, farming all their land themselves. **Cottagers** owned only a small allotment big enough to grow vegetables on.

Tenants

Most of the land was therefore farmed by **tenant farmers**. They rented from the landowners and hoped to produce enough food to feed their families and sell a small surplus to pay their rent. The vast majority of tenants rented less than 20 acres and many less than 5.

Labourers and squatters

Landowners and tenant farmers paid wages to **labourers** who worked on their land. They might be full-time employees on the larger farms, or part-time or seasonal workers for the smaller farmers. **Squatters** could be labourers. They were people who had moved on to marginal or waste ground and built homes. They might have kept small plots of land for generations, but they had no legal rights to them.

SOURCE A

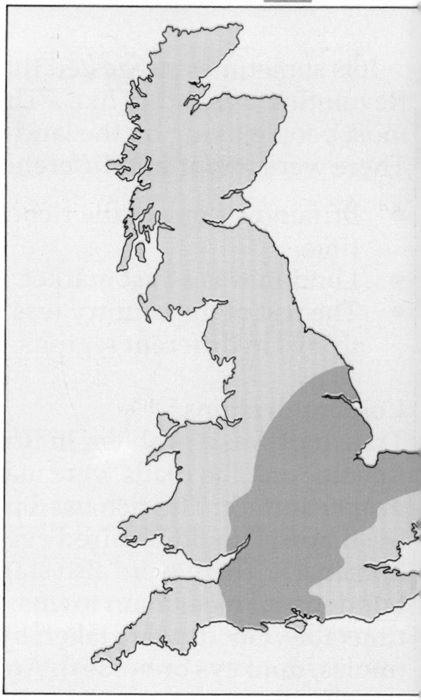

The main area of open field farming.

SOURCE B

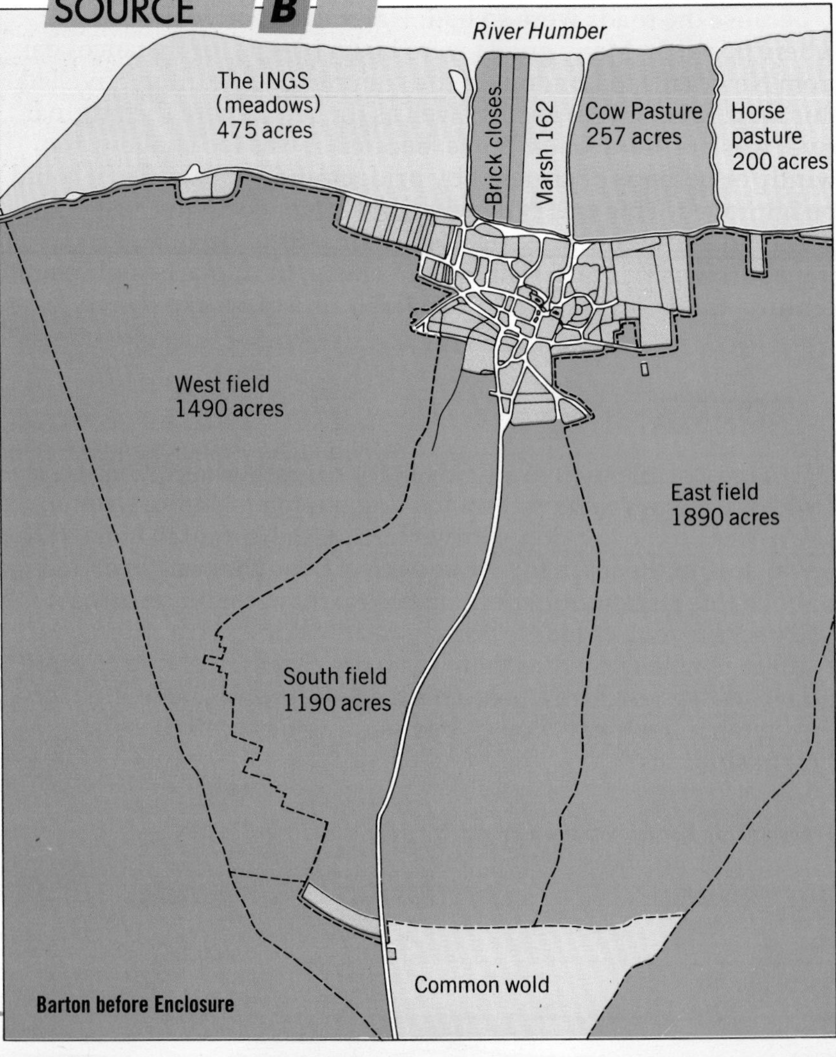

Barton before Enclosure

SOURCE C

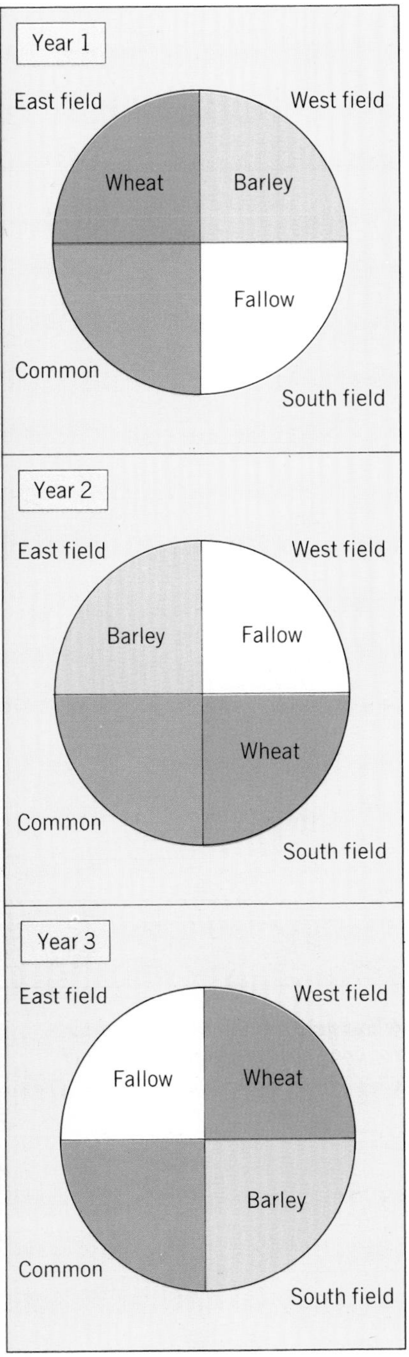

Rotations in the open fields.

The open field system

In 1700 about half of the land in Britain was farmed. About 60 per cent of cultivated land was organized under the **open field system**. There were regional variations. This system had never been popular, and had been replaced in the south-east, the south-west and the north of England, and in Scotland and Wales. But it was still the usual arrangement in the rest of England, particularly the Midlands (see Source A).

Under the open field system, all of the cultivated land in an area was divided into small **strips**, traditionally a furrow long (a **furlong**, or about 200 metres) and a **chain** wide (about 20 metres), and the strips were grouped together into three great fields. Each farmer had strips of land in each of the great fields and had to grow the same crops in his strips as all the other farmers in that field. There was normally a strict annual **rotation** of crops, involving a year of **wheat**, then a year of **barley** or **oats** and then a third year **fallow** (empty) in each field in turn (see Source C). The wheat was intended to provide flour for bread, and the barley was for ale or fodder for the livestock. The fallow year was to allow the soil to recover its fertility; for, if the same types of crop were grown year after year, the soil's nutrients would be used up, causing poorer and poorer yield. Cattle and sheep were let loose to graze on the stubble of the wheat and barley in winter.

The **common land** was an essential part of the open field system. This was a large area of waste land, sometimes partly wooded, which all of the local people who had **common rights** could use. This was an important bonus for them. They paid no rent for the common land, but could collect firewood or dig peat for fuel there, take fruit or berries, catch rabbits or hares and, most important, use it to graze their cattle, sheep, pigs, geese or chickens.

QUESTIONS

1 a What were the main differences between the aristocracy and gentry and the yeomen farmers?

b What were the main differences between the aristocracy and gentry and the tenant farmers?

c What were the main differences between the yeomen farmers and the tenant farmers?

d What were the main differences between the labourers and the squatters?

e Which of the distinctions you have just written about do you think people at the time would have felt was most important?

3.2 THE OPEN FIELD SYSTEM UNDER PRESSURE

Advantages of the open field system

The open field system developed during the Middle Ages. It was suitable for **arable** (crop) farming and **pastural** farming (grazing animals). At that time the population grew only slowly, and people were happy to produce mainly for **subsistence** (for their own needs) rather than needing large surpluses for sale at the markets. The system tended to produce an atmosphere of **co-operation** in the villages, because communal decisions were needed about which crops to grow, and farmers tended to share tools and labour. Because all of the farmers had strips in all the fields, the best and worst land was usually shared out fairly. Because each farmer had fields scattered over a large area, the houses were mostly clustered together at the centre, creating a **village community**.

However, the open field system also had disadvantages.

Disadvantages of the open field system

First of all, the open field system **wasted time and space**. When working their land, farmers constantly had to walk large distances between their strips, often hundreds of metres apart. The need for a fallow year meant that one-third of the arable land was wasted each year, and the potential arable land on the commons was also wasted. Farmers often left uncultivated borders or baulks between strips, and this was also a waste. But without such boundaries, the strips were so close together that weeds from one strip easily spread to neighbouring strips.

Secondly, **innovation was stifled**. All of the farmers had to grow the same crops in each field. Any enterprising farmer who wanted to grow a new crop such as clover, turnips or swedes to feed his cattle was not allowed to. The use of new improved tools was often impossible. The horse-drawn seed drill, intended to replace the wasteful practice of 'broadcasting', was not practical on the small strips. Ploughing across slopes to reduce soil erosion was also impossible on some narrow strips.

Thirdly, **livestock also suffered**. There was little shelter on the open fields and commons, and selective breeding was impossible. Herds sank to the quality of their poorest members. Disease spread unchecked, and fodder crops were always in short supply. The normal practice was to kill most livestock every autumn and salt the meat to eat in the winter, because farmers didn't have enough fodder to feed animals through the winter months. This 'autumn slaughter' prevented the build-up of large herds of livestock.

Motivation for change

The disadvantages of open field farming had been well known for many years. In some areas, the open fields had been replaced. But for most farmers there just wasn't the need to change the open field system until after 1700.

Then the **population** began to rise. England and Wales contained approximately 5.5 million people in 1700. But by the time of the first census in 1801, the population was 9.25 million.

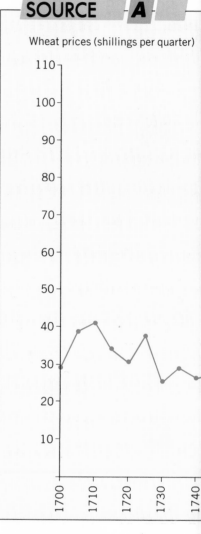

SOURCE A

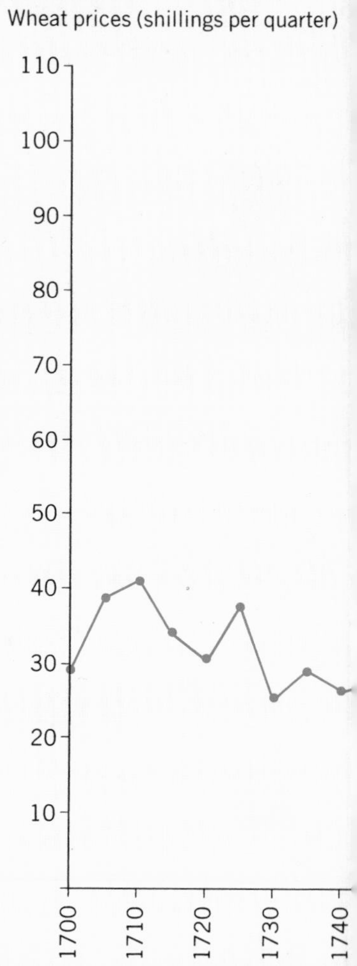

Wheat prices, 1700–1810. A quarter was one-fourth of a hundredweight of wheat (about 12.5 kilogrammes).

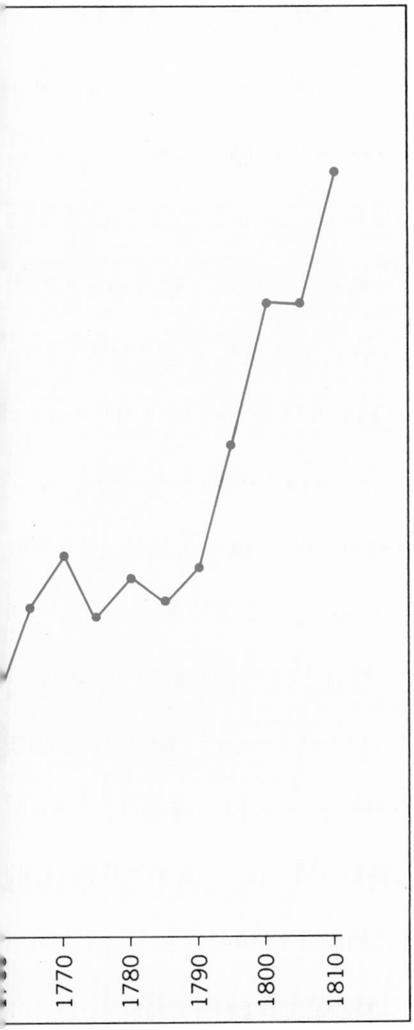

SOURCE B

Meat prices, 1750–1810. A stone was 14lbs, or 6.3 kilogrammes.

This increase in people meant an increase in the **demand for food**, and this caused **food prices** to rise. Wheat, which sold at less than 30 shillings per quarter in the 1730s, was averaging 45 shillings in the 1780s and almost 50 shillings by 1790. Sources A and B give details of wheat and meat prices.

Increased food prices meant the prospect of increased **profits** for farmers. The more efficient the farmers were and the larger their output, the greater those profits would be. The open field system stood in the way of efficiency and of increased production. As prices rose, so pressure mounted to end the open field system and replace it with another system called **enclosed fields**.

Arthur Young, an eighteenth-century traveller and writer, held out an enticing picture of the advantages to be gained if the restrictions of the open fields could be removed. He wrote in 1771: 'There is an amazing superiority of profit in enclosed counties to open ones. The profit (per sheep) in enclosed grounds is 11 shillings but in open ones only 2s and 6d. In the Vale of Evesham, the average fleece is 9 lb in the enclosures, but only 3 lb in the open fields. Can there be a stronger argument for enclosing?'

QUESTIONS

1. How did the open field system limit the amount of food that farmers could produce?
2. Study Sources A and B.
   - **a** At what date do you think that *many* farmers began to be seriously interested in enclosure schemes?
   - **b** At what date do you think that *most* farmers would have been convinced that enclosure schemes were a good thing?

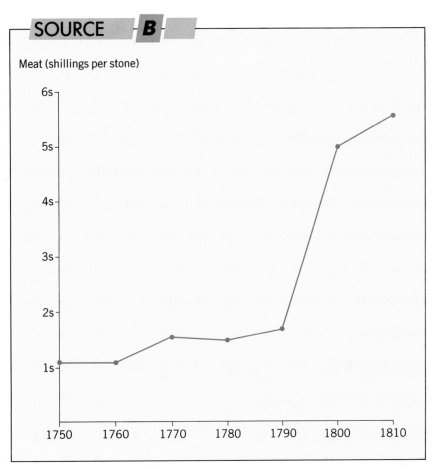

3.3 ENCLOSURE

Enclosure was the process of taking all of the scattered strips in the open fields or the common land, or both, and rearranging them into separate small fields. This meant that instead of having a large number of strips separated by great distances, and shared access to the common, each farmer's land was packaged into a single farm and fenced off from his neighbours.

Enclosures were not new. In the sixteenth century many landowners had enclosed their land for more efficient sheep farming. The first enclosures in the eighteenth century were **voluntary enclosures**. This could happen when landowners made private agreements among themselves to exchange strips, or when one landowner bought up a large number of strips. In either case, one landowner could gather together enough land to fence off from the rest, to farm separately. But there was a limit to what could be done by private agreement.

Parliamentary enclosures

From about 1740 **parliamentary enclosures** became more common. This was where landowners who wanted to enclose their land got the permission of Parliament to force enclosure upon their neighbours. This became increasingly common, reaching its peak between 1790 and 1810. Between 1760 and 1820 there were 4,000 Acts of Parliament passed, enclosing over 5 million acres.

The method of getting a parliamentary enclosure was slow and expensive, and some people thought it unfair. If the owners of 80 per cent of the land in an area wanted enclosure, they could petition Parliament to enforce it. Because, as we have seen, landownership was concentrated in the hands of a small minority of the population, this could mean that three or four people held the 80 per cent of land necessary. A counter-petition was possible; but this would probably involve only the smaller, poorer landowners, so it rarely occurred. Parliament usually agreed, and an enclosure Bill was prepared and passed.

To ensure that the legal rights of all the landowners were observed, **commissioners** were appointed to carry out the division of the land. These were usually experienced local land agents or surveyors; they were experts, but people often believed they were biased in favour of the wealthier landowners. The commissioners surveyed each landowner's strips to work out how much enclosed land each deserved. They also gave land to all those who had held common rights, to compensate for their loss. The problem was that smaller landowners often had no legal proof of their common rights, and squatters by definition had no legal rights at all – they were usually evicted. When their survey was complete, the commissioners made their award. Landowners were then required to have their new land hedged or fenced in.

This was not a cheap process. The **cost of enclosure** (see Source B) included organizing the petition and getting a Bill through Parliament, paying the commissioners, surveyors and map-makers and building the new roads, fences, hedges, barns and houses on the new farm.

SOURCE A

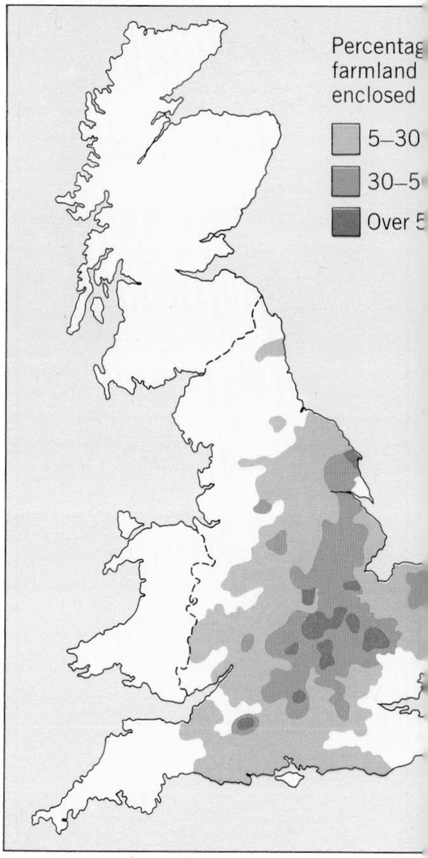

Enclosures in the eighteenth and nineteenth centuries.

SOURCE B

The costs of enclosure

	£	s	d
Legal charges	876	9	0
Parliamentary expenses	219	11	8
Commissioners' fees	1,284	9	4
Commissioners' expenses	251	7	10
Surveyors' fees	934	18	0
Roads and paths	1,030	11	4
Stakes and fences	184	1	1
Miscellaneous	916	2	3
Total	5,697	10	6

Common land in Sheffield was enclosed by an Act of Parliament in 1791. The costs involved in this enclosure are shown above.

SOURCE C

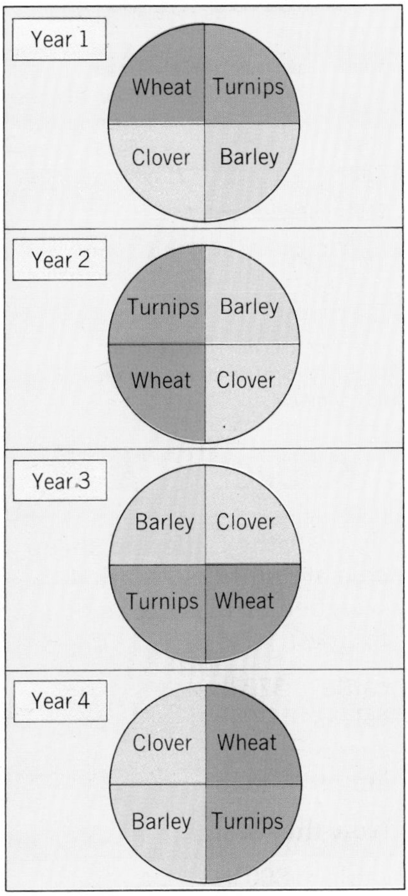

The Norfolk rotation.

SOURCE D

T.W. Coke of Holkham with a Devon ox, an example of selective breeding.

The results of enclosures – improved farming methods

Enclosures were a significant change. The new patchwork appearance of the land they brought about still dominates the English countryside. Landowners adopted enclosed fields because of the **improved methods of farming** they made possible.

One important innovation was **new crop rotations**. Once farmers had freedom to choose their own crops, they could get away from the fixed three-field rotation of wheat, barley and fallow. A popular alternative was the **Norfolk rotation** of wheat, turnips, barley and then clover (see Source C). The turnips (or sometimes swedes) extracted nutrients from a different level of soil from the grain crops, and the clover (or sometimes sainfoin or other grasses) returned to the soil nitrogen compounds which acted as fertilizers. This meant that there was no need for a fallow year. Also, livestock could be put out to graze on the grasses, and the root crops could be kept for fodder during the winter – so there was no need for an autumn slaughter. The animals would also manure the fields while they grazed and further benefit the crops. This rotation was popularized by **Viscount Townshend**.

Another area of improvement was **selective breeding**. Animals used for building up herds were now specially chosen for their best features, like the quality of their meat or wool. Enclosed fields made it possible for all farmers to adopt careful breeding policies, and some farmers created important new breeds. For example, **Robert Bakewell** developed the New Leicester sheep, Leicester longhorn cattle and Leicester horses, all bred for their strong bodies and short stocky legs. **Robert and Charles Colling** later developed shorthorn cattle which grew to two or three times the weight of traditional breeds.

Enterprising farmers could also turn to other improvements on the enclosed fields. Townshend did much to popularize the use of **marl**, a clay with a high lime content which helped to keep moisture in very light sandy soil. **Drainage trenches** could be used where soils were very heavy. Some farmers experimented with **new seeds** or **new crops**, or a variety of **fertilizers** like crushed bones and soot, whilst others adopted **new tools**. **Jethro Tull**, for example, invented a new tool to make seeding more efficient. The traditional method was 'broadcasting', whereby a farmer would walk in a careful pattern through a field, scattering seed around as evenly as possible. However, the seed was inevitably crowded in some areas and sparse in others, so the crop grew unevenly. Tull's **seed drill** was simply a seed container on wheels which could be pulled through the fields by a horse. The container had rows of holes in the base which methodically released the seed in even rows. This wasted less seed and allowed more even growth. Later Tull invented a **horse-drawn hoe** which could be pulled around the fields to clear weeds between the even rows of seedlings.

There is more detail about the role of the people who pioneered these improvements on pages 26–7.

3.4 SOCIAL AND ECONOMIC EFFECTS OF AGRARIAN CHANGE

We have seen how enclosures affected methods of farming, but the impact of all of these changes combined on the **economy** and **society** as a whole were even more significant. The removal of the fallow fields and the ploughing of the commons had greatly increased the **area** of land under cultivation. Between 1770 and 1810, for example, 350,000 extra acres of wheat were added. **Yields** were higher because of the improvements in seeds, tools, drainage and fertilizers. More land under production and higher yields led to huge increases in agricultural output (see Source A).

In Source B, Sir John Sinclair, president of the Board of Agriculture, describes how the **quality** as well as the quantity of produce had improved. This increase in output was matched by an increase in **profits**. Tenant farmers could therefore afford increased **rents**. Landowners' income from rents doubled during 1710–90 and doubled again between 1790 and 1810.

These were benefits which enclosures brought almost all farmers. Some of the smaller **yeomen farmers**, however, could not afford the costs involved in enclosures, or were unable to prove their common rights. In any case, some smaller farmers complained that the tiny amounts of extra land they were awarded were poor compensation for the loss of the huge benefits they had previously enjoyed from the commons. Some may have been forced to sell up and become tenant farmers or move to the towns. A popular rhyme of the period went:

> 'The Law locks up the man or woman,
> Who steals the goose from the common,
> But leaves the greater villain loose,
> Who steals the common from the goose.'

Yeoman farmers who survived enclosure – and this was the majority – enjoyed the same benefits of enclosure as other farmers. But there is no doubt that the new farming methods favoured the largest farms, and this may have widened the gap in rural society between the rich and poor.

For example, landlords began to realize that some of their tenants were more efficient than others – usually those with bigger areas of land. Some **tenant farmers** may thus have been evicted, after which their farms were combined with others to make bigger, more profitable ones. These farmers may then have had to take work as labourers.

For farm **labourers**, the hedging and ditching work which followed enclosure, and the extra acres brought into production, probably meant more work. As the population grew, the extra labour produced may have had to go to the towns in search of work, but there was no fall in the number of workers needed on the land. However, the new larger farms tended to need full-time rather than casual labour. It became rarer for a labourer, even more so for a farmer, to work some of the time on a small patch of land and some of the time in a craft cottage industry such as weaving. Agriculture, like industry, was becoming more business-like.

SOURCE A

Wheat output in England and Wales

1700	13 million quarters
1750	15 million quarters
1790	19 million quarters
1820	25 million quarters

Sheep on British farms

1700	11 million
1800	26 million

A quarter was one-fourth of a hundredweight of wheat (about 12.5 kilogrammes).

SOURCE B

'In 1710, the cattle and sheep sold at Smithfield Market weighed on average as follows:

cattle	370 lb
calves	70 lb
sheep	28 lb
lambs	18 lb

Now they weigh:

cattle	800 lb
calves	143 lb
sheep	80 lb
lambs	50 lb

Sir John Sinclair, president of the Board of Agriculture, giving evidence in 1795 to a parliamentary inquiry.

The most frequent sufferers were the **squatters**, who had no legal claim to the land they lived on and were usually evicted. On rare occasions, sympathetic commissioners accepted twenty years' occupation as a legal claim to land, but this was not the rule. In some places, there were fears the villages would disappear as farmers moved their houses and labourers' lodgings on to their farms. But the rising population meant that, in fact, villages generally grew rather than declined.

It would be misleading to overestimate the hardships caused by agrarian change. The majority of the farming community benefited. Landowners gained from higher rents; tenants enjoyed increased profits; and labourers benefited from more work. The whole of society could rely upon extra food, and this allowed the population to grow. In fact, farmers were providing food for the public with an ever declining proportion of the workforce. As the rural population increased, many people moved from the countryside to the towns. In this way industry gained a labour force and benefited from reasonable food prices, which enabled employers to keep wages, their biggest cost, under control.

SOURCE C

Surveyors planning the enclosure of the fields around Henlow, a village in Bedfordshire.

3.5 THE AGRICULTURAL REVOLUTION AND THE ROLE OF THE INDIVIDUAL

The word **revolution** applied to changes which took place in agriculture in the eighteenth century implies a sudden, dramatic transformation. There were certainly dramatic changes in this agrarian revolution, as we have seen, but they were by no means sudden. In fact, what is sometimes striking is how **slowly** the changes occurred. Change was sometimes so slow that the people usually given credit for improvements lived long after the first farmers to use them.

Let us take new crop rotations and marl as examples. **Lord Townshend** and **Thomas Coke** are the people most associated with these. Read Source A. It clearly shows that the historian G. M. Trevelyan gave these men the credit for introducing these to Norfolk. However, none of these ideas were new. **Sir Richard Weston** had seen four-field rotations in the Netherlands and described the system in a book published in the 1650s, nearly a century before. **Andrew Yarranton** had used clover to improve mixed arable and pastural farming in the 1660s (see Source B). **Sir Robert Walpole** senior had used turnips and clover on his estates at Houghton in Norfolk from the 1670s. The **Duke of Bedford** was just as famous for his sheep shearings at Woburn in Bedfordshire (see Source C) as Coke was for his in Norfolk.

Robert Bakewell, another person usually given credit for innovation, also perhaps barely deserves his fame. He used selective breeding to develop new breeds of sheep, cattle and horses. Source D shows how important one historian believed him to be. However, Bakewell's New Leicester sheep produced only very fatty meat and had a very short fleece. Southdown sheep, not the New Leicesters, came to dominate British herds by 1850. Similarly, Bakewell's cattle gave only fatty meat, and what they gained in weight they lost in milk. Farmers came to prefer the Durham Shorthorns developed by the **Colling brothers** in County Durham much later in the century. The Collings sold one of these bulls for £1,050 in 1810.

Other traditional 'heroes' of the agricultural revolution also need to be carefully assessed. **Jethro Tull** introduced his seed drill as early as 1701. His book, *Horse-Hoeing Husbandry*, was widely read, and in the third edition (see Source E) he claimed that his new tools would double a crop using only one-third of the seed. But the seed drill was never widely used until well into the nineteenth century, over 100 years after its invention.

Arthur Young is yet another example. From 1767 he travelled the country, writing articles about agricultural improvements. He became editor of *The Annals of Agriculture* in 1784 and secretary of the Board of Agriculture in 1793. He possibly did more to spread the ideas of the agricultural revolution than anyone. But he had failed as a farmer himself and had once paid someone £100 to take over a 300-acre farm which later proved perfectly profitable.

So we need to think carefully about the role of key personalities in the agricultural revolution. The questions in this unit are intended to focus on this.

SOURCE A

'Owners of large compact estates took the lead – men like 'Turnip Townshend' (who retired from politics to concentrate on his estates in 1730), and forty years later Coke of Norfolk. They introduced into Norfolk new crops and new methods – above all, root crops and the marling of light land. Their example put their backward county at the lead of English agriculture. Between 1776 and 1816 Coke so improved his land as to raise the rental of his Holkham estates from £2,200 to £20,000 a year. He granted his tenants the security of long leases but laid down strict terms about cultivation (he insisted on new crop rotations, for example). His 'sheep shearings' (agricultural shows) at Holkham were attended by experts from all over the country who gathered to see how land should be farmed and sheep fed.'

G. M. Trevelyan, 'English Social History', 1944.

SOURCE B

The Improvement improved
BY
A SECOND EDITION
OF
The great Improvement of Land
BY
CLOVER:
OR,
The Wonderful Advantage by and right management of CLOVER.

BY
ANDREW YARRANTON
of *Astley*, in the County of *Worcester*.

LONDON:
Printed by *J. C.* for *Francis Rea*, Bookseller in *Worcester*. 1663.

Title page of a book by Andrew Yarranton, published in 1663, describing the merits of clover.

SOURCE D

'By 1760 the appearance and use of horses, sheep and cattle had been changed in Leicestershire. Bakewell replaced the old breeds of sheep, which had been of use mainly for producing wool and providing manure, with new breeds selectively reared for meat. They were heaviest in the best butcher's joints and came to their peak in two seasons and not four. Others followed. Within a century the average weight of sheep at Smithfield Market rose from 28 lb to 80 lb.'

J. Steven Watson, 'The Reign of George III', 1960.

SOURCE E

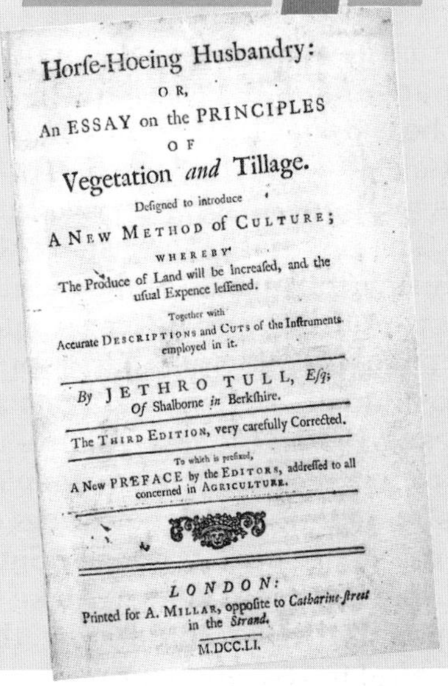

Horse-Hoeing Husbandry:
OR,
An ESSAY on the PRINCIPLES
OF
Vegetation *and* Tillage.
Designed to introduce
A NEW METHOD of CULTURE;
WHEREBY
The Produce of Land will be increased, and the usual Expence lessened.
Together with
Accurate DESCRIPTIONS and CUTS of the Instruments employed in it.

By JETHRO TULL, *Esq*;
Of Shalborne *in* Berkshire.

The THIRD EDITION, very carefully Corrected.

To which is prefixed,
A New PREFACE by the EDITORS, addressed to all concerned in AGRICULTURE.

LONDON:
Printed for A. MILLAR, opposite to *Catharine-street* in the *Strand*.
M.DCC.LI.

Title page of Jethro Tull's book 'Horse-Hoeing Husbandry', 1751.

SOURCE C

The sheep shearings at Woburn, 1804.

QUESTIONS

1 What are these people famous for in the agricultural revolution? Historians differ in their views about these people. Use the sources carefully to form your own opinion.
   - **a** Viscount Townshend.
   - **b** Thomas Coke.
   - **c** Robert Bakewell.
   - **d** Jethro Tull.
   - **e** Arthur Young.

2 Would you describe them as *innovators* (people who started new practices) or *propagandists* (people who convinced others about the new practices)?

3 Who were more important to the agricultural revolution, the innovators or propagandists? Explain your answer.

4 Why did Townshend, Bakewell and others in the eighteenth century become the leaders of the agricultural revolution, and not Weston, Walpole and others in the seventeenth century?

3.6 AGRICULTURE DURING THE WARS AGAINST FRANCE, 1793–1815

Napoleonic War.

From 1793 until 1815 Britain was almost continuously at war with France, and this war had far-reaching effects on the economy. The changes taking place in farming speeded up and reached their peak during these years, bringing the agricultural revolution (or agrarian revolution) to the end of its first phase.

The **population** of Britain, which had been growing steadily during the middle of the eighteenth century, was rising rapidly by the 1790s. Our best estimates suggest that the population rose from about 8.5 million to about 12.5 million during the war years, so **demand** for food was constantly growing. Also, **imports** were restricted by the war in Europe, so the **supply** of food was limited. More and more people competing for limited supplies of food meant that higher prices could be charged, and farmers' **profits** rose even more (see Source A).

Farmers were keen to make the most of this opportunity. The more grain they could grow, the more profit they could make. Many farmers and landowners borrowed money to extend or improve their land. Since the government was also borrowing heavily to finance the war, farmers had to pay very high interest rates to get loans, but their profits were high enough to make it worth their while. This period, then, became the most rapid period of change in the agricultural revolution.

Loans were spent on new equipment, better stock and seeds, drainage, fertilizers and, most of all, **enclosures**. The number of enclosure Acts during the war years was greater than at any other period, and the common land rapidly disappeared (see Source B). Grain output increased by 40 per cent during the three wartime decades, from 20 million quarters in 1790 to 28 million quarters in 1820. But, as always, not everyone benefited equally.

Landowners could charge more rent to tenant farmers as well as making bigger profits on land they farmed themselves. **Tenant farmers** had to pay higher rents, but enjoyed higher profits and came out better off overall. But **farm labourers** were lucky if their wages increased as fast as food prices. During the years of bad harvests, bread prices rose much faster than wages. In 1812, for example, the price of wheat rose to 155 shillings per quarter for several weeks. This caused serious public unrest (see Source C). High food prices also came with the loss of common land during enclosures, and this created more hardship for some farm labourers. On the other hand, there was full employment during the war years.

The wars thus speeded up changes in farming and magnified their effects. But this period of prosperity was followed by at least two decades of depression, and enclosures virtually finished at the end of the war. The first phase of the agricultural revolution was at an end.

SOURCE A

Average wheat prices over five-year periods (in shillings per quarter):

1780–4	47 shillings
1785–9	44 shillings
1790–4	49 shillings
1795–9	65 shillings
1800–4	84 shillings
1805–9	84 shillings
1810–14	102 shillings

From B. R. Mitchell and P. Deane, 'Abstract of Annual Historical Statistics', 1962.

SOURCE B

Enclosure Acts

1700–60	about 4 per year
1760–92	about 40 per year
1792–1815	about 80 per year

From Edmund Seddon, 'Modern Economic History', 1966.

SOURCE C

Sporadic local riots were caused by bad feelings about enclosures in the eighteenth century. But much more serious was public opposition to high bread prices, especially during the war years. This cartoon records a time in 1795 when King George III's carriage was attacked by angry crowds demanding an end to the war and cheaper bread. William Pitt the younger, who was then Prime Minister, is the coach driver.

QUESTIONS

1 Match the people in List A with the developments they are most associated with in List B.

List A	*List B*
Jethro Tull	The use of clover
Viscount Townshend	Durham Shorthorn cattle
Robert Bakewell	*The Annals of Agriculture*
Thomas Coke	New Leicester sheep
Arthur Young	The Norfolk rotation
Andrew Yarranton	The seed drill
The Colling brothers	The Holkham sheepshearings

2 The following list refers to some of the most important influences on the agricultural revolution. Write a short paragraph which includes all of the words and phrases, and explains the role of each and the connections between them.

Food prices / farmers' profits / population / demand for food / enclosures / output of food / farming methods / efficient production.

3 One historian suggests that, between 1700 and 1800:

- grain output in England increased by 45 per cent;
- the area sown with grain increased by 28 per cent;
- the yield of grain per acre increased by 12 per cent.

Assuming that this is true, does it tell us anything about the relative importance of the following changes which took place in the agricultural revolution?

a Enclosures.
b New rotations.
c New seeds.
d Better drainage.
e Marling and fertilizers.
f Selective breeding.
g New tools.

3.7 THE CORN LAWS

EVIDENCE

The end of the wars against France also brought an end to prosperity for British farmers. **Imports** increased from 1814, and this coincided with two bumper harvests. The **supply** of grain thus overtook **demand**, and **prices** began to tumble. The average price of grain in London fell from 112 shillings per quarter in 1812 to 74 shillings in 1814 and 63s in 1815.

The public enjoyed these cheaper food prices. But **farmers** had to sell their produce at lower prices while their costs remained high. Even if tenant farmers could persuade the landowners to lower their rents, they were still burdened with high rates and high interest repayments on the large loans taken out during the war. Lower incomes and high costs meant smaller profits. Many yeomen farmers went bankrupt and lost their farms. **Labourers** suffered too. Wages were slashed, and many lost their jobs as farmers tried to cut their costs.

British politics were at this time dominated by the landed classes. **Voters** among the public, **MPs** in the House of Commons and **peers** in the House of Lords were almost always landowners. Not surprisingly, the government came under heavy pressure to do something to help agriculture (see Source B). There were strong arguments for this besides just looking after the selfish interests of the landowners. Agriculture was the country's biggest **employer**, and was essential to feed the nation during wartime **blockades**. So the whole country's interests seemed threatened. The government introduced a **Corn Bill** to protect agriculture from foreign competition.

The Corn Law of 1815

Thus the **Corn Law of 1815** was passed. It set out to keep wheat prices at about 80 shillings (£4) per quarter by controlling **imports**. It stated that whenever the price of wheat was at or above 80s, imports of wheat were allowed. But that whenever the price was below 80s, then imports were **banned** for at least three months. The theory was that a price above 80s was unfair to the public, and cheap imports would increase supplies and reduce prices; but when the price was below 80s, farmers couldn't make reasonable profits, so cheap imports should be banned, encouraging prices to rise. In theory, the price of wheat would thus average out at 80 shillings per quarter, a price fair to farmers and the public. There were similar arrangements for all of the other grains, like barley and oats.

The Corn Law was unpopular with the public. The government was keeping the price of grain artificially high by keeping cheap foreign grain out of Britain. High grain prices meant high bread prices. At a time of widespread unemployment in many industries this seemed a heartless policy, and the Corn Law was hated by the poorer classes (see Source D). There were riots for several days around Westminster while the Bill was debated in Parliament. In Dundee over 100 shops were plundered as a protest against high food prices.

Unfortunately, the Corn Law didn't please the farmers either. At first it was assumed that **imports** were to blame for the low

SOURCE A

Average wheat prices over five-year periods (in shillings per quarter):

1810–14	102 shillings
1815–19	99 shillings
1820–4	57 shillings
1825–9	62 shillings
1830–4	57 shillings
1835–9	55 shillings
1840–4	57 shillings

From B.R. Mitchell and P. Deane, 'Abstract of Annual Historical Statistics', 1962.

SOURCE B

'In the depressed state of agriculture some relief is surely necessary. Numbers of people have been turned out of employment and most enormous losses have been suffered. If some speedy remedy is not administered, the agricultural interest of the country might soon be completely ruined.'

Lord Binning, speaking in Parliament in the Corn Law debates, 1815.

SOURCE C

SOURCE D

'Betwixt Corn Lords and
the Poor
I've not a slightest
hesitation.
The people must starve
to ensure
The Land its due
remuneration.'

A contemporary rhyme by Thomas Moore. He is saying that the landlords who rely on corn for their wealth have no pity for the poor. The landlords will get their remuneration (money), even if it means that the poor must starve.

SOURCE E

Examples of points on the sliding scale for wheat

Wheat price in London	Import tariff charged
73 shillings	1s 0d
70 shillings	10s 8d
66 shillings	20s 8d
62 shillings	25s 8d

From B.R. Mitchell and P. Deane, 'Abstract of Annual Historical Statistics', 1962.

prices and that banning imports would mean higher prices and better profits. Unfortunately this was not true. British farmers had expanded **domestic production** of grain during the war so much that, except in years of poor harvests, they were producing more grain than was needed. **Supply exceeded demand**, even without imports. Banning imports didn't cause a shortage and therefore didn't make prices rise to the expected levels. The ban did keep out cheap French grain, priced at about 50 shillings per quarter (see Source C), thus annoying the public, but it never raised wheat prices to the level which the farmers wanted. Bad harvests between 1815 and 1819 kept prices up for a while, but they soon slumped to an average of about 58 shillings and stayed stubbornly there for decades (see Source A). The Corn Laws, then, annoyed the public and disappointed the farmers.

Attempts to amend the Corn Laws

The government amended the Corn Laws in 1822, 1828 and 1842 to try to make them more effective, but without success. The change in 1828 was the biggest. Instead of a blanket ban on imported grain, the government introduced a **sliding scale** of import tariffs or duties (taxes). This meant that when grain prices were low, high tariffs kept imports down to safeguard British farmers; as grain prices rose, so the import tariffs fell on a sliding scale, gradually allowing in cheap imports (see Source E). This was a more subtle system for controlling imports, but it didn't change the fact that Britain was producing more grain than it needed, so it had no effect on the depression in farming.

EXERCISE

1. Look at the statistics in Source A. If you were a historian, what would you want to know about them before you would feel confident about using them as evidence?
2. Assuming that you can trust the figures in Source A, can they tell you:
   - **a** the price of wheat in 1812?
   - **b** whether it was easier for people to afford food in 1840–4 than in 1810–14?
   - **c** whether the price of wheat was going up or down between 1810–44?
3. Study Sources B, C and D. How far do they agree about *why* the Corn Laws were passed?
4. Study Source C again. Did George Cruikshank support or oppose the Corn Laws? Explain your answer.
5. 'Source C is clearly biased, so it is useless to historians of the Corn Laws.' Do you agree with this statement?

A Cruikshank cartoon, 1815. The landlords standing nearest to the boat refuse the French corn, and one says: 'We won't have it at any price – we are determined to keep up our own to 80s., and if the poor can't buy it at that price, why they must starve. We love money too much to lower our rents again.' The family on the right prepare to emigrate: 'No, no, masters, I'll not starve but I'll quit my native country where the poor are crushed by those they labour to support.'

3.8 FROM DEPRESSION TO RECOVERY, 1815–45

The period after 1815 was a difficult one for farmers and labourers alike. The huge growth of food production during the war years meant that there was constantly a **surplus of food** on the market. This kept prices low. There was also a **depression in industry** which meant that working people had very little money to spend on food, and this kept food sales down. This was therefore a period of low prices, low profits and low wages in farming.

Tenant farmers also had more than low prices to worry about. **High rents** had been fixed on long leases during the prosperous war period. They also had **tithes** to pay. These were local taxes amounting to one-tenth of each tenant's produce, which they had to pay to the church. Tenants also had **rates** to pay. These were local taxes paid to the parish which were used, among other things, to help the local poor. Tenant farmers' only simple way of keeping costs down was to reduce the wages of their labourers or to sack them.

The **wages** of farm labourers went down, and **unemployment** increased. Wages fell from an average of 15 shillings per week in 1815 to 10 shillings per week in 1822. Before **enclosures**, labourers had been able to make use of the common land. They could keep chickens, geese, pigs, and even a cow to provide them with their own source of eggs, milk and meat in hard times. Before the spread of **factories**, labourers could turn their hands to spinning or weaving in cottage industries to add to their farm wages. But the common land had mostly disappeared, and cottage industry was in decline by the 1820s.

Some labourers turned to **poaching** to fend off starvation. Under the **Game Laws** poaching was punished by whipping, imprisonment or transportation. Poachers using violence against gamekeepers were hanged. Gamekeepers used mantraps to protect their land. Nevertheless, many desperate men were tempted. Two brothers named Lilley were accused of shooting at a gamekeeper in 1829. The elder was 28, married with two children, living on 7 shillings poor relief per week. His brother, aged 22, was earning 6d per day from the parish for his work. They were both convicted and hanged.

The only other protection against starvation was **poor relief** from the parish. Sometimes this took the form of money hand-outs, sometimes shelter in a workhouse, sometimes a poorly paid job (see page 142 for details). Parish poor relief was regarded as degrading and could involve splitting up families. People put up with great suffering rather than go for help to the parish (see Source A).

The harsh winter of 1830 saw the start of widespread rioting called the **Swing Riots**. Bands of labourers attacked the property of landowners, burning hay-ricks and smashing threshing machines which were used by some farmers to separate corn from the straw. Rioting was worst in the south-east and east of England, the main wheat-growing areas (see map). Rumours spread of a mysterious 'Captain Swing' who planned to lead the rioters to revolution. But there was no such leader. The Swing Riots were the desperate protests of starving people with little

SOURCE A

'Leicester, 26 April 1830: Look at the miserable sheds in which the labourers reside, made of mud and straw, bits of glass without frames or hinges merely stuck in the mud wall. Enter them and look at the bits of chairs or stools; the wretched boards tacked together to serve for a table; the floor of pebble, broken brick or bare ground; and survey the rags on the backs of the wretched inhabitants. Wonder if you can why the jails increase.'

From William Cobbett's 'Rural Rides', 1830.

SOURCE B

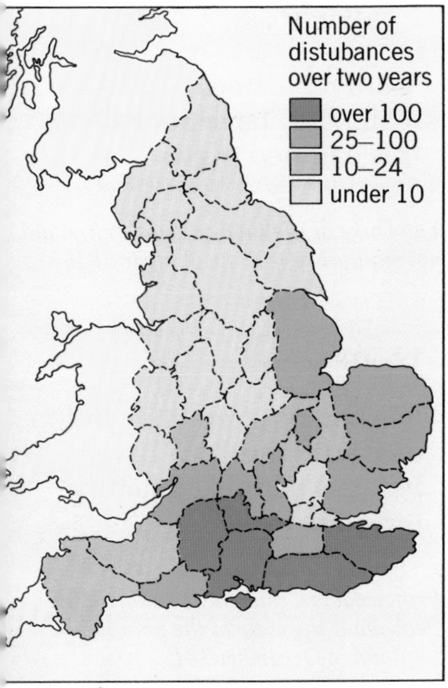

The Swing Riots. Areas of England where rural riots took place, 1830–2.

thought of political change on their minds. However, the landowners were frightened by the possibility of revolution (see Source C). They took strong action. Hundreds of arrests were made; nine men were hanged, 457 transported to far-off colonies and hundreds more imprisoned.

Slowly, however, improvement came. The first relief came to farmers on the lightest soils who could switch away from wheat farming to more profitable vegetables or livestock. But gradually matters improved even for wheat farmers on heavy clay soils unsuited to other crops. **Costs** began to fall. Leases taken out at high wartime rents eventually finished, to be replaced by lower rents. Loans were eventually paid off. The **Poor Law Amendment Act of 1834** reduced the cost of helping the poor, and so rates fell. The **Tithe Commutation Act of 1836** made the payment of rates even easier. Then **prices** began to rise. By 1841 the population of Britain stood at 18.5 million (compared to 12.5 million in 1811), and this meant more demand for farm produce. By the 1840s falling costs and slight upturn in prices meant that profits and prosperity returned to the farms.

SOURCE C

▲ *A cartoon published at the height of the Swing Riots, showing rioters on the left, farmers guarding their hay-rick in the centre and a meeting of landowners on the right.*

◀ *This cartoon, published in January 1830, shows the sorry state of Farmer Giles. His letter says: 'This is to inform you that the children have been received into the workhouse.'*

3.9 REPEAL OF THE CORN LAWS

CAUSATION

The Corn Laws taxed imports of grain to protect farmers from foreign competition. People had argued about these laws ever since they were passed in 1815 (see pages 30–1). But pressure to repeal (abolish) them came to a head in the 1840s.

Manufacturers in industry particularly disliked the Corn Laws. Industry enjoyed **'free trade'** (unrestricted trade, not hindered by tariffs), and industrialists wanted to 'free' trade in grain from the restrictions of the Corn Laws. In 1839 two factory owners, **Richard Cobden** of Manchester and **John Bright** of Rochdale, set up the **Anti-Corn Law League**. It was a well-financed organisation with headquarters in Manchester which sent out newspaper articles, pamphlets and speakers to campaign against the Corn Laws. It used the penny post and railways to send pamphlets to every voter in the country.

The Anti-Corn Law League had a range of arguments. The Corn Laws kept bread prices higher than necessary, it said, which was unfair to the poor. Abolish the Corn Laws, and other countries could sell their cheap grain in Britain, lowering the cost of living. People could then spend more money on more expensive foods, like meat, improving their diet and helping farmers. They could spend money on industrial goods too, helping British industry and creating jobs. The countries which sold their grain in Britain would also then have money to spend on British industrial goods, and this would be good for exports. The Leaguers also said that all of this trade would encourage peace by making countries trading partners rather than rivals.

Cobden became MP for Stockport in 1841 and John Bright MP for Durham in 1843. They campaigned in Parliament for repeal. The Prime Minister was **Sir Robert Peel**, himself the son of a factory owner. He agreed with reducing restrictions on trade. He had cut tariffs on industrial goods in his budgets, so he was a supporter of free trade. But he could not go as fast as Cobden wanted him to (see Source C). He was leader of the **Conservative Party**, the party of most agricultural landowners who almost all opposed repeal.

Landowners said that, if the Corn Laws were abolished, then cheap grain from abroad would flood into Britain. British farmers would be unable to make a profit and would go bankrupt, putting thousands of farm labourers out of work. They said the real reason why the manufacturers wanted cheaper food prices was because they wanted to be able to cut the wages of their workers.

Despite this opposition, Peel decided to repeal the Corn Laws. He didn't think that British farmers needed the protection as much as they had in 1815. He doubted that there were huge stocks of cheap grain in Europe. He also felt that if British farmers were protected from foreign competition for too long, they would become inefficient. Two events in 1845 finally made up his mind. Firstly, about 70 per cent of the **Irish potato crop** was destroyed by a disease. A quarter of the Irish population, 2 million people, relied entirely upon potatoes for survival; mass starvation was threatened. Yet the Corn Laws made it impossible to import

SOURCE A

'Rotten potatoes have done it all. They have put Peel in this damned fright.'

The Duke of Wellington, who at first did not support repeal, speaking in 1845.

SOURCE B

'He had no alternative but to deal with the Corn Laws before a national calamity forced it on us.'

Prince Albert, referring to a talk with Peel about the state of the poor in England in December 1845.

EXERCISE

Here are some causes of the repeal of the Corn Laws in 1846:

- **a** The Corn Laws kept bread prices high, harming the poor.
- **b** Because they kept bread prices high, sales of more expensive foods were low. This harmed farmers.
- **c** They kept bread prices high. This reduced the spare money in people's pockets, keeping sales of manufactured goods low, harming industry.
- **d** They reduced the trade between nations. This reduced friendly ties and made war more likely.
- **e** They had been needed in 1815 to protect farmers but by 1846 were not necessary.
- **f** They protected farmers from competition and thus made them become inefficient.
- **g** They made it harder to help the Irish when the famine started in 1845.
- **h** They made it harder to help the poor in England after the bad 1845 harvest.

SOURCE C

'Papa Cobden taking Master Robert for a free trade walk'. 'Punch' cartoon by Richard Doyle, 1845. Papa Cobden: 'Come along now, Master Robert, do step out.' Master Robert: 'That's all very well, but you know I cannot go as fast as you do.' ▶

1 Group these causes under the following headings:
- Humanitarian causes.
- Economic causes.
- Short-term causes.
- Long-term causes.

(Some may go under more than one heading.) Give reasons for your answers.

2 Which reasons for repeal were most important to:
a the Anti-Corn Law League?
b Sir Robert Peel?

3 Do you think any of the causes given above were *not* important at all?

4 Look at Sources A to C. What do they suggest lay behind repeal according to:
a the Duke of Wellington?
b Prince Albert?
c *Punch* magazine?

5 Why do *you* think the Corn Laws were repealed? In your answer, refer to as many possible causes as you can, showing how the part played by each cause was different.

cheap grain to feed them (see Source A). Secondly, the **harvest in England** was bad; farmers laid off labourers, and food prices began to rise. Reports of terrible suffering in the countryside began to reach London. Again, the Corn Laws kept cheap food out and threatened starvation in England too (see Source B). Peel braved the storm of protest from landowners and repealed the Corn Laws in 1846.

The effects of repeal

The repeal had disastrous effects for **Peel**. The Conservative Party was bitterly split by his actions. He had to resign as Prime Minister.

Neither did the repeal help the **Irish**. Povery in Ireland was so great that many people could not even afford cheaper grain. By 1849 one million Irish had died, and a further one million emigrated to avoid famine.

But the results for **farming** were not bad. Peel had been right. There was no flood of grain from Europe, where the population was rising fast and using up food supplies. Imports of grain did increase slowly, but prices fell only a little. The average price of wheat in the years 1820–46 was 58 shillings per quarter, and this fell only to 53 shillings in 1846–76. Prices of barley, oats and meat actually rose as the population continued to increase. Farm profits and wages therefore did not crash; they improved. Landowners gained too, increasing rents by 25 per cent by 1870. Farmers responded to foreign competition by becoming more efficient, and British agriculture entered a new phase of prosperity called **'high farming'**.

3.10 HIGH FARMING

The fears of widespread bankruptcy in farming after the repeal of the Corn Laws were unfounded. Agriculture enjoyed a period of prosperity after 1846 sometimes called the **'golden age of farming'**.

This was partly because of favourable conditions outside the farmers' control. The size of the **population** of Britain continued to grow rapidly from 18.5 million to 26 million between 1841 and 1871. This meant a bigger market for food. The **economy** was booming too, with rising wages and employment, so people had more money to spend on food. This benefited farmers, as did the new **railway system** which provided a cheap form of transport for farm produce. There were also no huge imports of cheap wheat or meat from abroad at this time to compete with British produce.

But farmers also contributed to their new prosperity. Without the protection of the Corn Laws they couldn't be complacent. They had to keep improving their farming methods to remain efficient. Many farmers followed the advice of a writer, **James Caird**, who described the improvements possible in his book, *High Farming, the Best Substitute for Protection.*

'High farming' involved more **intensive** production using **scientific** methods. New machinery, new fertilizers and better drainage methods were the most common changes. They were intended to increase production without using more land, and using less labourers.

Machinery was introduced to save labour. For example, Dr Patrick Bell's reaping machine (see Source A) had been invented in 1828, but was now improved by manufacturers and sold widely. Other machines which became more commonly used were seed drills and threshers. From about 1850 **steam power** was harnessed to farm work (see Source B). Steam-powered reapers and threshers could do the work of many labourers.

Better **drainage** methods were used to increase yields by stopping seed and crops rotting in the ground. Steam engines could pump excess water from the black silts of the Fens in Cambridgeshire for just 2s 6d (12½p) per acre per year. Factories could produce clay pipes for drainage trenches at a cost of less than £1 per thousand, and Fowler's mole plough (see Source D) could lay them for less than £5 per acre. From 1846, under the Drainage Act, the government could offer farmers help to drain their land.

Fertilizers were also used to increase yields. Guano (bird droppings rich in phosphates) was imported from Peru at a rate of over 100,000 tons a year in the 1850s. Crushed bones and soot were natural substances, but superphosphates, nitrates and other artificial fertilizers were imported from Germany or bought from factories at home. In 1842 Sir John Lawes opened a chemical fertilizer factory in London.

Scientific research lay behind much of this progress. The Royal Agricultural Society was set up in 1838. It financed research and publicized progress in its huge agricultural shows. From 1843 the Royal College of Agriculture at Cirencester provided a scientific

SOURCE A

Bell's reaping machine.

SOURCE B

education to young farmers. In the same year Sir John Lawes set up a scientific research station at Rothamsted.

As a result of all of these developments, **farm production** grew by 70 per cent between 1840 and 1880. Not only was this achieved without using more land, but the number of farm labourers used actually fell by 300,000. With demand booming and transport costs falling, this added up to a period of record profits for farmers. However, it all depended upon profits in a small number of products – cereals and meat – and unfortunately this didn't last long.

SOURCE C

'The farmer need never unyoke his horses from the fields as far as his threshing is concerned. He has only to light his furnace in the morning, by breakfast the steam is up, and before dinner as much grain is thrashed, cleaned and ready for sale as a dozen men could have prepared in a month.'

'Chamber's Journal', 1845.

SOURCE D

'Two horses went to work by the side of a field on a capstan which, by an invisible wire-rope, draws towards itself a low framework, leaving but the trace of a narrow slit on the surface. But it has been dragging after it a string of pipes, following the plough's snout that burrows all the while four feet below ground, twisting itself like a gigantic red worm. So when the framework has reached the capstan, the wire is withdrawn and you are assured that a drain has been invisibly formed under your feet.'

The 'Journal of the Royal Agricultural Society' describing a demonstration of Fowler's mole plough in 1851.

Steam-powered threshing machine and seed drill exhibited at the Great Exhibition, 1851.

3.11 DEPRESSION: 1870–1900

The golden age of farming lasted from 1846 to 1870. The period which followed, from 1870 to 1900, brought so many problems that it is known as the **great depression**. What went wrong?

The big new factor was **foreign competition**. In the middle of the nineteenth century new areas of wheat production were developed abroad. The North American prairies began to yield huge crops of corn. Argentina, Australia and New Zealand began to produce massive quantities of meat, dairy produce and wool. Farmers there had immense areas of cheap land and they used **extensive farming** methods to mass-produce very cheap food.

At first these competitors were no threat to British farmers. Transport costs to Europe were high and it was difficult to keep meat and dairy produce in good condition over such long distances. But this also changed after 1870. **Transport** became cheaper. Railways began to open up the interior of the large continents. Steamships provided cheap transport across the oceans. Shipping wheat across the Atlantic cost 33 cents per bushel in 1870, but only 14 cents by 1881 and a mere 2 cents by 1904. **Refrigeration** became possible. Reece's freezing machine was invented in 1868, and the first cargo of frozen meat left New Zealand for Britain in 1882. **Canning** plants were opened abroad, and tinned meat from South America began to compete with British produce. Food prices began to tumble. Wheat prices, for example, fell by half in thirty years (see Source A).

As if this extra competition was not bad enough, British farmers also had other problems. Between 1874 and 1882 there were only two good harvests of grain (see Source B), and **bad weather** led to pastural farmers losing 3 million sheep with foot rot in 1879 alone. In previous decades, problems like these would have led to shortages, pushing up prices, so farmers' profits would have been protected. But with cheap produce pouring in from abroad, prices stayed low. This meant less profit for British farmers. To make things worse, most farms were rented on long leases, and so farmers' **rents** stayed high.

Wealthy landowners complained loudly to Parliament about the problems of farmers, and **Royal Commissions** were set up in 1879 and 1893 to investigate matters. In 1889 the **Ministry of Agriculture** was set up, providing the government with a permanent department to look after the affairs of farmers. However, there was little the government could do. Cheap imports meant cheap food to the public. No one living in the towns complained about imported food. Many working-class people had the vote by the 1880s, so no government would seriously consider bringing import tariffs like the Corn Laws back to protect the farmers.

But the picture wasn't completely bleak. The effect of cheap imports was worse for some farmers than for others. Pastural farmers found that there was always a market for fresh meat as well as frozen and tinned imported meat. They could also diversify and produce **milk**, which could still not be imported. Better still, the cheap foreign grain which was ruining British arable farmers was a bonus for pastural farmers. It was cheap

SOURCE A

Average wheat prices (in shillings per quarter) 1870–99

1870–4	55 shillings
1875–9	47 shillings
1880–4	42 shillings
1885–9	31 shillings
1890–4	29 shillings
1895–9	27 shillings

From B.R. Mitchell and P. Deane, 'Abstract of Annual Historical Statistics', 1962.

SOURCE B

'A very heavy rainfall began in the early spring which continued without stopping until the end of September. All mechanical work in the fields was blocked by the water and the mud. Barley went to the dogs badly in June and disappeared in July. It first turned yellow and then faded away. Wheat, instead of ripening, turned black. Towards the end of September, the disastrous weather came to an end, leaving ricks of mouldy hay; corn stacks hardly worth threshing; our sheepfolds wiped out or badly depleted; and the farmers' bank balance seriously on the wrong side.'

Mr Kendall, a farmer in Somerset, writing in 1879.

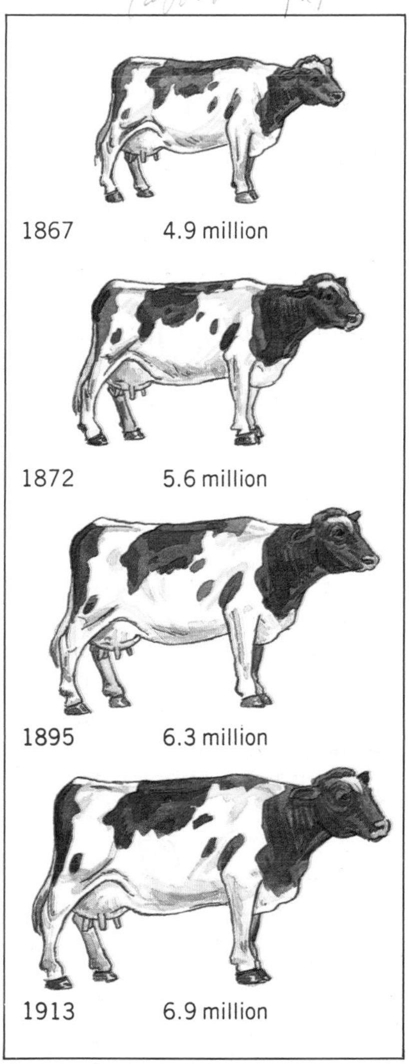

Cattle in Great Britain 1867–1913.

fodder for their animals, reducing their costs. Even some arable farmers had soil suitable for **vegetables** and could switch away from grain. There was a good market for milk and vegetables. The growth of industrial towns meant that many millions of people who did not have access to allotments or gardens could no longer produce their own vegetables or milk. The Anglo-Swiss Condensed Milk Company (later Nestlé) set up a milk-processing factory in 1873, and Wiltshire United Dairies was formed in 1896.

So the great depression in farming wasn't a depression for everyone. It was also a period of adjustment. **Landowners** found that their land was less of an asset than it had been before. Because farm profits fell, so the selling prices of land fell by about a half. Rents fell by about a third. Some of the huge estates of the aristocracy were broken up as their owners began to look for more profitable investments.

Arable farmers suffered if they could not switch to products other than grain. This was the case in many southern counties, especially Essex. The area under wheat was cut by half between 1867 and 1913, more than 1.5 million acres going out of production. However, **pastural farmers** increased their land by 6 million acres in the same period. The population of cattle increased by 2 million. Other types of farming like vegetable production, market gardening and forestry all expanded.

The fate of **agricultural labourers** varied. For those who worked for arable farmers, wages fell, and some labourers lost their jobs. But their food cost less. For labourers who worked in areas of pastural farming, wages held up better. (Although much less labour was required on pastural farming.) Overall, the number of people employed in agriculture decreased by about 300,000 between 1871 and 1911.

These changes in farming caused terrible disruption of lives in the early years of the great depression. By the late 1890s, though, the necessary adjustments had been made, and the decade before 1914 was a much happier one.

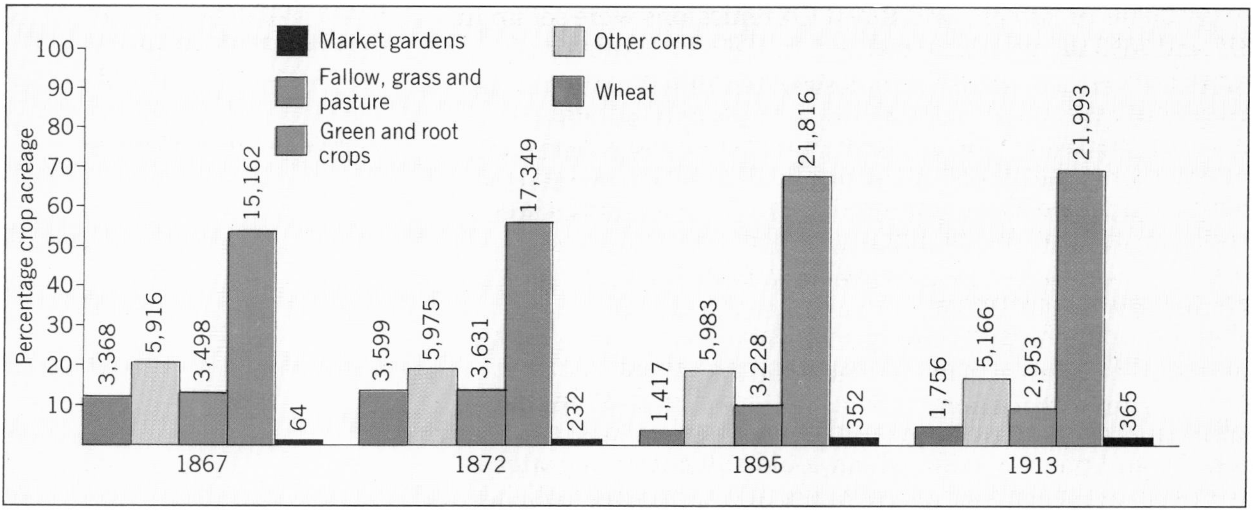

Crop acreage in Great Britain (in thousands of acres).

3.12 AGRICULTURE DURING THE TWENTIETH CENTURY

The First World War

In 1914 **war** broke out in Europe. People in Britain expected the fighting to be over in a few weeks. But as the months went by, it became clear that this would be a long war – and the longer it went on, the more important the role of agriculture became. The German navy had U-boats (submarines) which sank the merchant ships bringing food from abroad. Britain would have to feed itself or starve.

The greatest need was for **staple foods** high in calories (energy value), like wheat and potatoes, rather than luxury foods like meat and butter. Yet it was just these staple foods for which Britain most relied upon foreign supplies. In 1914, 80 per cent of the country's wheat had been imported.

This situation demanded urgent **government action**. In 1915 the Board of Education gave permission for children to miss school to help farmers. In 1916 **War Agricultural Committees** were set up to increase food supplies, and soon parks and playing fields were being ploughed up for planting. The **Corn Production Act** was passed in 1917. This encouraged grain production by guaranteeing minimum prices for corn and minimum wages for farm workers. Some farmers were made to plough up their pastures and plant cereals.

The war changed the face of British agriculture. Huge numbers of women, children and prisoners of war were set to work in the fields to replace the labourers who had gone into the forces. It was a prosperous time for farmers. Limited imports meant shortages and higher prices. Farmers began to use lorries on their farms; and by 1916, 1,000 tractors were in use. The switch to pastural farming since 1870 was sharply reversed (see Source A).

The country had every reason to thank its farmers by the end of the war in 1918. The calorific value of British food production had been increased by 25 per cent in four years, and rationing was avoided until February 1918. However, it was a very artificial prosperity, based on wartime conditions. As soon as the war ended, then the prosperity ended too.

The inter-war years

The **1920s** were a bad decade for British farming. The end of the war brought the return of cheap imports, and prices therefore fell. The Corn Production Act was soon costing the government £35 million in subsidies and it was repealed in 1921. Farmers who had been selling wheat for 86 shillings per quarter in 1920 found that they received only 40 shillings by 1922. Profits slumped; wages were dragged down with them; and there was a rare strike of farm labourers in 1923. This encouraged the Labour government of 1924 to reintroduce **minimum wages** – better for the labourers, but it was the farmers who had to pay.

Once again **competition** from cheap imports was worse in arable products, and so the grain farmers suffered most. The area under grain fell to about one million acres, enough to produce only 15 per cent of British needs. Many arable farmers went out of business; large numbers switched to other products.

SOURCE A

	Output	
	1909–13 average	1918
Wheat	7 m. qtrs	11.6 m. qtrs
Oats	21 m. qtrs	31 m. qtrs
Potatoes	6 m. tons	9 m. tons
Milk	1,900 gallons	1,500 gallons
Beef and Mutton	1 m. tons	0.85 m. tons

The switch back to arable farming, 1914–18.

SOURCE B

A tractor reaping corn, 1928.

SOURCE C

A Buckinghamshire farmer still dependent upon horses for reaping his corn, 1936.

For a while, between 1924 and 1929, switching to dairy products, poultry, pigs, fruit and vegetables allowed some farmers to prosper. But the **world depression** brought a slump in prices after 1929. Wheat prices, which averaged 44 shillings per quarter in the years 1920–4, fell to only 6 shillings 1930–4. This was a general fall in world food prices – farmers worldwide were faced with hardship.

These circumstances led the government to act to help farmers. No government would wish to ban imports to protect agriculture because this would cause unacceptable price rises for the public. But the First World War had shown that it was dangerous to be too dependent upon imports. Britain needed a healthy farming industry. So the intention was to cushion British farmers against the worst effects of foreign competition and at the same time to improve their efficiency.

In 1929 the **Local Government Act** made farmland and buildings exempt from the payment of rates. In 1931 and 1933 two **Agricultural Marketing Acts** allowed farmers to elect **marketing boards** to control the production, price, sales and imports of all milk, hops, potatoes, bacon and pork. These boards set a guaranteed price for each product to ensure farmers a reasonable income. But they also set a maximum output to prevent too much being produced. For example, the **Milk Marketing Board** was set up in 1933. Farmers sold all their milk to the Board at an agreed price; the Board advertised and distributed the milk and sold it to retailers and other outlets such as butter and chocolate manufacturers. This guaranteed farmers a reliable income and gave them the marketing advantages of a large group. The **Wheat Quota Act of 1932** made similar arrangements for wheat farmers, with a guaranteed price of 45 shillings for a limited amount of wheat (the 'quota'), paid by the Wheat Commission. **Subsidies** (government grants), were also offered to encourage production of certain **key crops**. Sugar-beet was the first target; a ten-year subsidy was introduced in 1925, and £30 million had been paid out by 1934. Subsidies and guaranteed prices had the effect of allowing farmers to invest in **machinery** which saved on labour costs and made production more efficient. Combine harvesters and milking machines were introduced, and the number of tractors in British farms increased from 6,000 in 1921 to 50,000 in 1939.

These measures did not reverse the trends which had started in the 1870s but only slowed them down. Cheap imports, particularly of grains, made arable farming less and less attractive to farmers. By 1939 the wheat acreage was down by 800,000. The drift to meat, milk, vegetables and fruit continued (see graph below). By 1939 sales of milk were valued at £68 million while domestic wheat sold for only £9 million, including the subsidy.

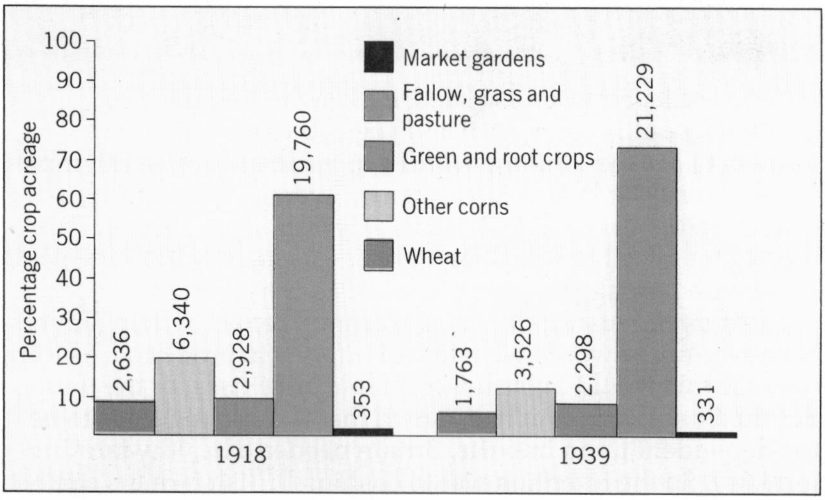

The continued drift away from arable farming. Crop acreage in Great Britain 1918 and 1939. (Figures are in thousands of acres.)

SOURCE D

A 'land girl' ploughing the fields, March 1942. 21-year-old Peggy Ayres was a factory worker from Watford.

Helping agriculture was expensive. State assistance to agriculture stood at £45 million in 1934; by 1939 it had reached £100 million. The prices fixed by the marketing boards were often criticized as too high. However, the importance of ensuring that Britain had its own food supply was obvious once war broke out in 1939.

The Second World War

By 1939 Britain still produced only about 30 per cent of the food it used. Once the war began, German U-boats renewed their attacks on merchant shipping bringing food to Britain. The need for the government to increase efficiency and organization was undeniable.

War Agricultural Committees, organized by the Ministry of Agriculture, were again set up in every county to increase food production. They provided money, fertilizers and machines, but they could also tell farmers what to produce and put parks and gardens under cultivation. Subsidies of £2 an acre were paid to plough up pastoral land and plant grain. An **Agricultural Research Council** investigated ideas for increasing efficiency, and an **Improvements Council** financed the spread of these ideas among farmers. The **Women's Land Army** was formed to train women to replace the labourers who had gone to war (see Source D). By 1944, 25,000 **prisoners of war** had also been put to work on the land. The **Ministry of Food** was set up to ration food supplies.

Once again it had taken a war to bring prosperity back to the farms. Farmers enjoyed the twin benefits of increased output and rising prices. Wheat output rose from 1.6 to 3.4 million tons between 1938 and 1944, and its price returned to 64 shillings per quarter in 1945, a price which hadn't been normal for a hundred years.

SOURCE **E**

These government posters emphasize how important the production and consumption of food became in the Second World War.

3.12

Since 1945

Governments since the Second World War have been keen to protect agriculture. This has been partly for strategic reasons and partly because the cost of imported food has begun to rise. The era of plentiful and cheap imports ended, and so British farmers had to become more efficient and better organized to provide an affordable and reliable food supply for the public.

The **Agriculture Act of 1947** continued the idea of guaranteed prices for farm produce. Prices were to be decided by the Minister of Agriculture in an annual price review. The **Hill Farming Act of 1946** gave subsidies to Scottish hill farmers for improvements in pastural production. Measures like these encouraged farmers to produce more. The **Agriculture Act of 1967** set up the Meat and Livestock Commission to improve the production and marketing of meat and started the Central Council for Agricultural Co-operatives to encourage smaller farmers to form co-operative groups. These were measures to improve the efficiency of farming.

Membership of the **European Economic Community** since 1973 has increased the protection of farming. The EEC has a **Common Agricultural Policy (CAP)** for all of the member states, which Britain has to implement. Under this policy there is a tariff on farm produce imported from outside the Community. This gives farmers in Europe an advantage over foreign producers. Within the Community however, there can be no tariffs on trade between member countries. Small, inefficient farms in some member countries would be ruined by competition from the better organized areas of the Community if they were not helped. So to protect these less efficient farmers, the Community buys up any **surpluses** at a guaranteed price. This gives farmers security and prevents hardship but it has also led to the wheat and butter 'mountains' and the wine 'lake'. Sometimes the Community has had to sell some of this surplus produce at very low prices to other countries, such as the Soviet Union. There has been much criticism of the CAP. Some people feel that it protects farmers too much and reduces the need for efficiency.

SOURCE **F**

By the 1950s a wide variety of machinery was common on British farms.

AGRICULTURE AND SOCIETY

The changes that took place in agriculture after 1700 were all connected with many other changes taking place in society. It is important to be aware of these connections.

Agriculture and population

The rapid growth of the **population** between 1700 and 1870 was a **cause** of agricultural change. More people meant more demand for food; this led to a rise in food prices and thus bigger profits. Farmers who could meet this demand for food could make more money. They changed their methods of production and increased their output.

On the other hand, it would have been impossible for the population to grow so rapidly if British farmers had not been able to increase the size of the food supply. So, in this sense, population increase was also a **result** of agricultural change.

But the rate of population increase slowed dramatically after 1870. Therefore the growth in domestic demand for food slowed down. Since 1870 the problem for farmers has been overabundance of food, made worse by cheap imports. The dominant change has thus been the switch to higher-profit, higher-quality and often perishable foods, like meat and milk.

Agriculture and industry

Agriculture has managed to feed Britain's population with an ever decreasing proportion of the labour force. In 1700 about 75 per cent of the population was employed in agriculture. By the early twentieth century the figure had fallen to less than 10 per cent. This has released a huge share of the labour force to work in **industry**.

On the other hand, industry has also benefited agriculture. The machinery which has been introduced in to farms increasingly since about 1830 has often been pioneered by British industry, like Ferguson tractors, developed in the 1920s.

Agriculture and war

The wars against France (1793–1815) and the First and Second World Wars (1914–18 and 1939–45) had immense effects upon farmers (see pages 28–9 and 40–4 for details). Sometimes these effects have been temporary, like the switch back to wheat farming in the First and Second World Wars; sometimes permanent, like the enclosures of the 1790s.

Agriculture and the government

The story of the past 200 years has been one of increasing **government intervention** in farming. In the eighteenth century the government hardly interfered at all in the lives of farmers. The 1815 Corn Laws were intervention in a crisis. Similarly, during the world wars, the government took sweeping emergency powers. However, since 1945 the government has seen it as its role to manage the development of agriculture for the benefit of the nation.

CONCLUSION

1 Draw a time line representing the years 1700 to the present day. Then:
   - a divide your time line into *sections* so that each section is a period in the history of farming with its own distinct features. (For example, you might choose 1815 to 1845 as a period.)
   - b discuss your divisions with other people and try to justify any differences.
   - c write notes on your time line to show the distinctive features of each period. (For example, for the period 1815–45 you could write: 'low grain prices', 'Corn Laws in force', 'low incomes for landowners, tenant farmers and labourers', 'sliding scale', 'Swing Riots'.)

2 Put yourself in the position of a tenant farmer renting a farm with a mixed output of grain and livestock in the Midlands. Choose a year between 1700 and the present day when you would be at your most prosperous and contented. Explain why you have chosen that year in contrast to others.

3 The text on this page shows the connections between agriculture and other areas of society since 1700. Write paragraphs showing the links since 1700 between:
   - a farming and *science*.
   - b farming and *transport*.

4.1 POWER

Windmills

Windmills had been used in Europe since the twelfth century, and they had some advantages over other sources of power. They were cheap to build and cost virtually nothing to run. Plenty of people understood how to make and run them. There were improvements in the eighteenth century. In 1745 Lee invented the **fan tail** which kept the sails pointing to the wind; while in 1772 Meikle improved the design of the sails themselves, so they could be adjusted to wind strength. Earlier, in 1754, Smeaton had started using metal rather than wood in the construction of windmills. Finally Mead's invention of the **centrifugal governor** (1787) made their operation almost automatic.

However, the advantages of windmills were outweighed by their disadvantages. They did not produce much power, about 15 horsepower at best, and they worked only on windy days.

Water power

The Romans had been the first to use **water power** in Europe, and, like wind power, its use was improved in the eighteenth century. In 1759 Smeaton showed that the **undershot** wheel was only 22 per cent efficient, whereas the **overshot** wheel was nearly 60 per cent efficient. Later, the **breastshot** wheel was developed, which was 65 per cent efficient. Wheels came to be made of iron, so they could be bigger and produce more power. The largest early nineteenth-century wheel could produce up to 200 horsepower – more than any steam engine at the time.

Water power also had its disadvantages, however. Dry summers and ice in winter could stop the wheels. Water-mills were often expensive to make, and other mills upstream could interfere with the flow of water. Worst of all, it was possible to build a water-mill only near a fast-flowing stream or river.

Early steam power – Savery and Newcomen

Thomas Savery patented the first British **steam engine** in 1698, designed to pump water out of mines. However, it didn't work very well. In 1712 Thomas Newcomen invented a **steam pump** which did work. Because of Savery's patent he had to join with Savery to sell it. Newcomen's engine produced **vertical motion** – it could drive something up and down. This was ideal for working a pump, and his engine was adapted to blow the bellows of blast furnaces as well. However, most machines wanted power in the form of **rotary motion**, where something could be turned round. Both wind and water power produced rotary motion. In all about 300 Newcomen steam engines were in use by 1800, most of them powering pumps which drained coal mines. Newcomen's engine was very expensive to run, because it used vast amounts of coal.

The development of steam power – Watt and Boulton

James Watt was a scientific instrument maker at Glasgow University. Given a model of Newcomen's steam engine to repair, he began to think about ways of improving it. By 1765 he

SOURCE A

'13 July 1733. Yesterday I was obliged to blow out the new furnace, our water being quite gone . . .'

From letters written by Richard Ford, manager of Coalbrookdale Ironworks.

SOURCE B

'I had two motives in offering you my assistance, friendship for you and love of an ingenious money-getting project. I presume your engine would require money, very accurate workmanship and extensive correspondence with customers to make it turn out to the best advantage. To keep the work out of the hands of the multitude of practical engineers, who from ignorance would affect its reputation, and to produce the most profit, my idea was to settle a manufactory near my own, by the side of the canal. From this manufactory we would serve all the world with engines of all sizes. We could engage and instruct some excellent workmen, with more excellent tools than it would be worth any man's while to get for one single engine. We could make the engine 20 per cent cheaper than otherwise, and with as great a difference in accuracy as there is between the blacksmith and the mathematical instrument maker.'

Letter from Boulton to Watt, 1769.

had an idea: use less fuel by cooling the steam in a separate condenser. He went into partnership with John Roebuck to make the engine, and they took out a patent in 1769. However, their engine did not work. Probably the craftmanship of the workers who built it was not accurate enough.

In 1773 Roebuck went bankrupt, and Watt's idea could have died. However, Matthew Boulton took over Roebuck's share of the patent and persuaded Watt to come to Birmingham to try again. Birmingham was in the middle of an area where great advances in metalworking were happening. New techniques were used to build an engine to Watt's design, and in 1776 the first working engine was installed in Bloomfield Colliery. With Boulton's encouragement, and the help of his foreman William Murdock, Watt improved the engine. In 1781 he developed **sun and planet gear** which gave his engine rotary as well as vertical motion. The next year saw the **double action** engine, where steam both pushed the piston up and, from the other side, pushed it down. **Parallel motion** (1784) and the **centrifugal governor** (1788) made sure the output of power was even.

Boulton concentrated on selling the engines. Before their patent ran out in 1800, 496 had been sold. Bad payers, and piracy of their ideas by other firms, meant they did not make vast profits, but by the 1790s they were financially successful. The big selling points of Watt and Boulton's engine were rotary motion and its cheapness to run (it used a quarter of the coal used by a Newcomen engine). Boulton charged one-third of the savings in running costs between the two engines rather than a fixed price to encourage people to change to his engine. Even so, in 1800 there were probably fewer Watt and Boulton engines in use than others.

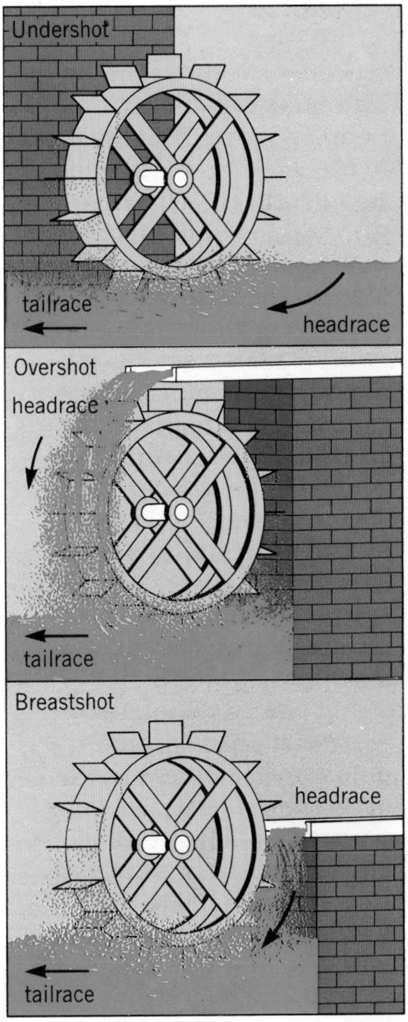

Importance of the steam engine

The steam engine was one of the key developments of the Industrial Revolution.

- It provided constant power, unlike wind and water, and it provided more power than muscle power ever could.
- It could be used in many different industries. By 1800 steam power was used in mines and brewing and in the manufacture of sugar, malt, textiles, iron, flour and pottery.
- It encouraged the growth of factories. The cost of setting up a steam engine was high, and it was better to have it drive several machines rather than one.
- It allowed factories to be built anywhere, not just beside fast-flowing streams and rivers.
- The manufacture of steam engines became an important industry in itself.
- The use of steam engines had a 'knock-on' effect for other industries. More coal was needed as fuel. More iron was used as people found wooden machines were not strong enough to be run by steam engines.

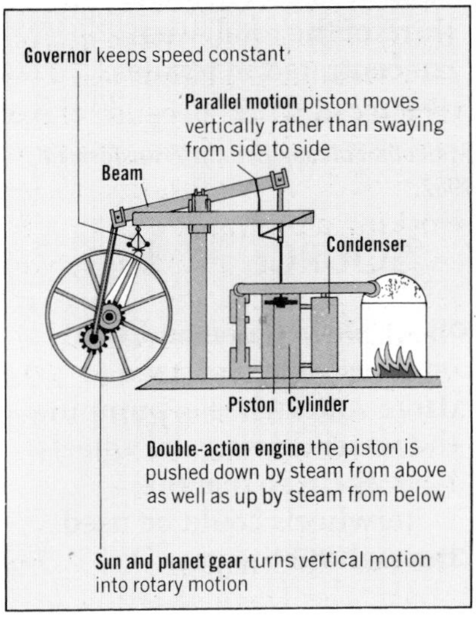

The 1787 version of Watt and Boulton's engine.

4.2 THE SPREAD OF THE STEAM ENGINE

SOURCE A

'The first steam-driven cotton factory was at Papplewick in 1785; the first in Manchester was opened in 1792 and by 1802 there were said to be 52 steam-powered cotton mills in the Manchester district. Yet these were all spinning mills. Cotton weaving remained a handicraft industry, and not until the 1830s did the quantity of cotton cloth woven on steam-powered looms exceed that produced by handloom weavers. Even for spinning, more yarn was produced by water-driven machines in 1800 than by steam power, although by 1815 steam had become dominant. In other branches of textiles, such as woollens, worsteds and linens, the advance of steam power was slower, and outside the textile factories, its adoption was very limited. As late as 1870, of a total steam horsepower of 1,980,000, about 580,000, nearly a third of the total, was concentrated in textiles.'

Malcolm Falkus, 'Britain Transformed', 1987.

SOURCE B

'Both Newcomen and Watt engines were also used to drive waterwheels, pumping the water driving the wheels back again so that the waterwheels could be used throughout the year.'

Malcolm Falkus, 'Britain Transformed', 1987.

SOURCE C

Pithead scene about 1820, including a Newcomen engine.

SOURCE D

The Severn valley.

SOURCE E

Heckington Mill, Lincolnshire, built in 1830.

SOURCE F

'It is not too much to say that steam engines are found in far greater numbers in England, than are water and windmills with us. Also they are found in all possible sizes, of better or worse construction. Those around Swansea are used for different purposes. Some pumped the water out of the coal mines, others hauled coal to the surface, and still others set rolling mills, stamping machines etc. in motion. Several of them were of older design, had a less pleasing appearance and consumed much fuel.'

Diary of a Swedish traveller and industrial spy, 1802–3.

EXERCISE

1 Study the information about steam engines on pages 46–7. When was the steam engine fully developed? Explain your answer.

2 Does your answer to question **1** agree with, or contradict, the evidence of Source F? Explain your answer.

3 What sorts of power are being used in Source D? Give reasons for your answer.

4 What does Source C tell you about the use of steam engines?

5 What do Sources E and G suggest about the uses of power in the nineteenth century? Give reasons for your answer.

6 'As soon as they were technically perfect, steam engines became the most important and the most common source of power for industry.' Do you agree? Give reasons for your answer.

SOURCE G

Killhope Lead Mill, built about 1860.

4.3 CAPITAL, INVENTORS AND ENTREPRENEURS

Source A shows how much it cost the Kennet & Avon Canal Company to put one steam engine in one pumping station. This was quite a small cost for the company, which also had to buy the land the canal ran through, dig the canal, make locks, build bridges, build lock-keepers' houses and build warehouses, to say nothing of paying an engineer to design the canal. All this before it made one penny in charges for using the canal. Having the right money available at the right time was just as important in the Industrial Revolution as having the power to run machines.

Definitions

Capital is the money used to pay for setting up a business or buying a new machine. The Kennet & Avon Canal Company spent £785 19s 2d of its capital on buying the steam engine. All the time the company owned the engine it could, if it was desperate for money, sell it. So the second-hand value of the engine became part of the company's **assets**. These were things which could be turned into money if needed. If capital was borrowed from a bank, then **interest** would be paid on the money borrowed.

Some businesses (like canals) cost so much to set up that one person could not afford it by themselves. People grouping together to run businesses were called **trusts** (like the Turnpike Trusts) or **joint stock companies** (like the Kennet & Avon Canal Company) (see pages 82 and 89). People could buy **shares** in companies. When the company made a profit they would get as many shares in the profit as they owned shares in the company. Some companies were **limited liability companies**. This meant that if the company went bankrupt the shareholders could loose only the money they had paid for their shares. In ordinary companies people who owned shares could loose everything else they owned if the company had debts it could not pay. Limited liability companies could be set up only by a special Act of Parliament before 1862, and there were only a few, mainly railways.

Some new inventions were granted **patents**. Boulton and Watt had a patent on their steam engine until 1800. This meant they were the only people allowed to make and sell them. If anyone else started to sell a steam engine with the same principles, Boulton and Watt could, and did, take them to court and get them stopped. Patents encouraged people to risk their money backing a new invention, because if it was successful the patent would allow them to make a lot of profit.

Entrepreneur is the name often given to the men who ran the businesses of the Industrial Revolution. They had to decide how much capital to invest, what to make and how to try and sell it. Many of them made vast fortunes. Others finished their lives bankrupt. They were not always the men who invented the new machines and systems, but rather the people who made them work. In the partnership between Boulton and Watt, Boulton was the main entrepreneur, while Watt was the inventor.

SOURCE A

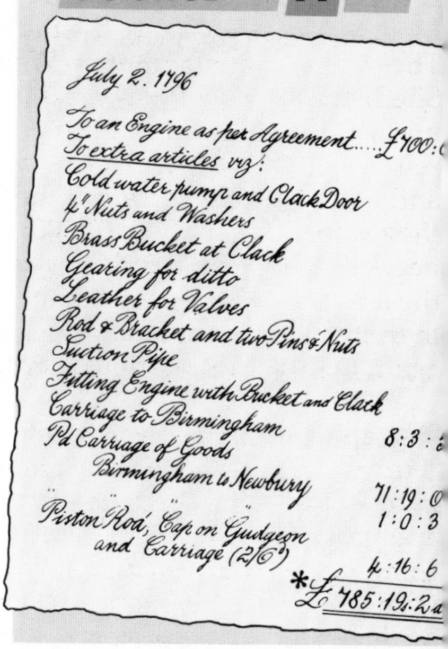

July 2. 1796

To an Engine as per Agreement.... £700:

To extra articles viz:

Cold water pump and Clack Door

4" Nuts and Washers

Brass Bucket at Clack

Gearing for ditto

Leather for Valves

Rod & Bracket and two Pins & Nuts

Suction Pipe

Fitting Engine with Bucket and Clack

Carriage to Birmingham 8:3:

Pd Carriage of Goods

Birmingham to Newbury 71:19:0

" " " 1:0:3

Piston Rod, Cap on Gudgeon and Carriage (2/6) 4:16:6

*£785:19:2d

A bill from Boulton and Watt to the Kennet & Avon Canal Company, 1796.

SOURCE B

'Get rid of the dronish, sleepy and stupid indifference, which enchains men in the exact paths of their forefathers, without enquiry, without thought and without ambition, and you are sure of doing good. What trains of thought, what a spirit of exertion, what a mass of power of effort have sprung in every path of life from the works of such men as Brindley, Watt, Arkwright?'

Arthur Young, 'Tours in England and Wales' about 1800.

Industry – capital investment

Most businesses during the Industrial Revolution started small. The capital needed to set up Walker Brothers' iron foundry near Sheffield in 1741 was about £10. Their foundry shows the way many businesses grew. Each year most of the profits were reinvested in the foundry, to provide new and better machines and buildings. The assets of the foundry grew quickly: by 1746 they were £600; in 1750, £2,500; and in 1760, £10,000. The factories needed in the textile industry cost more. A large factory using all the latest techniques, like Jedediah Strutt's in Belper, cost £5,000 to build, as much again to stock with machinery and as much again to buy the material to start production with.

Transport – capital investment

Turnpikes, canals and (later) railways needed much more capital investments than industry did. They could not easily start small and grow by reinvesting their profits. They needed to be complete to attract business. Only the Bridgewater Canal was small enough to be financed by one man, the Duke of Bridgewater. The original canal was only seven miles long and cost about £200,000 to build. It made profits of about £80,000 a year. These profits encouraged many people to invest in canal companies in the next few years. In all about £20 million of capital was invested in canal companies before 1830, much more than was invested in industry. This was a small sum compared with the money invested in railways in the following fifty years. Because transport needed so much capital, people got used to companies rather than family businesses.

Inventors and entrepreneurs

Part of the success of the Industrial Revolution was due to the new inventions. Machines changed the way people worked, and often increased profits. Some of the inventors were also successful entrepreneurs. Richard Arkwright may or may not have really invented the machines his name was linked with, but he was certainly a great entrepreneur. He had faith in the inventions; he risked his money and persuaded other people to risk theirs. He got very rich in the process. When he died he left about £500,000, which was a vast fortune.

Without the inventors, industry as we know it could not have started. Without the entrepreneurs, it could not have developed. They decided which risks to take. When they were successful they laid the foundations for our industry today.

SOURCE C

Arkwright's mill, Cromford, Derbyshire.

ACTIVITIES

1 Do you think the attitudes expressed in Source B were important to the success of the Industrial Revolution? Explain your answer.

2 Compare Source C with Source C on page 48. Which industry do you think had the higher capital costs at the time, textiles or mining?

3 How much capital was needed to set up Strutt's mill in Belper?

4 a Why were the capital needs of the Kennet & Avon Canal Company and the Walker Brothers so different?
  b Does this explain why only one of these businesses was a company? Explain your answer.

4.4 THE DOMESTIC SYSTEM

EVIDENCE

The **domestic system** was common before the Industrial Revolution. Nails, shoes, stockings, lace, chains, hats and gloves were all made this way. Because **textiles** were the biggest industry however, we usually think of the domestic system in textiles.

Wool goes through various processes on its way to becoming cloth. First the wool was **washed**, then **carded** to make all the fibres run the same way, then **spun** into thread. The thread was then **woven** into cloth, and the cloth was **cropped** and **fulled** (processes which made it thicker and improved the quality). In the domestic system most of these processes would be done by families in their own homes. Clothiers were merchants who had the capital to buy the wool. They arranged for it to be taken to **outworkers**, who would wash, card, spin and weave it. The clothier would then have the wool collected, pay the outworkers, take the wool somewhere else to be finished and then market it (see page 15).

The whole family would usually take part in the work. Children washed and carded, women spun, and men wove. Sometimes the family would rent the tools they needed, such as a weaving loom, from the clothier. The family would often have a small plot of land, and maybe keep a few animals as well. Work was usually collected on a Saturday; it was common for families to work very long hours just before it was collected, and not work at all early in the week. They called an extra day on their weekend **Saint Monday**.

SOURCE A

'The family were at that time chiefly employed by Samuel and James Broadbent of Cannon Street. The work was for the most part handkerchiefs, and occasionally silk and cotton garments or handkerchiefs. The 'bearing-home' wallet was often both bulky and heavy; and when it happened to be too much so for one person to carry, a neighbour's wallet would be borrowed and the burden divided in two, and I would go with my uncle.

'The warehouse of Messers Broadbent was nearly at the top of Cannon Street. We mounted some steps to a landing place, one side of which was railed off with a banister, and the other furnished with a seat for weavers to rest upon when they arrived. Here we should probably find half a dozen weavers and winders waiting their turn to deliver work and receive fresh material. The business between workmen and putter-out was generally done in an amicable, reasonable way. If the work was really faulty, the weaver was shown the fault, and cautioned against repeating it. If the length or weight were not what it should be, he was told of it, and would be expected to set it right, or account for it, at his next bearing home.

'It would sometimes happen that warp or weft would not be ready until after dinner, and on such occasions my uncle would go downstairs, get paid at the counting house, and from there go to the public house where we lunched on bread and cheese or cold meat, bread and ale. After which, my uncle would go again to the warehouse, and getting what material he wanted, would buy a few groceries and tobacco in town and we wended our way towards home.'

Samuel Bamford, 'Early Days', 1849, describing his life as a silk weaver about 1800.

SOURCE B

▼ *Domestic workers, c.1780.*

SOURCE C

'Within we saw the houses full of lusty fellows, some at the dye vat, some at the loom, others dressing the cloths. The women and children carding, or spinning. All employed from the youngest to the oldest. Scarce any thing above four years old, but its hands were sufficient for its own support. The people in general live long; they enjoy a good air. Under such circumstances hard labour is naturally attended with the blessing of health, if not riches.'

Daniel Defoe, 'A Tour through the Whole Island of Great Britain', 1724.

SOURCE D

'Their children grew up in the fresh country air. If they could help their parents at work it was only occasionally. Of eight or twelve hours' work for them, there was no question.'

Friedrich Engels, 'The Condition of the Working Class in England', 1845.

SOURCE E

Weavers' cottages, built about 1800.

SOURCE F

Outworkers in Yorkshire, 1814.

SOURCE G

'I have been in many dwellings of weavers, in remote, vile courts and alleys, usually in cellars. Often half-a-dozen of these handloom weavers, several of them married, live together in a cottage with one or two work rooms, and one large sleeping room. Their food consists almost exclusively of potatoes, with perhaps oatmeal porridge, rarely milk, and scarcely ever meat. "See," cries the bourgeois, triumphantly, "see how these poor creatures must famish, while the mill workers are thriving, and then judge the factory system."'

Friedrich Engels, 'The Condition of the Working Class in England', 1845.

EXERCISE

1 Did Samuel Bamford approve of the domestic system? Give reasons for your answer.

2 Do you think the artist of Source B had an attitude about the domestic system? Explain your answer.

3 Do Sources C and D agree about the domestic system?

4 **a** What is unusual about the weavers' cottages in Source E?
b How do you think this was linked to the domestic system?
c Is this the sort of cottage Samuel Bamford would have lived in? Give reasons for your answer.

5 **a** What industry did the people in Source F work in?
b Do you think this is a reliable source about their working lives? Give reasons for your answer.

6 How can you explain the two different views of the domestic system given in Sources F and G?

7 Copy each of the following statements, and then say how far you think it is supported or contradicted by the sources in this unit.
a The domestic system was always pleasant to work in.
b The domestic system died out as soon as the first factories were built in the late eighteenth century.
c Conditions for workers in the domestic system differed according to the industry they worked in, the area they lived in and the time being described.

4.5 INVENTIONS IN THE TEXTILE INDUSTRY

While the domestic system applied to both cotton and woollen textiles, the developments of the eighteenth century affected the cotton industry first. Some of the techniques were more suited to cotton, and the woollen industry was more set in its ways.

John Kay's flying shuttle, 1733 If cloth being woven was wider than the weaver's arms could reach (called broadcloth) two weavers were needed to pass the shuttle back and forth. The flying shuttle used hammers to knock the shuttle back and forth, so broadcloth could be woven by one person and not two.

Strutt's improved stocking frame, 1759 The stocking frame was a machine for knitting socks. Ribbed socks, which were more fashionable, could be knitted only by hand until Strutt's improved stocking frame, which could produce both ribbed and plain knitting.

Robert Kay's drop box, 1760 Robert, John's son, improved the flying shuttle with the drop box. This allowed different coloured threads to be used and changed automatically, and so patterned cloth could be woven.

James Hargreaves's spinning jenny, 1765 The previous three inventions increased the demand for spun thread, and it was hard for spinners to keep up with demand. It took five spinners, each working on a one-thread spinning wheel, to supply one weaver. The spinning jenny spun 8 threads at a time. Later modifications increased the number of threads to 12, then 16, then 20, and then, with power-driven machines, to 80 and 100. The smaller versions (up to 20 threads) were hand-powered and used at home. Larger versions were water-powered and used in factories. The thread produced was rather soft, and suitable only for weft.

Arkwright's water frame, 1769 This produced stronger and coarser thread. It was suitable for the warp, but not for the weft. A much larger machine than the jenny, the first was horse-powered, but Arkwright switched to water power. They could be used only in factories. In 1790 Arkwright adapted the water frame so that it could be driven by a steam engine.

Crompton's mule, 1779 A cross between the water frame and the jenny, this produced thread that was soft but strong and could be used for both the weft and the warp. The first version was hand-powered, but Crompton did not patent the idea, and it was soon adapted to factory use. In 1790 William Kelly produced a water-powered version which spun 300 threads at once.

Cartwright's power loom, 1785 Now that spinning was mechanized, there was a weaving bottleneck. Cartwright's loom did not work well at first, and it became fully reliable only after Horrocks produced a metal version in 1803. Richard Roberts significantly improved the design further in 1822.

Witney's cotton gin, 1793 This speeded the processing of raw cotton in North America before it was shipped to Britain.

Robert's self-acting mule, 1825 This mule, which spun 2,000 threads, did not need to be supervised by a skilled spinner. A child could be employed instead.

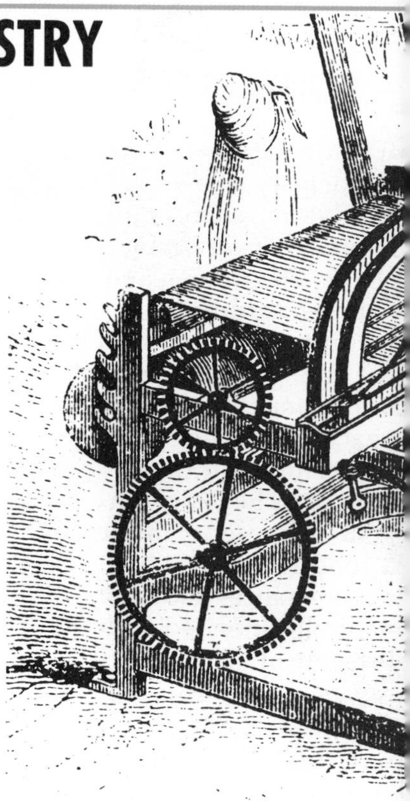

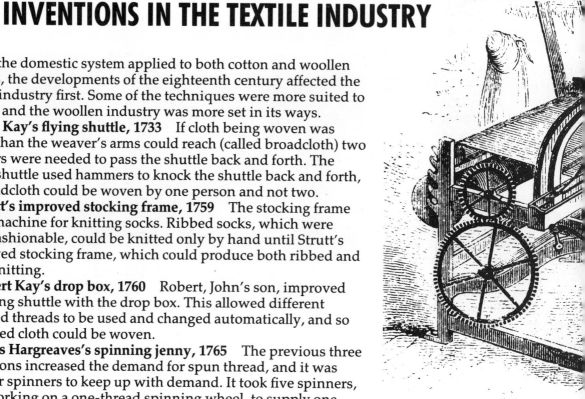

Nineteenth-century power loom.

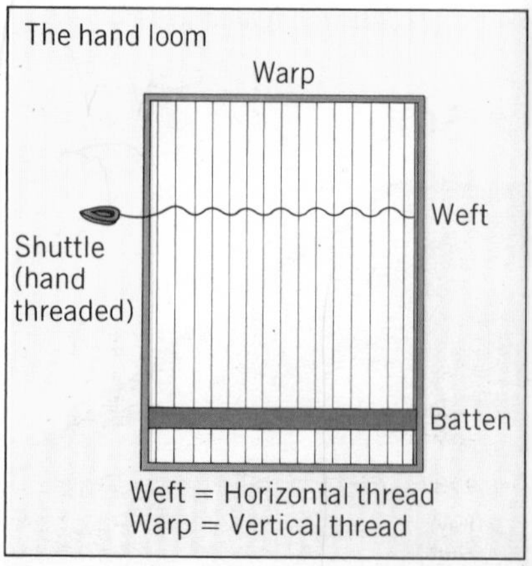

Terms used in weaving. The weft, which is the vertical thread, has to be strong enough not to break while being stretched on the loom.

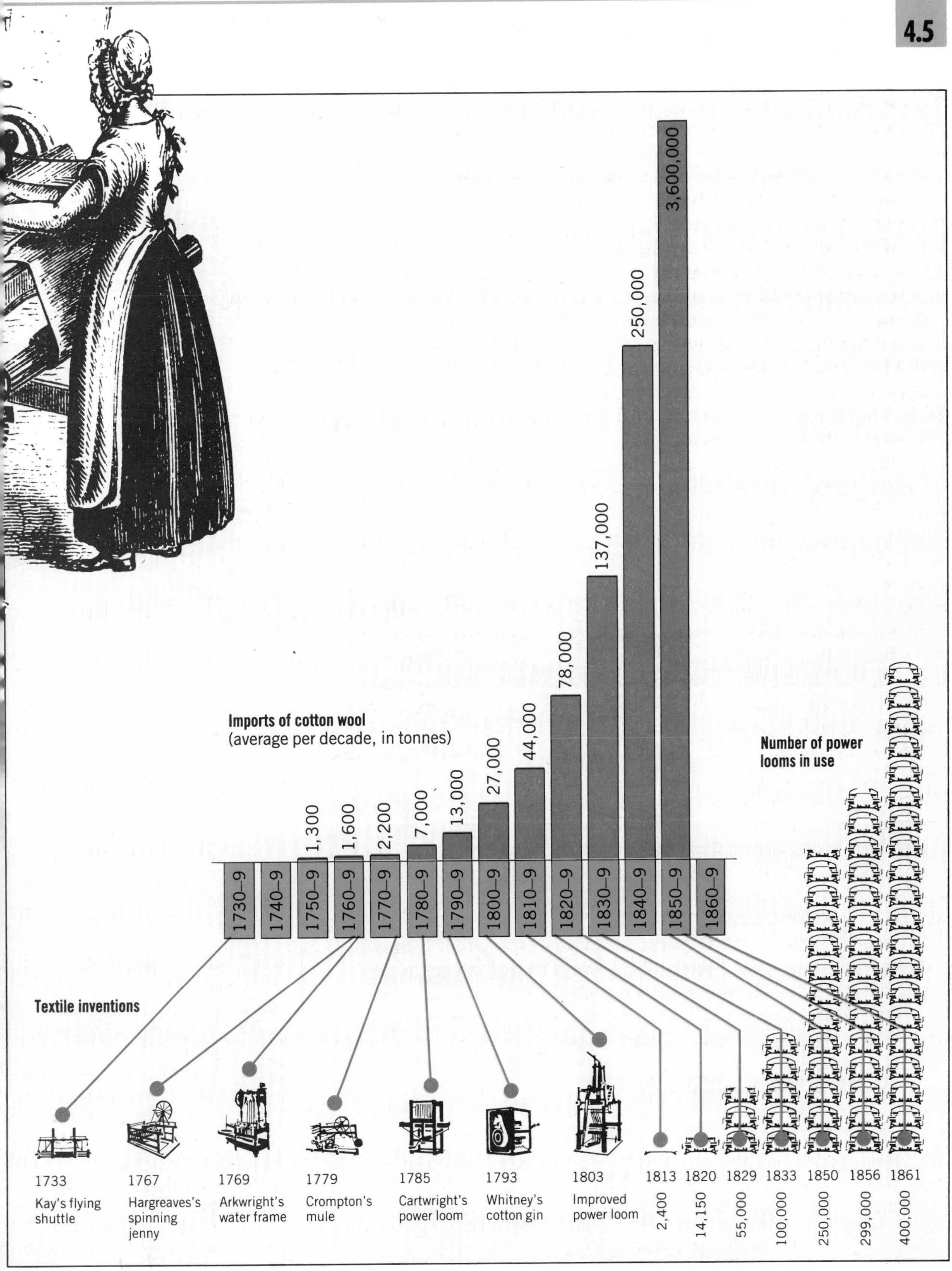

The inventions, the use of power looms and the import of raw cotton. Since all cotton had to be imported, the figure for imports shows us how much was made over a ten-year period.

4.6 THE FACTORY SYSTEM

CAUSATION

In 1750 most people worked in small groups. If they did not work in agriculture they probably worked at home or in small workshops. There were some larger employers – shipbuilding yards, breweries and some silk mills, for instance. Few places employed more than 100 people. By 1850 this had changed. Large factories were common places of work. The most important industry had changed too. In 1750 it had been the woollen industry, but by 1850 it was the cotton industry.

This unit looks at some of the causes and consequences of this change to the **factory system**. It was not a simple change which happened overnight. The cotton industry was almost completely factory-based by 1850. The first cotton factories had been built in the 1780s, and by 1800 most cotton spinning was done in factories. However, it was not until the 1830s that cotton weaving was dominated by factories.

SOURCE A

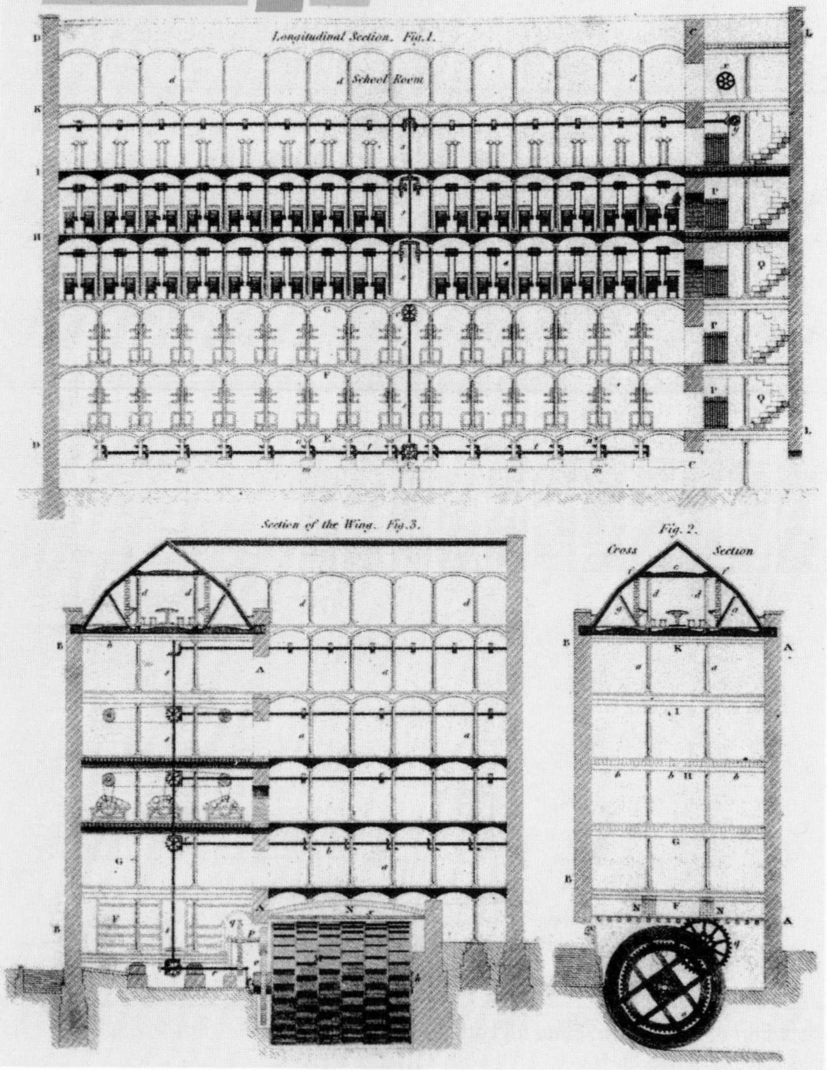

Plans of Jedediah Strutt's cotton mill in Belper, 1819.

SOURCE B

1780 40 shillings

1812 13 shillings

1860 5 shillings

Price of a length of cotton.

The inventions

1733	John Kay's flying shuttle
1759	Strutt's improved stocking frame
1760	Robert Kay's drop box
1765	Hargreaves's spinning jenny
1769	Arkwright's water frame
1779	Crompton's mule
1785	Cartwright's power loom
1803	Horrocks's metal power loom
1822	Roberts's improved power loom
1825	Roberts's self-acting mule

Note: for details of these inventions, see pages 54–5.

SOURCE C

'The Hebble Mill in Wheatley near Halifax, being three stories high containing three rooms each 26 m long and 10 m wide and three other rooms. Each with drums for machinery turned by a water-wheel 7 m in diameter and 2 m wide, and a crank steam engine, cylinder 1 m in diameter with two large boilers. The water-wheel is supplied by Hebble Brook and a spacious dam, the fall of water 7 m. A warehouse adjoining 41 m by 7 m and four stories high with a smith's shop at the end of it. A dyehouse 64 m long and 5.5 m wide and at the end of it a building 2 stories high, 6 m by 5.5 m.'

Advertisement describing a factory for sale, 'Leeds Intelligencer', 13 August 1804.

SOURCE D

RULES
TO BE OBSERVED
By the Hands Employed in
THIS MILL.

RULE 1. All the Overlookers shall be on the premises first and last.

2. Any Person coming too late shall be fined as follows:—for 5 minutes 2d, 10 minutes 4d, and 15 minutes 6d, &c.
3. For any Bobbins found on the floor 1d for each Bobbin.
4. For single Drawing, Slubbing, or Roving 2d for each single end.
5. For Waste on the floor 2d.
6. For any Oil wasted or spilled on the floor 2d each offence, besides paying for the value of the Oil.
7. For any broken Bobbins, they shall be paid for according to their value, and if there is any difficulty in ascertaining the guilty party, the same shall be paid for by the whole using such Bobbins.
8. Any person neglecting to Oil at the proper times shall be fined 2d.
9. Any person leaving their Work and found Talking with any of the other workpeople shall be fined 2d for each offence.
10. For every Oath or insolent language, 3d for the first offence, and if repeated they shall be dismissed.
11. The Machinery shall be swept and cleaned down every meal time.
12. All persons in our employ shall serve Four Weeks' Notice before leaving their employ; but L. WHITAKER & SONS, shall and will turn any person off without notice being given.
13. If two persons are known to be in one Necessary together they shall be fined 3d each; and if any Man or Boy go into the Women's Necessary he shall be instantly dismissed.
14. Any person wilfully or negligently breaking the Machinery, damaging the Brushes, making too much Waste, &c., they shall pay for the same to its full value.
15. Any person hanging anything on the Gas Pendants will be fined 2d.
16. The Masters would recommend that all their workpeople Wash themselves every morning, but they shall Wash themselves at least twice every week, Monday Morning and Thursday morning; and any found not washed will be fined 3d for each offence.
17. The Grinders, Drawers, Slubbers and Rovers shall sweep at least eight times in the day as follows, in the Morning at 7½, 9½, 11 and 12; and in the Afternoon at 1½, 2½, 3½, 4½ and 5½ o'clock; and to notice the Board hung up, when the black side is turned that is the time to sweep, and only quarter of an hour will be allowed for sweeping. The Spinners shall sweep as follows, in the Morning at 7½, 10 and 12; in the Afternoon at 3 and 5½ o'clock. Any neglecting to sweep at the time will be fined 2d for each offence.
18. Any persons found Smoking on the premises will be instantly dismissed.
19. Any person found away from their usual place of work, except for necessary purposes, or Talking with any one out of their own Alley will be fined 2d for each offence.
20. Any person bringing dirty Bobbins will be fined 1d for each Bobbin.
21. Any person wilfully damaging this Notice will be dismissed.

The Overlookers are strictly enjoined to attend to these Rules, and they will be responsible to the Masters for the Workpeople observing them.

WATER-FOOT MILL, NEAR HASLINGDEN,
SEPTEMBER, 1851.

J. Read, Printer, and Bookbinder, Haslingden.

EXERCISE

1. Do you think one, some or all of the textile inventions can have been a cause of the factory system? Explain your answer.
2. What cause of the factory system does Source B suggest? Give reasons for your answer.
3. Some historians have suggested that the need to use power was a cause of the factory system. Do Sources A and C suggest that this is true?
4. Are the causes of the factory system you have written about in answer to questions **1**, **2** and **3** linked in any way? Explain your answer.
5. The following statements all describe features of working life after 1850. In each case say whether you think this was a consequence of the factory system, and give reasons for your answer.
   - **a** Workers lost their freedom to take odd days off, particularly 'Saint Monday'.
   - **b** Workers couldn't choose when during the day they would work.
   - **c** Workers could not easily chat while they worked.
   - **d** Workers needed to be clean.
   - **e** Workers all had to start and stop work at the same time.

4.7 THE DARBYS OF COALBROOKDALE

Early eighteenth-century ironmaking

At the start of the eighteenth century the British **iron industry** was in decline. There was plenty of iron ore and limestone, but charcoal was needed to fuel the blast furnaces. The great forests were gradually being eaten up by the demands of wood for building, shipbuilding and fuel, so wood for charcoal was harder to get and more expensive. Iron was traditionally made in well-wooded areas, because wood was the bulkiest thing to transport. These areas, the Weald of Kent and Sussex, Shropshire, the Forest of Dean, the north-east and the Scottish highlands, were not close to the big markets. Iron-making also needed water power to work the bellows and hammers used. With streams drying up in summer and icing over in winter, this usually meant iron could not be made all the year round.

One family, the **Darbys**, and their works in **Coalbrookdale**, were to have a hand in solving all these problems.

Abraham Darby I (1677–1717) Darby's first job was in the malt trade, where he will have known that coke was used to dry malt rather than coal, because of the gases caused by burning coal. He bought the Coalbrookdale works on the river Severn in 1709. It was an ideal site. The Severn provided a transport route; there was iron ore and limestone nearby; there was also a high-quality coalfield; and it was a traditional iron-making area, so there were plenty of skilled workers. Darby soon experimented with the local coal for smelting, but without success. He then tried coke (coal which has been burned once, with many of the impurities removed). Coke producded pig iron, which could be used for cast iron, but was not good enough for use as wrought iron. Darby kept his discovery quiet and most of his competitors continued to use charcoal.

The process of iron-making

Smelting Iron ore and limestone were heated in blast furnaces. Smelting had to be done with charcoal. If coal was used the gases released by the burning coal made the iron too impure to use.

Pig iron The moulten iron was drained out of the blast furnace into moulds called **pigs**. As the iron cooled in them, the slabs which solidified were called pig iron.

Cast iron Cast iron, was made by pouring the iron when still liquid into a mould. Sometimes cast iron was made straight from the blast furnace, but usually the pigs were melted again. Cast iron was rather brittle, because there were still many impurities in it from smelting.

Wrought iron Wrought iron was made by reheating the pig iron and hammering it to remove impurities. This was called forging. Wrought iron was less brittle but also softer than cast iron.

SOURCE A

The Upper Works at Coalbrookdale, 1758.

SOURCE B

'He tried to smelt the iron from the ore in the blast furnace with Pit Coal. He first tried with raw coal as it came out of the mines, but it did not answer. He, not discouraged, had the coal coked into cinder, as is done for drying Malt, and it then succeeded to his satisfaction. My husband was but six years old when his father died, but he inherited his genius and made many improvements. Had not these discoveries been made, the iron trade would have dwindled away, for wood for charcoal became very scarce, and the prices of wood exceeding high.'

From a letter written in 1763 by Abiah Darby, wife of Abraham Darby II.

Abraham Darby II (1711–63) took over the works in 1732. He introduced three key developments. He bought a Newcomen steam engine, which was used to pump water back above the water wheel, so that there would not be slack times when the forges could not work. He improved coke-making by burning coal in ovens; this coke produced pig iron good enough for wrought iron. Finally, the company became expert at casting boilers for steam engines.

Richard Reynolds Darby died while his son was too young to take over, so the works were managed by Reynolds. He linked the various forges and furnaces together with a railway, and developed a method of making cast-iron rails. When Boulton and Watt produced their steam engine with rotary motion, Reynolds was one of their first customers.

Abraham Darby III (1750–91) found new uses for iron. In the late eighteenth century ironmasters had solved their production problems. They could now make as much iron as they could sell. The new task was to find new uses for iron. One of the most successful new uses was the building of an iron bridge across the Severn. It became a tourist attraction and helped convince people almost anything could be made from iron. Coalbrookdale Iron Company was a great success. In 1785 it had eight blast furnaces and seven forges, all linked by railway, with sixteen steam engines in use. The production of iron increased from 30,000 tonnes in 1750 to 68,000 in 1788 and 272,000 by 1806.

SOURCE C

The iron bridge at Ironbridge, painted in 1788.

4.8 DEVELOPMENTS IN THE IRON AND STEEL INDUSTRIES

The Darbys had not solved all the iron industry's problems. Charcoal was still needed to reheat pig iron while turning it into wrought iron. This process was slow and expensive, taking twelve hours to produce one tonne of wrought iron. Britain could not produce enough, and imported wrought iron from Sweden and Russia. Various ironworks around the country were working on ways to improve the production of wrought iron. The race was won by **Henry Cort**.

Henry Cort: the reverberatory furnace and rolling mill, 1783

Cort was a business man supplying the navy. He bought an ironworks near Portsmouth in 1775 and by 1783 had succeeded in making wrought iron by new, cheaper and faster methods. Cort used coal to melt the pig iron, but kept the coal away from the iron in the furnace. The iron was stirred (**puddled**) while in the furnace, and this helped get rid of the impurities. When ready the iron was stirred into balls called **blooms** by the puddler. These blooms were taken out of the furnace and rolled into bars or sheets between grooved or flat rollers.

Cort's process produced 15 tonnes of wrought iron an hour, and used the cheaper coal rather than scarce and expensive charcoal. The last reason against locating the iron industry on the coalfields had gone.

SOURCE A

Puddlers at work.

SOURCE B

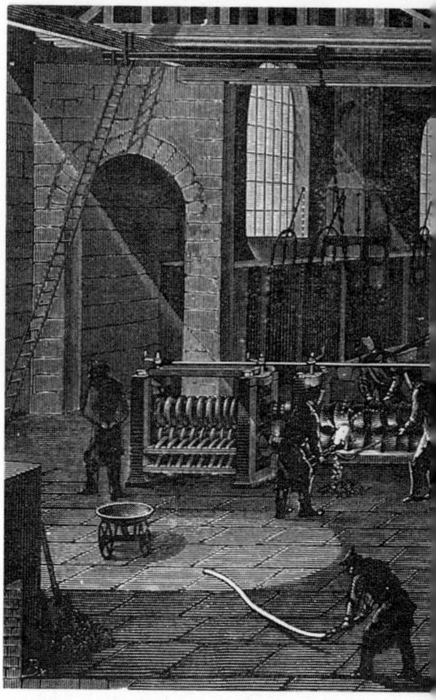

Rolling mills and a steam hammer.

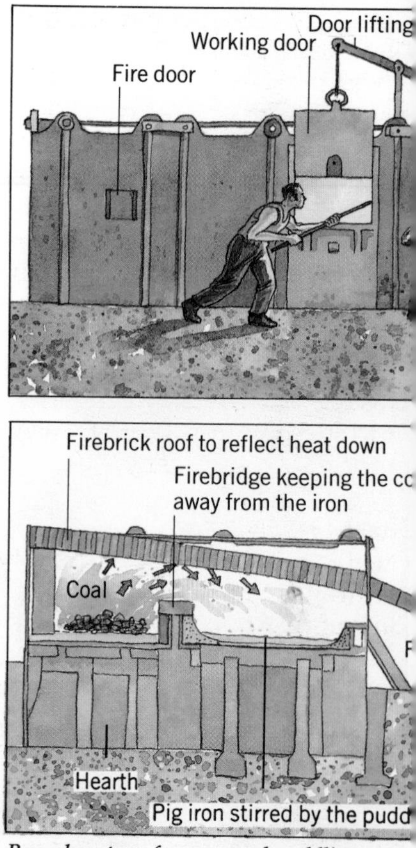

Reverberatory furnace and puddling and rolling.

The iron industry in South Wales

In South Wales puddling and rolling were adopted almost immediately. Richard Crawshay made 500 tonnes of wrought iron at the **Cyfarthfa Ironworks** in 1787. That year he introduced Cort's processes, and by 1812 production was over 10,000 tonnes a year. There were other firms, including John Guest's **Dowlais Ironworks**, and by the 1830s there were 191 blast furnaces in the area.

SOURCE **C**

Water-powered tilt hammers, 1785.

SOURCE **D**

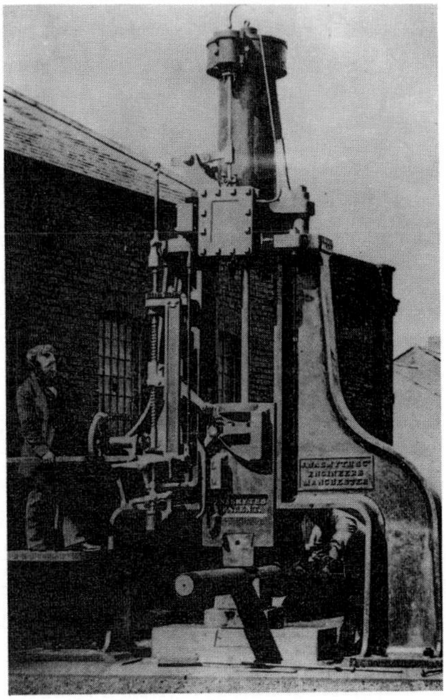

A Nasmyth steam hammer, photographed in 1855.

James Neilson: the hot blast, 1829
Neilson improved the smelting of iron by **heating** the **air** before it was pumped into the blast furnace. Using this method cut the use of coke by two-thirds. Yet the technique took a number of years to spread from Neilson's native Scotland and become common in the English and Welsh ironworks.

James Nasmyth: the steam hammer, 1840
Very large or complicated wrought iron could not be produced by the rolling mills, and tilt hammers were used to shape it. Tilt hammers were not very accurate, and could not work on very large pieces of iron. Nasmyth's **steam hammer** was so accurate it was claimed that an ironworker could use it either to crack an egg or to shape a piece of metal weighing many tonnes. It could also work on much larger jobs.

Steel-making
Steel is harder and more flexible than wrought iron. It was used for things like swords and cutlery. Steel is made by mixing some carbon in with iron. In 1700 the process was very slow, and steel was very expensive. There was only one important change in the steel industry before 1850, **Benjamin Huntsman's crucible process**, developed in 1740. A little charcoal and high-quality wrought iron were heated together in a crucible. When the slag was removed, this produced better-quality steel, with the carbon well mixed throughout the metal. Steel could be made this way only in small quantities, however, and the industry was at this time not as important as iron.

ACTIVITIES

1 a What jobs are the three people in Source A doing? Give reasons for your answer.
b The troughs in the front in Source A were filled with water. What do you think they were for? Give reasons for your answer.

2 In Source B there are four rolling mills and a steam hammer. What is each one doing?

3 What are the differences between the tilt hammers (Source C) and Nasmyth's steam hammer (Source D)?

4 Which of these sources do you think are the most useful for historians studying the iron industry?

4.9 WEDGWOOD AND POTTERY

CAUSATION

In the early eighteenth century pottery was not an important industry in Britain. Most people ate and drank from pewter (an alloy of tin and lead) or wood rather than china. Most English pottery was fairly crude earthenware. It was made using the domestic system; potters often farmed a little land as well.

Josiah Wedgwood was one of a family of potters in Burslem in Staffordshire. Born in 1730, he started work in the family pottery at the age of 9. While a teenager still apprenticed to his brother, he started experimenting with ways of improving the quality of pottery. By 1759 he had saved enough money to open his own pottery works. Pottery quickly became a major industry, and the area around Stoke-on-Trent where Wedgwood worked is still known as **The Potteries**. This unit looks at how much of the credit for this development should be given to Wedgwood.

Background

- Trade with China was growing. Chinese porcelain (fine pottery) was expensive but very fashionable.
- Tea and coffee drinking were becoming increasingly popular, and fine china was considered to be the most suitable thing to drink them from.
- In the 1750s Thomas Whieldon, an English potter, made fine-quality china which was almost as good as Chinese porcelain. He made services in the shape of cauliflowers and pineapples. Wedgwood worked for him at this time.
- About 1760 it was discovered that cornish clay (**kaolin**) could be mixed with other materials to make good-quality china.
- In 1761 the Bridgewater Canal was opened and was an immediate success (see pages 86–7).

Manufacturing

- In 1763, after many experiments, Wedgwood produced a new type of pottery, called **Queen's ware**. It was cream-coloured, with scenes painted on it, thin, shiny and tough.
- Wedgwood organized his works on the principle of **division of labour**. This greatly increased the amount of pottery produced.
- When he could not get enough skilled painters, Wedgwood arranged with a firm in Liverpool to produce **paper patterns**, so a plate could be decorated by someone who was not a fine artist.
- In 1769 Wedgwood opened a new works at **Etruria**. He built a village for his workers to live in next to the site.
- In 1774 Wedgwood developed **Jasper ware**, a fine-coloured pottery with decoration in white.
- In 1782 Wedgwood used a **Boulton and Watt engine** to grind flints used in his pottery; by 1800 there were four engines at Etruria.

SOURCE A

'To Staffordshire, to see them making the fine teapots, cups and saucers of fine red earth, in imitation of that which comes from China.'

Celia Fiennes, a traveller and writer, 1697.

SOURCE B

'The present price of freight and carriage for clay and flint for pottery in Staffordshire which is 15 shillings per Ton on average, will be reduced to 2 shillings per Ton on about 4,000 Tons. The carriage and freight on pottery in return, will be reduced from 28 shillings to about 12 shillings per Ton.'

Wedgwood's calculations about the benefit to his pottery of the Trent-Mersey Canal.

SOURCE C

'The Great People have had these vases in their palaces for long enough for them to be seen and admired by the Middling Class, who are vastly superior in number to the Great. Although a great price was at first necessary to make the vases esteemed Ornaments for palaces, that reason no longer exists. The middling people would probably buy quantities of them at a reduced price.'

From a letter Wedgwood wrote to Thomas Bentley, his partner in the manufacture of ornamental pottery.

SOURCE D

The Trent–Mersey Canal and the Etruria works.

Marketing

- Wedgwood opened **show-rooms** in other parts of the country to sell his pottery. There were rooms in London, Dublin, Bath and Bristol.
- Wedgwood concentrated on getting **well-known people** to use his pottery. Queen's ware was so called because he sent a sample to the Queen, who asked for a whole service. Wedgwood always put 'Queen's Potter' on his bills and letters after this.
- Wedgwood employed three travelling **sales representatives** to get orders.
- Wedgwood took out **newspaper advertisements** and published **catalogues**.
- Wedgwood worked hard at selling pottery **abroad**. The catalogues were translated into various European languages, and services were produced decorated with the Pope's head, for sale in Catholic countries. He got ambassadors to take samples of his pottery abroad, and in this way got a famous order from Catherine the Great, Empress of Russia.

Transport

- Wedgwood was involved in setting up **turnpikes** (toll roads) around the Potteries.
- In 1766 he was one of the backers of the **Trent and Mersey Canal** which opened in 1777. This canal linked these two navigable rivers, and it ran past Etruria. It provided cheap transport for kaolin from Cornwall (around the coast to Liverpool and then down the canal), and also gentle transport for finished pottery.

EXERCISE

1. Are any of the factors in the 'Background' section causes of the growth of the pottery industry?
2. What contribution did Wedgwood make to the manufacture of pottery?
3. What contribution did Wedgwood make to the marketing of pottery?
4. What contribution did Wedgwood make to the scene shown in Source D?
5. Did Wedgwood's interest in transport help his business?
6. 'Wedgwood was the father of the English pottery industry. Without him it would have been crude and unimportant.' Do you agree with this statement? Give reasons for your answer.

4.10 COAL MINING

Coal mining in the early eighteenth century

Many **coal mines** in the early eighteenth century were very small, often worked by one or two families. Most worked coal only near the surface, using either **bell pits** or **drift mines**. Demand for coal was growing, and the only way to increase production was to get at the coal which was further down by using **shaft mines**. The shaft mines of the early eighteenth century were never more than 400 feet deep, and most were less.

There were a number of problems facing the coal industry. Most were associated with shaft mining, but some applied to all types. **Safety, drainage** and **ventilation** were problems that most affected the shaft mines. **Haulage** (getting the coal to the surface) and **transport** (getting it to the market) affected all types of mining. The success of the coal industry during the Industrial Revolution was based on its ability to solve these problems and increase production by using much deeper shaft mines.

Drainage

Any hole dug in the ground is liable to collect water. In bell pits the problems were small scale. In drift mines digging a drainage channel called an **adit** helped. The problem was more serious in shaft mines; the deeper the mines, the greater the problem. Drainage more than anything else limited the depth of the shaft mines and therefore the amount of coal that could be obtained.

Early attempts to drain mines with chains of buckets raised by horse-power were unsuccessful because horses were not powerful enough. The Newcomen engine, first used in a coal mine in 1712, was a breakthrough. By 1733 there were 78 **steam engines** on coalfields, and by 1775 the number had risen to 399. The more efficient Watt and Boulton engine was first used in 1776. It was more powerful and therefore allowed the mines to go much deeper.

Ventilation

As shafts got deeper the miners came across pockets of two carbonic gasses, known as **choke-damp** and **fire-damp**. Choke-damp could suffocate miners unless they got out of it quickly. Fire-damp was even worse; if it came into contact with a flame it would explode. Even without these two gases, shaft mines needed ventilation to get fresh air to the areas where miners worked. An early attempt to deal with the problems of gas was lighting a candle at the end of a long pole and, by pushing the pole ahead, hoping to explode the gas without hurting anyone. Another idea was taking a bird in a cage into the mine and using it as an 'early-warning device', since it would stop singing or even die when there was a build-up of dangerous gases. Neither approach was very satisfactory.

The **furnace method** was the first scientific attempt to solve the problem. A second shaft was dug and this shaft, known as the upshaft, would have a fire lit at the bottom of it. The upshaft became a chimney as the hot air rose, and fresh air was drawn down the main shaft to feed the fire.

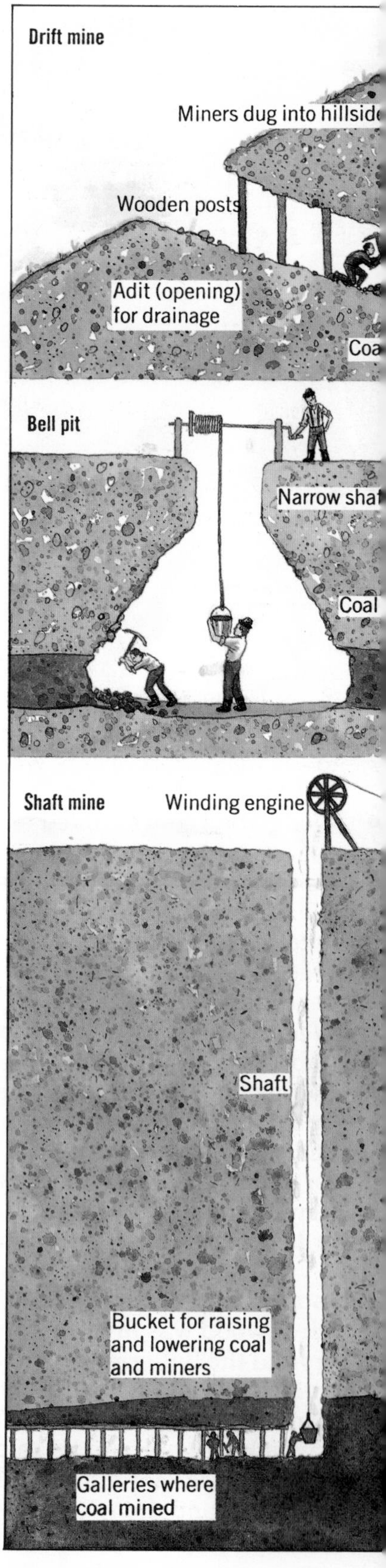

This method was improved by making a series of airtight trapdoors in the mine so that fresh air was usually channelled through all the workings. The trapdoors were minded by children called **trappers** who often sat in the dark all day, opening and closing the doors when someone needed to pass through. If the trapper fell asleep and left the door open, the system would be much less effective. At best this system could keep the mines well-ventilated, but at worst the fire could explode the fire-damp.

Experiments were made with **steam-powered fans** which would suck the foul air and gasses out of the mines. The first was installed by John Buddle at Hebburn Colliery in 1807, but they were not as effective as the furnace method. Exhaust fans were gradually improved, but only in the 1860s did they come to be the usual method of ventilating mines.

Safety

Miners used candles for light, and the candle flame could explode the fire-damp. After a particularly bad explosion in 1812 in which ninety miners were killed the **Sunderland Society for the Prevention of Accidents in Coal Mines** was formed. In 1815 the society asked **Sir Humphrey Davy**, a well-known scientist and inventor, to look at the problem. He produced the **Davy safety lamp**, with the flame inside a wire gauze. This stopped the flame coming into contact with any fire-damp that was present, so there would be no explosion. The flame changed colour if any gas was present, giving miners a warning.

The safety lamp was widely used, but it did not eliminate all danger of explosion. It gave only a dim light, and miners would sometimes use candles instead, or take the top off the lamp, which could allow gas to reach the flame. Sometimes, too, draughts could blow the flame outside the gauze. As a result of the safety lamp, deeper mines were worked, and the percentage of miners killed in explosions was reduced, but not eliminated.

Mine ventilation system

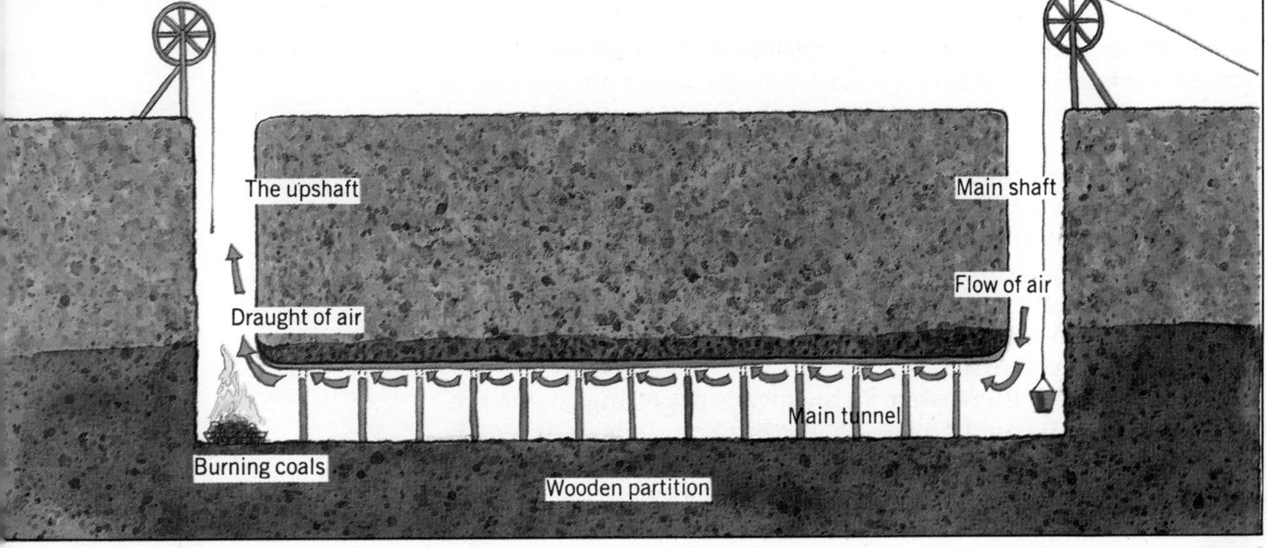

Cutting the coal

The earliest shaft mines were worked using the **bord-and-pillar** method. Roadways were cut from the bottom of the shaft, and large squares of coal (the 'pillars') were left to keep the roof up. This method left much of the coal uncut and was replaced by the **longwall** method. In this system a miner undercut the coal seam while it was propped up; then the props were removed, and the rest of the seam collapsed. Apart from gunpowder, first used in 1825, mining remained a job done with simple tools until the late nineteenth century.

SOURCE A

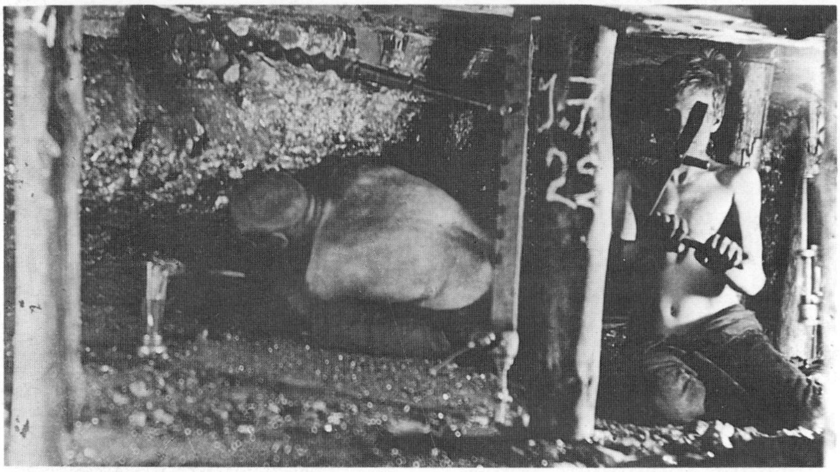

Man and boy working in a pit in the late nineteenth century. The man is undercutting the seam, while the boy drills a hole for a gunpowder charge which will bring down the rest of the seam.

SOURCE B

Modern open-cast mining, which takes off the earth and rock above the coal, has revealed an old bord-and-pillar mine. Notice the scale of the picture, and the amount of coal wasted.

Haulage

There were two tasks once coal was cut: to get the coal from the face to the shaft, and to get the coal up the shaft to the surface. It was also necessary to get miners from the surface to the face and back again.

Ladders were the simplest way. In some mines coal was carried. Women and children would drag the coal from the face to the shaft and climb ladders while carrying baskets of coal to get it to the surface.

In bell pits a **windlass**, similar to the device for raising and lowering buckets in a well, was sometimes used to bring up the coal. This would not work for deeper mines, nor were ladders really satisfactory. A **horse whim gin** was the usual answer. This used horse-power to turn a large wheel, around which rope was wound. The rope could be used to lift coal up the shaft and also to lift miners up and down.

In the mine itself there were various ways of getting coal to the foot of the shaft. It could be carried, dragged on sleds or dragged along rails in trucks. The dragging was often done by **women and children**, though in the bigger mines **pit ponies** were used (see pages 128–9).

SOURCE **C**

Pithead near Brosely, Staffordshire, 1788, showing a horse whim gin, a wagonway and pack-horses. The chimney on the right was built over the upshaft to help improve the ventilation.

Gradually horse gins were replaced by **winding machines** driven by steam engines. In 1834 an **iron cage** was first used. Tubs of coal could be raised in it, and miners could also travel in it. The cage ran along guide-rails and was much safer than being lowered in a large tub or sitting on a seat. In the 1840s **iron wire ropes** were used, and it was possible to lift greater weights from deeper shafts.

Transport

Something as heavy as coal is not an easy thing to transport. Mine owners played a key role in the development of transport as they improved the ways they moved coal. The Duke of Bridgewater's canal was built to transport his coal cheaply to Manchester where it was sold, and it started the great boom in **canal building** (see pages 86–7). Mining was also involved in the early development of **railways**. Wooden railways, called **wagonways**, with the wagons pulled by horses, had been used by mine owners since the seventeenth century. Wooden rails, however, rotted and could be damaged by the heavy wagons. In 1767 the Coalbrookdale Iron Company produced the first cast-iron rails. These were in their turn replaced by wrought-iron rails, first made by John Birkinshaw in 1820.

The Mines Act of 1842

In 1840 a **Royal Commission on Conditions in the Mines** began work on a report which was published in 1842. The report, which was illustrated with drawings (including Source D), shocked people. They were worried about young children being forced to work in the dark as trappers; worried at the long hours and hard work forced on women and children; and worried about the possible consequences of men and women working together in mines which were so hot that many worked naked or naked from the waist up.

SOURCE **D**

Children being lowered down a mine shaft by a windlass, from the 1842 Royal Commission report.

4.11 INDUSTRIALIZATION

EVIDENCE

Between the years 1780 and 1850 Britain was **industrialized**. This means it became a country where industry, usually organized by **division of labour** in factories, was the most important part of the economy. At the same time there was urbanization – towns grew quickly, and living in towns became much more common.

Historians have tried to work out whether industrialization and urbanization were good for the people who lived through these changes. They have disagreed. Some say things improved, others that things got worse. They have usually tried to measure the changes in two ways, by thinking about the **quality of life** (which is hard to measure) or about the **cost of living** (which is hard to discover).

SOURCE A

'The children almost universally ill-looking, small, sickly, barefoot and ill-clad. Many *appeared* to be no older than seven. The men generally from 16 to 24, and none aged, were almost as pallid and thin as the children. The women were the most respectable in appearance. I saw, or thought I saw, a degenerate race – human beings stunted and enfeebled men and women that were not to be aged – children that were not to be healthy adults.'

Turner Thackrah, a Leeds doctor, describing cotton spinners in 1832.

SOURCE B

Changes in prices and wages

Years	*Money wages*	*Price changes*	*Real wages*
1740–1815	+63.1%	+74.1%	−11.0%
1815–25	−10.6%	−29.3%	+18.7%
1825–50	+9.8%	−19.4%	+29.2%

From Malcolm Falkus, 'Britain Transformed', 1987.

SOURCE E

Average age at death in 1842

Area	*Gentry*	*Trades people*	*Labourers*
Rutlandshire	52	41	38
Truro	40	33	28
Derby	49	38	21
Bethnal Green	45	26	16
Leeds	44	27	19
Liverpool	35	22	15

From a report on the Sanitary Conditions of the Labouring Population, 1842.

SOURCE C

Cartoon about a cotton factory. Peel was a Tory politician.

SOURCE D

SOURCE F

Factory girls during their lunch break. Painting by Eyre Crowe, 1874.

'Tremendous Sacrifice', a cartoon by George Cruikshank, about 1840. The workers queuing to be fed into the mincer are saying: 'I understand that it is impossible to get a living at this work'. 'So I have heard, never the less we must try'. In the shop a lady is saying: 'I cannot imagine how they can possibly be made for the price'.

EXERCISE

1 Does Source B help you decide whether Source A is reliable?

2 **a** Is Source C biased? Explain your answer.
b Is Source C useful for a historian studying this problem?

3 Sources C and F are both about factory life in the nineteenth century. How can they be so different?

4 Source F is a realistic painting, while Source D is a cartoon. Does this mean Source D must be less reliable than Source F?

5 Clothes were not made by putting workers through the mincer.
a Does this mean a historian will decide Source D is not reliable? Give reasons for your answer.
b Does this mean a historian will decide Source D is not useful? Give reasons for your answer.

6 Do the sources here prove that life got worse during the Industrial Revolution? Give reasons for your answer.

4.12 THE WORKSHOP OF THE WORLD

The Great Exhibition of 1851

The 1840s had been a difficult decade for Britain. The economy had gone through two slumps; there was famine in Ireland, and there were high food prices elsewhere. In 1848 many had expected the **Chartist protests** to spill over into revolution (see pages 138–9). There had been revolutions that year in many European countries including France. However, the crisis passed. There was no revolution. The economy improved.

In 1849 a commission, which included Prince Albert, husband of Queen Victoria, began to plan a great exhibition which would celebrate the achievements of British and foreign industry. There was some opposition to the idea, but the planners pushed ahead. They chose a radical design for the exhibition building, made out of iron and glass, which gave it its name, **The Crystal Palace**. The advantage was that this building was **prefabricated** – the difficult work was done in the factories, and the building was put together on site. Mass production was the key. All the measurements were standard. The glaziers used trolleys which ran along the metal ribs as if they were railways.

SOURCE A

'That miserable Crystal Palace, the wretched place, where every species of fraud and immorality will be practised. Let the Britisher beware, they will have all their food robbed – they will have a piebald generation, half black, half white. They might look for assassinations – for being stabbed in the dark; but careless of that, I am determined to pursue an even straightforward course, and I would say that the dearest wish of my heart is that the confounded building called the Crystal Palace should be dashed to pieces.'

From an attack on the idea of the Great Exhibition by Colonel Sibthorpe MP, 1850.

The **Great Exhibition** was a great success. Opened by Queen Victoria on 1 May and lasting to 15 October, it was seen by 6.2 million people. There were 7,000 British exhibitors and 6,000 from abroad. On some days admission was a shilling, on others 5 shillings and sometimes even £1. This was so the upper classes would go on the more expensive days and not have to mix with the rest. The **railway companies** organized cheap excursion trains from all over the country. The London and North-West Railway Company alone took 750,000 passengers on its special trains.

The Victorians were proud of the exhibition and collected bizarre statistics such as '2 million buns were eaten' or '1 million bottles of mineral water were sold'. More important, it helped to bring the country together. Londoners saw that northern factory workers were not brutish savages, and millions of people visited London without any trouble. The exhibition was also a good shop-window for British goods, and for the next twenty years Britain dominated world trade, being known as the **workshop of the world**.

SOURCE B

'The first real event in my life came in 1851, when I was six. My mother took me up to London to see the Great Exhibition. Our special train from Thirsk to King's Cross was a wonder to me. The train was of enormous length and drawn by six locomotives. Every seat was occupied.

From the autobiography of R. E. Crompton, published in 1928.

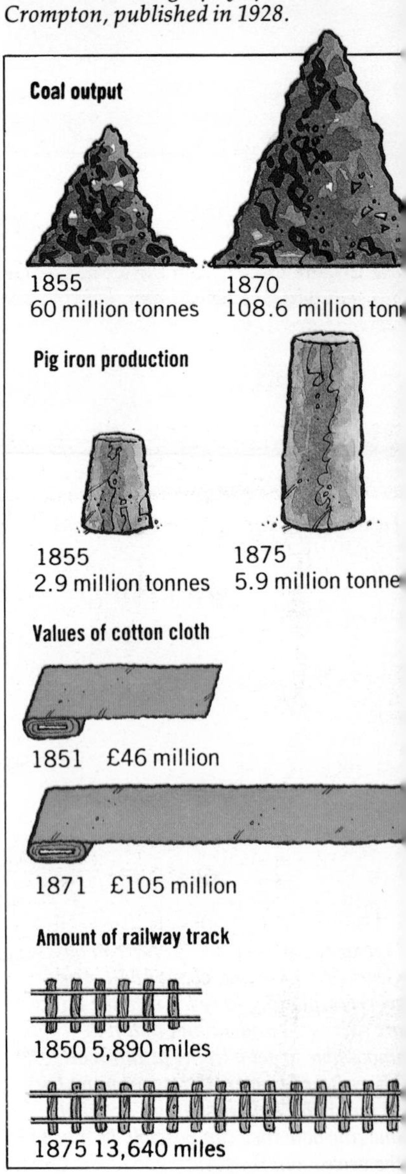

The Crystal Palace itself was so popular that it was taken down from its site in Hyde Park after the exhibition and re-erected in Sydenham, where it stayed until destroyed by fire in 1936.

SOURCE C

The Crystal Palace from the west. The west and east naves were divided by the transept with the domed roof. British goods were in the western nave, foreign in the eastern nave.

SOURCE D

Looking down the west nave at the Great Exhibition.

4.13 THE TRIUMPH AND DECLINE OF THE 'OLD' INDUSTRIES

Textiles

Before the First World War
Textiles, especially **cottons**, were a major and successful industry. The British textile industry dominated the world. In 1900, 67 per cent of the entire world's cottons were produced in Britain. However, during this period there were also worrying signs. The British cotton industry was no longer the place where new inventions were developed. Even worse, the industry was slow in developing new inventions from overseas. The key developments of the period both came from the USA. **Ring spinning**, a process which was faster and cheaper than mule spinning, had been invented in 1828. The first British mill to use it introduced it in the 1840s, but by 1914 only 19 per cent of British output was by ring spinning, while the figure was 87 per cent for the USA. The **Northrop loom**, which made weaving quicker and cheaper, was first introduced from the USA in 1892, but the take-up was slow.

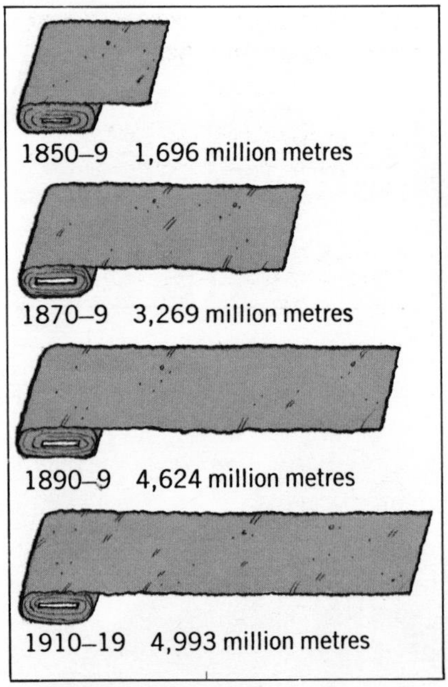

Average annual exports of cotton cloth in millions of metres, 1850–1919.

Iron and steel

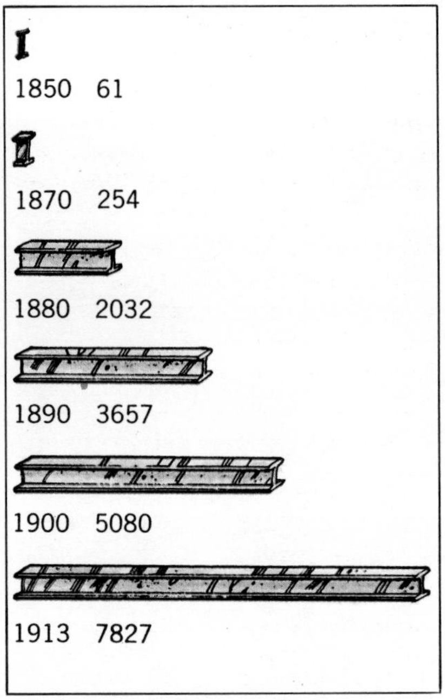

Steel production in thousands of tonnes, 1850–1913.

Before the First World War
Between 1850 and the First World War **steel** became the key section of the industry. New developments made steel production quicker and cheaper. **Bessemer's converter** (1856) halved the cost and got production up to 3 tonnes per hour, but it could work only with non-phosphorus iron ore. Most British ore was phosphorus. **Siemens's open-hearth process** (1867) would work with scrap iron as well as ore. Again, it could not work with phosphorus ore. The **Gilchrist Thomas basic process** (1879) did use phosphorus ore, separating the phosphorus so that it could be used in chemical fertilizer. This allowed the British steel industry to expand. New steelworks were opened in areas where there was coal and iron ore. The north-east was the most important area.

Steel became the metal used in building, shipbuilding and machine-making. Demand increased rapidly.

Shipbuilding

Before the First World War
In the second half of the nineteenth century **shipbuilding** changed as it became one of the country's most important industries. Ships themselves changed. Instead of building wooden sailing ships the industry built iron steamships. The important shipbuilding areas moved from places near forests to places near coal and iron ore deposits. The key places were on the rivers Tyne, Mersey and Clyde, and in Belfast and Barrow-in-Furness.

British shipbuilders dominated the world industry. In the 1890s, 80 per cent of all new ships were built in Britain. Shipbuilding was seen as being linked to a country's ability to have a strong navy, and Germany was determined before the First World War to have a much stronger navy. Germany did all it could to help its shipbuilding industry grow. Between 1910 and 1914 only 60 per cent of the world's new ships were built in Britain.

SOURCE A

A shipyard on the Tyne, 1910.

Textiles

Between the wars
The First World War changed the textile industry. Much of the production was required for war work, and shipping was not easily available for exports. Many of the markets which usually got their cottons from Britain developed their own industries or found other sources of supply. In particular the industries in the **USA** and **Japan** grew. Both had factories with the latest machines. Japan had the further advantage of a low-wage economy, which kept the price of its exports low.

In their successful years British firms had not invested in **new machines**. After the war they could not get their old markets back. Because this meant they were not profitable, banks would not lend them money to invest in new machines. By 1938 British cotton was only 28 per cent of world production.

SOURCE B

'Never again let anybody in Lancashire hear you talk this childish stuff about foreign competition. It's just twaddle. In the first place we've got the only climate in the world where cotton piece goods in any quantity can ever be produced. In the second place, no foreign Johnnies can ever be bred that can spin and weave like Lancashire lasses and lads. In the third place, there are more spindles in Oldham than in all the world put together. And last of all, foreigners could never find the brains Lancashire cotton men have for the job.'

B. Bowker, 'Lancashire under the Hammer', 1928.

Iron and steel

Between the wars
The arms race before the war, and then the war itself, had kept the steel industry very busy. However, it had been overtaken by the steel industries of both **Germany** and the **USA** before the First World War. After the war there was a short boom, but from 1920 to 1933 the industry was in a slump. In the years when Britain had not been exporting steel, other countries had expanded their own industries. As a result, Britain did not win back many of its traditional **export markets**. Even worse, Britain did not put import tariffs on steel coming into the country, and some foreign steel-makers were selling steel here more cheaply than British firms could make it. Finally the **world depression** of 1929–34 meant that the industries which used steel, especially shipbuilding, needed much less.

In the later 1930s the steel industry began to recover. The government eventually set up **tariffs** to stop cheap imports. More importantly, the rise of Hitler and the possibility of another war led to government **rearmament** – modernization and re-equipment of the armed forces in case there should be another war. Tanks, guns and warships needed a great deal of steel, so the demand for steel went up.

Shipbuilding

Between the wars
During the First World War the British shipbuilding industry could not supply its traditional export markets. **Japan, Scandinavia** and the **USA** all expanded their shipbuilding industries to meet the demand for ships.

Immediately after the war there was plenty of work for all the shipyards, because all countries wanted to make good the losses of ships during the war. This didn't last long, however, and it soon became clear that British shipbuilders were not able to get back the markets they had lost during the war. The competitors, who had more modern yards and often cheaper labour as well, could build ships more quickly and more cheaply.

These problems lasted until the government passed the **North Atlantic Shipping Act** (1934) and the **British Shipping (Assistance) Act** (1935). These Acts made government money available to help shipowners buy new ships from British yards. In the late 1930s rearmament also increased the shipyards' business.

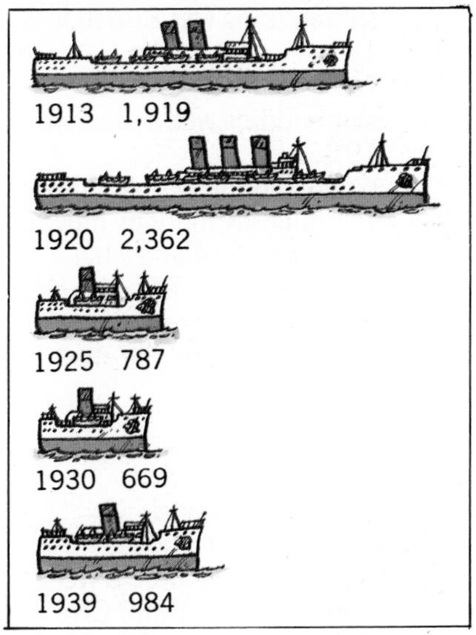

British shipbuilding in thousands of tonnes, 1913–39.

The Jarrow marchers of 1936.

ACTIVITIES

1 a What percentage of world textile production was British in 1900?
b What percentage of world textile production was British in 1938?
c Can any of the causes of the British textile industry's decline after 1918 be seen before 1914?

2 a Which was the most important development for British steel-making: the Bessemer converter, the Siemens open-hearth process or the Gilchrist Thomas basic process? Give reasons for your answer.
b Do the figures suggest that British steel-making was a success before 1914?
c What danger signs were there for the British steel industry before 1914?

3 a What percentage of world shipbuilding was British in 1890?
b What percentage of world shipbuilding was British in 1914?
c What percentage of world shipbuilding was British in 1986?
d Where did the British shipbuilding industry move to before 1914 and why?
e What area became important in both shipbuilding and the steel industry?

4 a What problems did the textile industry face between the wars?
b Do you think the ideas expressed in Source B were common at the time? Give reasons for your answer.

5 a What problems did the steel industry face between the wars?
b How did the steel industry recover in the late 1930s?

6 a What problems faced the shipbuilding industry between the wars?
b How did the shipbuilding industry recover in the late 1930s?

7 a Were there any common problems shared by these industries between the wars?
b Could it be said that Hitler was good for British industry in the 1930s?

8 a Why has the cotton industry declined since 1945?
b What has happened to the steel industry since 1945?
c What has happened to the shipbuilding industry since 1945?

9 In 1900 Britain was a great industrial nation. In the 1980s Britain is not a great industrial nation. Does this mean either that British industry has been run by bad managers or that it has had poor workers? Give reasons for your answer.

The world depression

The late 1920s and early 1930s were bad times for all three industries, and for the rest of British industry. This was the **world depression** – a time of high **unemployment, falling production** and terrible **poverty**. The slump that affected industry and trade was a vicious cycle. Since there was less trade, there were fewer exports, including cotton; with fewer exports, fewer ships were needed; fewer ships needed meant less steel needed; and so on. Trade and industry were so closely linked that the problems multiplied.

In one town, Jarrow on Tyneside, the shipyard was closed. It had no orders, and the owners were worried about **overcapacity** (producing more than could possibly be sold). Male unemployment in the town reached as high as 80 per cent. A march was organized from Jarrow to London in the hope the government would be persuaded to help. The **Jarrow March** failed to achieve this. The government said the workers must find jobs for themselves. A plan for a steelworks in the town fell through because the steel industry was also worried about overcapacity. Unemployment remained staggeringly high until the Second World War.

Textiles

People employed in the cotton industry, 1851–1987.

After the Second World War
Clothing was rationed after the end of the Second World War, and for a short time the British **cotton and woollen industries** could sell everything they produced. However, this did not last. Again the industry found it hard to compete with countries where mechanization was better or wages lower. Cotton suffered especially. Not only did Britain start to import cheap cotton from **India** and the **Far East**, but also there was competition from new **synthetic fibres**.

Synthetic fibres were by-products of the oil industry. The first was **nylon**, invented in the USA. A factory was set up in Britain to make nylon in 1940, but in Monmouthshire rather than the traditional textile districts. **Terylene** was developed by British chemists during the Second World War, but was not produced until after the war. Since the 1950s various other synthetic fibres have been developed. By 1960 they accounted for over 80 per cent of textile production in Britain. These fibres were usually made by large companies, so many fewer people were needed.

Iron and steel

After the Second World War
How the steel industry should be organized is something the Labour and Conservative parties have disagreed about. The Labour Party believed in **nationalization**. This means the industry is taken over and run by the state. Decisions about how much to produce and where to produce are controlled by the government through the managers it puts in charge. In the case of steel, the argument was that, because it employed so many people, because it made raw material for other industries including defence and because whole communities were built around steelworks, it was too important for private firms to run. The Conservative Party has generally been against nationalization. It felt that the steel industry would be more efficient if it was made up by firms which competed in the **free market**.

The steel industry was nationalized by Labour in 1949, privatized by the Conservatives in 1953 and re-nationalized by Labour in 1967. Production increased until the early 1970s. Then there was cheaper foreign competition and a fall-off in demand from customers like the car and shipbuilding industries. The industry lost a great deal of money during the 1970s and Mrs Thatcher's Conservative government brought in a manager from the US steel industry, Ian MacGregor, who closed many works and concentrated production on a few more efficient sites.

Shipbuilding

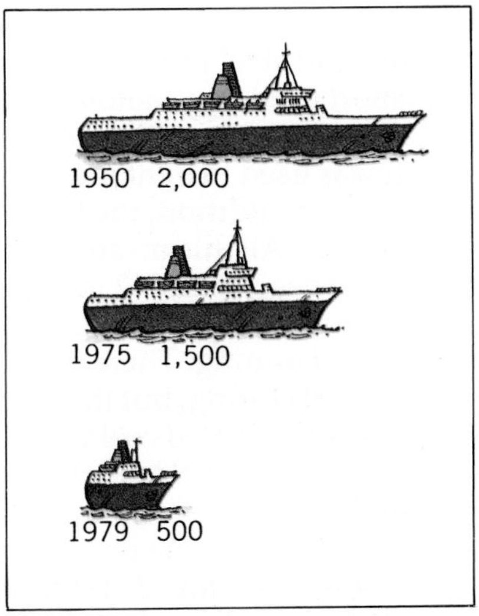

British shipbuilding in thousands of tonnes, 1950–79.

After the Second World War
Japan and **Germany** had been two of Britain's main competitors in shipbuilding. At the end of the war their yards were in ruins. While this gave the British industry a head start, which was further helped by the replacement of ships lost in the war, this did not last long.

British shipyards got a reputation for being expensive and for not meeting their delivery dates. This was often blamed on strikes and trouble with the **trade unions**. The British unions insisted on **demarcation**, where skilled craftsmen worked at their own trade only, long after this practice had died out in German and Japanese yards. The German and Japanese yards also had the advantage of **more modern machinery**.

British shipyards were nationalized to try to help them over their problems, but the attempt failed. By 1986 only 1 per cent of the world's new ships were built in British yards.

4.14 COAL MINING SINCE 1850

Before the First World War

Between 1850 and 1914 the demand for **coal** increased. Coal was the most common **domestic fuel**, and it was also used as fuel in the **iron and steel industries**, which were expanding rapidly. **Transport** used large amounts of coal as well, with both trains and ships running with coal-fired steam engines. Even **gas**, which was used to light most towns and many houses, was made from coal. In addition, the British coal industry had increasing **export sales**. All this meant that production increased: 1913 was the record year, with 282 million tonnes produced.

This growth in production was not brought about by new methods of mining. There were new machines which could be used in coal cutting, but they were rare in Britain. In 1900 only 1.5 per cent of mined coal was cut by machine, compared with 25 per cent in the USA. Part of the increase was due to **new coalfields** which were opened in Kent, south Yorkshire and Nottinghamshire. The rest can be explained because there were **more miners** employed. Yet there were problems in the industry. The **safety record** was bad, and **productivity** was falling. Average production per miner in 1913 was less than it had been in 1800.

Between the wars

During the First World War the mines had been run by the government as part of the war effort. After the war the industry struggled. There were over 1,400 separate colliery companies, most of them very small. They did not have the money needed to invest in new machines. They also found it hard to sell their coal because coal from the modern pits in the USA, Poland, Spain, the Netherlands and even Australia was cheaper. The coal owners' solution was to **increase** the number of **hours** the miners worked, and **cut** their **pay**. This led to two long and bitter disputes in 1921 and 1926, the second of which caused the **General Strike** (see pages 164–5).

There were other reasons why the coal industry did badly between the wars. **Other fuels** were becoming more popular. Ships were turning to oil, and many new locomotives were diesels not steam engines. Electricity was becoming more popular as a source of power in homes and factories, and some electricity was being made in oil-fired power stations or in hydro-electric schemes. The number of miners employed fell. In 1924 there had been 1.25 million; by 1930 there were only 1 million.

After the Second World War

During the Second World War the mines had again been run by the government. It had been difficult to keep up production levels. Miners were encouraged not to join the armed forces but to continue in the mines. Some men, called **Bevin boys** (Ernest Bevin was Minister of Labour) were conscripted to serve in the mines rather than in the forces.

SOURCE A

'This is the coal face. The gallery you are in is only as high as the ledge of coal itself, probably not much more than a yard. The first impression of all is the frightful, deafening din from the conveyor belt which carries the coal away. You cannot see very far, because the fog of coal dust throws back the beam of your lamp, but you can see either side of you a line of half-naked men driving their shovels under the fallen coal and flinging it swiftly over their left shoulders. They are feeding it on to the conveyor belt, which runs a yard or two behind them. They are not only shifting monstrous quantities of coal, they are also doing it in a position that doubles or trebles the work. They have got to remain kneeling all the while. And the other conditions do not make things easier. There is the heat and the coal dust that stuffs up your throat and nostrils and collects along your eyelids, and the unending noise of the conveyor belt, which in that confined space is rather like the rattle of a machine-gun.'

George Orwell, 'Road to Wigan Pier', 1937.

SOURCE B

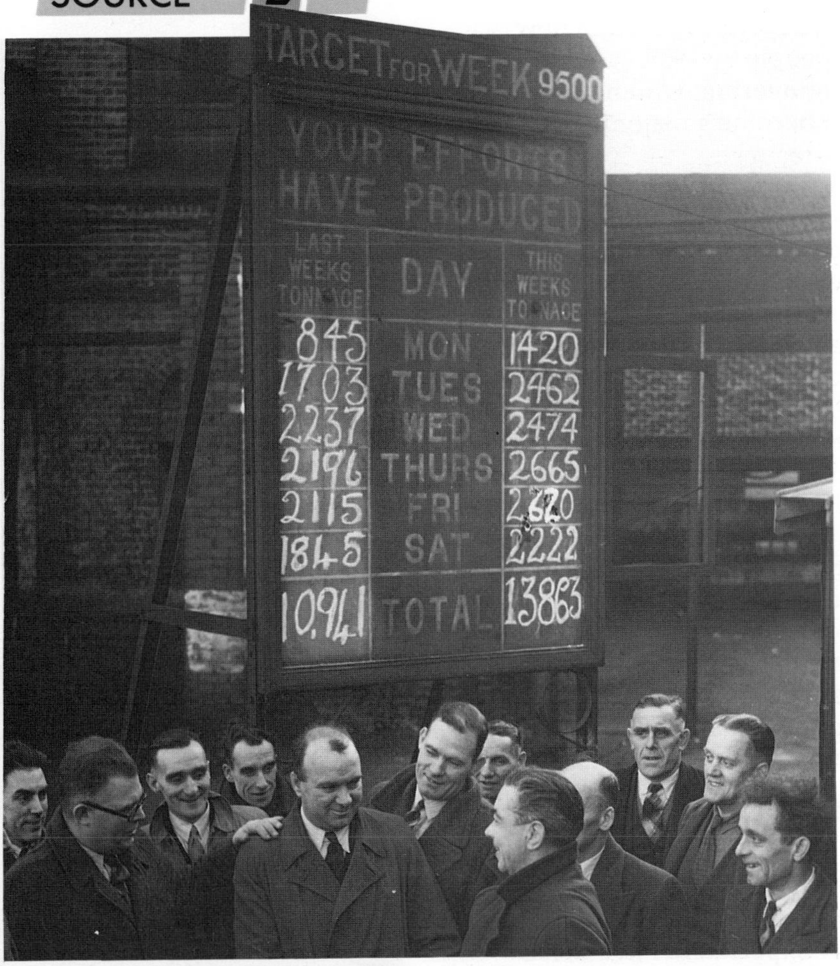

Miners congratulating themselves, 1946.

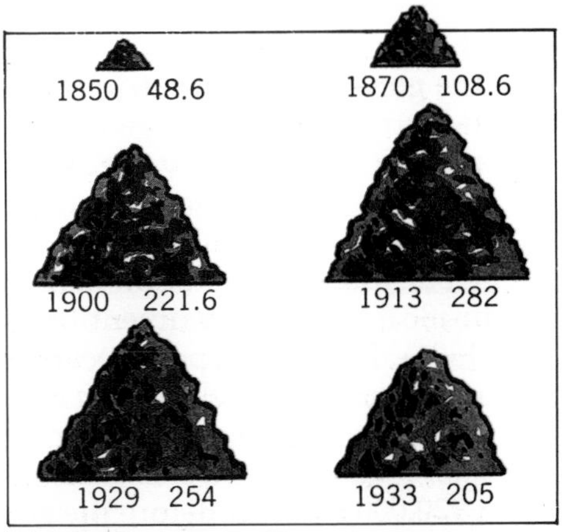

Coal production in millions of tonnes, 1850–1933.

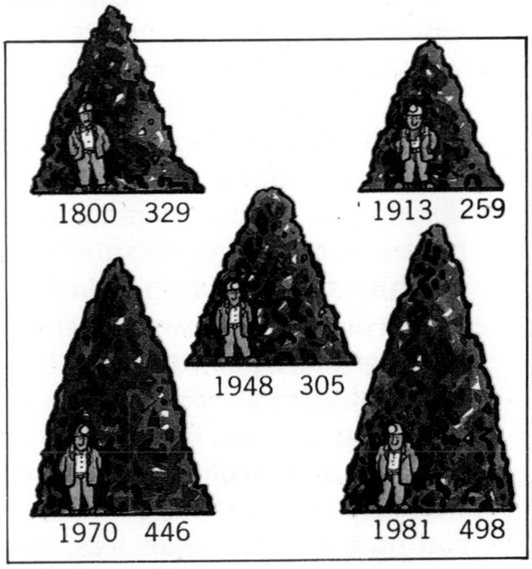

Average productivity per miner in tonnes, 1800–1981.

The Labour Party **nationalized** the coal industry in 1947, putting it under the control of the **National Coal Board**. The NCB had the difficult task of **modernizing** the industry and increasing output. Although there were many pit closures in the 1950s, the NCB succeeded. Conditions were improved: pithead baths were installed (these had been very rare before nationalization); transport was usually provided underground to take men from the shaft to the face; and mechanization was increased.

The coal industry received an unexpected boost when the 1973 **oil crisis** made coal a much more attractive fuel. In 1974 the NCB and the National Union of Mineworkers jointly published a *Plan for Coal* which looked forward to ten years of expansion. But in the late 1970s it was clear that these optimistic forecasts were not being fulfilled. Under pressure from the Conservative government the NCB began a programme of closing pits because they were expensive to mine rather than because they were exhausted. This led to the bitter **miners' strike** of 1984–5 in which the NUM was defeated. Since the end of that strike there have been many pit closures and redundancies.

SOURCE C

First day of nationalization, 1 January 1947.

4.15 NEW INDUSTRIES

Electricity

The **generation of electricity** and its **distribution** was a new industry which employed 100,000 people by 1938. It led to another new industry, **electrical engineering**, which produces electrical goods. Electricity has also become a major power source for the rest of British industry.

The first **power station** in Britain started generating electricity in 1881, but the key invention was **Parsons's steam turbine** (1884). This new type of steam engine was much more efficient and so generated electricity more economically. The 'take-off' period for the new industry came after the First World War. There were 730,000 electricity users in 1920, 2,844,000 in 1929 and 8,920,000 by 1938. Before the government set up the **Central Electricity Generating Board** in 1926, electricity was produced by many local companies, each working with its own voltages. The CEGB standardized voltages and constructed the **National Grid**, which allowed power to be shared by the country as a whole, wherever it was generated.

Without the common voltages it would have been almost impossible for the electrical engineering industry to have developed. Electricity made a whole range of new machines possible, including vacuum cleaners, refrigerators, washing machines, gramophones and radios. Mass production brought prices down, and lower prices, together with hire purchase, enabled more people to buy the new machines. In 1922 a radio had cost £30; in 1939 the price was £4, and 2 million sets a year were being made. By then the industry employed 350,000 people.

Consumer electronics grew rapidly after the Second World War. There were new products – radar, televisions and, later, computers, video recorders, calculators etc. More important, however, was that most people now expected to have these machines. Before the war washing machines and fridges were the luxuries of the richer middle class. Gradually after the war they became accepted parts of most households.

The British consumer electronics industry had geared itself to producing for the home market, and it lost out to competition from Japan and other Far Eastern countries, which had geared their production for world markets. Now **Japanese firms** own many of the factories that produce electronic goods in Britain. The consumer electronics industry has seen high-profile **entrepreneurs**, similar in some ways to the men who dominated the early Industrial Revolution. Both Sir Clive Sinclair and Alan Sugar have been highly successful. Sinclair Research, however, which was a company dominated by technical advances, did not survive, while Sugar's Amstrad, where the emphasis was as much on marketing, has gone from strength to strength.

There have been changes in the **generation of electricity** since the war. The CEGB opened its first **nuclear power station** in 1956, and by the late 1980s there were eighteen. There has been considerable opposition to nuclear power, particularly since serious accidents at nuclear power plants at Three Mile Island (USA) and Chernobyl (USSR).

A North Sea oil rig.

SOURCE A

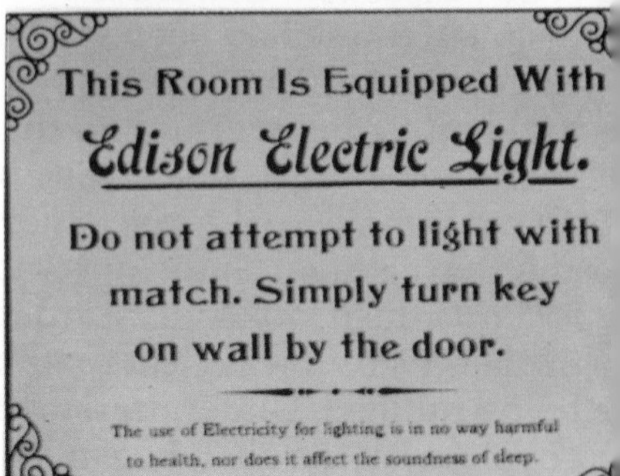
This Room Is Equipped With
Edison Electric Light.
Do not attempt to light with match. Simply turn key on wall by the door.
The use of Electricity for lighting is in no way harmful to health, nor does it affect the soundness of sleep.

ACTIVITIES

1 When do you think Source A was used? Give reasons for your answer.

2 What are the similarities between the growth of the electrical industry and the growth of the chemical industry?

3 What effect do you think war, or the possibility of war, has had on:
a the electrical industry?
b the chemical industry?

Chemicals

The heart of the **chemical industry** before the First World War was the production of **soda**, which was essential in making paper, soap and glass. The British chemical industry was not a success. A new method, the **Solway process**, was adopted in Germany and the USA. When war broke out in 1914 Britain could not manufacture the dye for uniforms or, more seriously, nitrogen to use in explosives. After the war the government helped the chemical industry to grow, in particular by import duties which made foreign chemical products very expensive. In 1926 the four largest firms in the industry formed **ICI** (Imperial Chemical Industries). The new firm dominated the industry at home, and was large enough to compete successfully abroad. ICI could also fund the very expensive research which the industry needed. New products such as fertilizers, plastic and celluloid helped expansion.

The industry has continued to expand since the Second World War. Most chemicals had been developed from coal tar between the wars, but **petrochemicals** (based on oil and its by-products) have become much more important. Penicillin had been discovered in 1928, yet no chemical firm was able to manufacture it in usable quantities until money was found for research as part of the war effort. Commercial quantities were produced by 1941. This is one of many examples of the boost given by wartime research. Since 1945 an alliance of research scientists and large chemical firms has produced a whole string of life-saving (and very profitable) drugs.

Oil refining itself has become a major industry. The oil companies found that crude oil was safer to transport than petrol, and there were a growing number of uses for the by-products. Governments of both political parties have encouraged the refining industry because of the strategic importance of oil supplies. During the Second World War oil and petrol shortages had been a constant threat. The refineries were sited on the coast, usually on estuaries, where the increasingly large tankers could dock easily.

In 1971 oil was found under the **North Sea** bed in commercial quantities. Getting this oil ashore presented one of the greatest engineering problems faced during the years covered by this book, but the increase in **oil prices** by the oil-exporting countries of OPEC in 1973 meant the challenge would be profitable. The first North Sea oil was piped ashore in 1975, and by 1981 Britain became an oil-exporting country, producing more than was consumed. During the 1980s falls in the price of oil have meant that North Sea oil, which is very expensive to bring ashore, has been less profitable than was at first hoped. It has, however, given the government and the economy a tremendous boost during the 1980s.

The motor industry

The first **motor car** was built in Germany in 1885. In Britain the motor industry developed after the repeal of the **Red Flag Act** in 1896. This Act had made it illegal for any self-propelled vehicle to go faster than four miles an hour, and had insisted that someone went in front waving a red flag. By 1914 there were 132,000 cars in Britain, but no real mass production.

The First World War helped the industry to grow. The war itself increased the demand for cars and lorries. After the war there were many more people who knew how to drive and how to repair engines. The two biggest British car firms, **Morris** (based in Oxford) and **Austin** (based near Birmingham), developed proper **assembly lines** in the 1920s, similar to those first used by Ford in the USA. This meant that cars could be made much more cheaply than before. Morris produced the first £100 car. Car making was dominated in Britain by six large firms: Austin, Morris, Ford, Standard, Vauxhall and Rootes. The firms were large enough to buy their raw materials in bulk (therefore cheaply) and to compete for export markets.

After the Second World War there were mergers to make bigger companies. Austin and Morris merged to form the British Motor Corporation, then the BMC merged with Leyland (which had specialized in bus and truck making) to form **British Leyland** (now called Austin Rover). The first few years saw success as British cars achieved good export sales, but slowly the industry

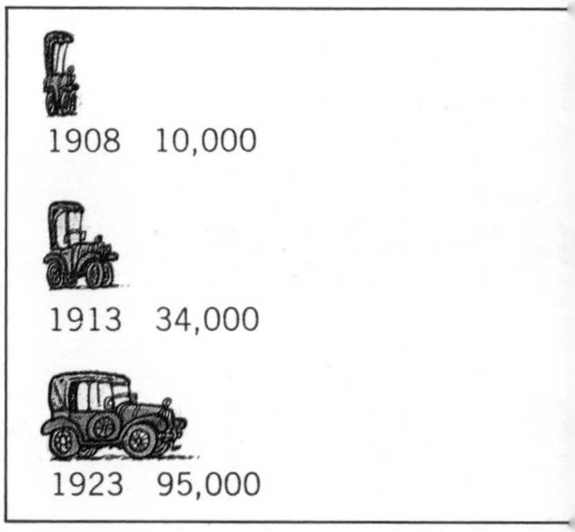

Number of motor vehicles produced, 1908–38.

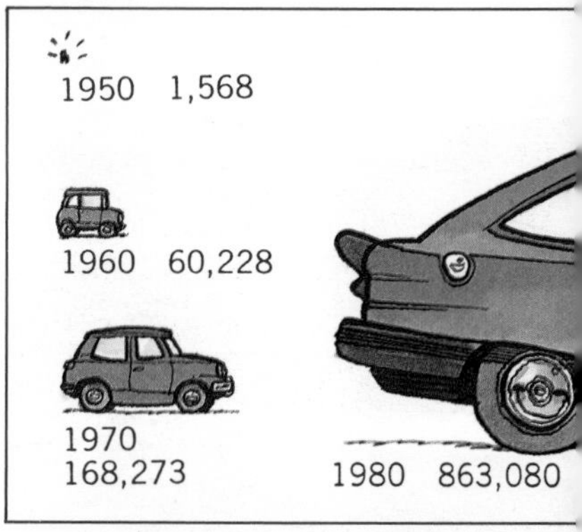

Number of cars imported, 1950–80.

SOURCE **B**

Assembly line, Morris Motors, Oxford 1930s.

SOURCE **C**

Assembly line, Austin Rover, Oxford 1980s.

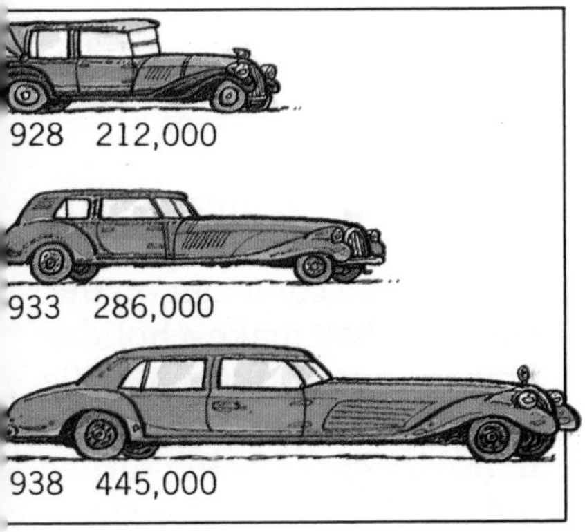

went into decline. It got a reputation for making unreliable cars, and labour relations were bad. Not only were export markets lost, but also imported cars took a larger and larger share of the home market. In 1986 the Japanese car firm **Nissan** opened its first British factory at Washington in the north-east. Cars are assembled there, but many of the parts are made in Japan. For Nissan the advantage is they can assemble and sell cars from this factory without paying duties for import into Britain or the EEC. The British government backed the plan because it brought some jobs to the north-east, a region badly hit by unemployment.

Aircraft

Making **aircraft** had not been an important industry before the First World War, but the use made of aircraft during the war meant that production increased rapidly. After the war the government was keen that Britain should have a strong aircraft industry because of the value of aircraft during wartime. In the mid-1930s it was still a relatively small industry, employing no more than 30,000 people, but rearmament before the Second World War led to rapid growth. The quality of the planes produced by the industry gave Britain a crucial advantage in the decisive air battles of the Second World War.

Since the Second World War the industry has had successes and failures. There have been many big projects like **Concorde**, which has been a success in terms of prestige, but not in terms of aircraft sold and profits. One large firm, **British Aerospace**, came to dominate the industry. Nationalized in 1978, it was privatized by the Conservative government in 1981.

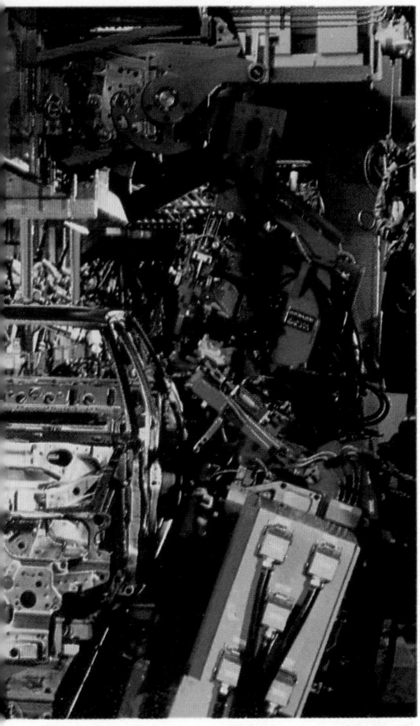

The new industries and the British economy

The new industries have a number of common features which distinguish them from the industries which dominated the early Industrial Revolution. They use **electricity** or **oil** as fuel, which means they have no need to set up near coalfields. Instead they have tended to set up near the biggest market, which is London and the south-east. They also tend to concentrate on **scientific** and **technical** processes. Most have concentrated on the home market, with export sales declining in the face of strong competition from other countries. The danger of this, apart from the loss of export sales, is that foreign companies have such large-scale production that they can compete successfully within Britain as well as in other markets.

Manufacturing industry is getting less important in terms of its share of the British economy. Instead **service industry** has come to dominate, and it now employs over 60 per cent of the workforce. Service industry, as its name implies, sells services rather than making and selling goods.

5.1 ROADS, TURNPIKES AND COACHES

Infrastructure

Infrastructure is the word economists use to describe the things a country needs if its economy is to be successful. **Roads** are a key part of the infrastructure. Without the ability to transport goods and people reliably, cheaply and efficiently, industry would find it hard to grow. During the Industrial Revolution roads were not always the most important form of transport, but the great improvements in road transport which took place during the period were essential to the success of industrialization.

Cheaper transport was most important for heavy and bulky goods such as coal or corn. Quicker and more reliable transport was important for moving high-quality goods, fresh foodstuffs and people. With a good transport system producers could reach a much larger market with their goods. It might be possible to sell to most of the country rather than just a local area. This allowed towns and regions to specialize in producing things they could do best, perhaps because of the raw materials available locally.

The great improvements in the transport system gave a further boost to the growth of economy. Transport itself became a big industry. In the 1838 the **turnpike trusts** (see below) alone employed some 23,500 people; many more were employed as coachmen and in the livery stables which supplied horses. The **canal system** was also a large employer, and **railways** were to become an even larger one. When the new roads, railways and canals were built they employed tens of thousands of workers and, in the case of railways, greatly increased the demand for iron.

Roads

Unless taken over by a turnpike trust, **roads** were the responsibility of the local parish. By law all men had to provide material or do six **statute days** as labourers repairing local roads. This was often resented, because the roads were used by people passing through a parish as well as by those who lived in it. The work was often not done very well. Not only did the labourers begrudge their time, but also the surveyor in charge of the work was unlikely to be an expert in roadmaking. Look back to page 17 for some of the problems faced by people travelling on these roads.

Turnpike trusts

Turnpike trusts were an alternative to the parish system for building and maintaining roads. The trusts were groups of local landowners and businessmen who banded together and took responsibility for a section of road. Each separate trust was set up by an Act of Parliament, and by 1838 there were 1,116 trusts. The trust was responsible either for building and maintaining a new road, or for maintaining existing roads. In order to finance this they could set up **toll gates** on their roads, charging different rates for horses, coaches, wagons, animals, and so on. In 1838 the trusts were running 22,000 miles of road with 7,796 toll gates. The parishes were responsible for the remaining 104,770 miles of

SOURCE A

'Five hired labourers will do as much work as ten or twelve who come out on the statute. They make a holiday of it, lounge about, and trifle away their time. As they are in no danger of being turned out of their work, they stand in no awe of the surveyor. It is a common saying among them that if a drop of sweat should happen to fall from any of them it will infallibly produce a quagmire. In short, statute work will never mend the roads effectively.'

Shrewsbury parish road surveyor writing in his minute book, 1788.

SOURCE B

Road menders, early nineteenth century.

SOURCE C

Turnpike Acts passed each decade, 1700–99.

1700–9	10
1710–19	23
1720–9	45
1730–9	25
1740–9	37
1750–9	170
1760–9	170
1770–9	75
1780–9	34
1790–9	59

road. The turnpikes were not a national system, but rather a series of local businesses. The great trunk roads which ran to London were usually operated by a series of small turnpike trusts.

Not all trusts were good at maintaining their roads. The new roadbuilding methods of Metcalfe, Telford and McAdam were used for only about 1,000 of the 22,000 miles of turnpiked road.

The great roadbuilders

'Blind Jack' Metcalfe (1717–1810) was the first man significantly to improve roadbuilding techniques. He built about 180 miles of turnpike road in Yorkshire and Lancashire between 1765 and 1797. Metcalfe used larger stones for a foundation and stone chippings rammed down hard as a surface, with a camber on the road to help drainage.

Thomas Telford (1757–1834) built the only turnpike road which was a 'through route', the London to Holyhead road, and worked for a number of other trusts. He believed foundations were the most important thing about a road, and used a flat foundation of larger stones, a layer of stones no larger than 6 cm and finally a layer of gravel on top, with a cambered surface. His roads were criticized as being very expensive, because of the stone foundations, and the surface sometimes broke up in heavy frost. However, they were much better than previous roads.

John McAdam (1756–1836) was the most influential of the roadbuilders. He believed that expensive foundations were not necessary, and that the 'native soil' would be fine as long as it was kept well drained. McAdam's roads also did not have a steep camber (only 3 inches), because he said water would drain off any slope.

The surface of McAdam's roads was made from small chips of stone, usually granite. He said the wheels of coaches and carts would crush these small chips together, and they would make a waterproof road surface. This system was much cheaper than Telford's. It is still used for many roads, but now tar is added to the top layer, and the system is called **tarmacadam**.

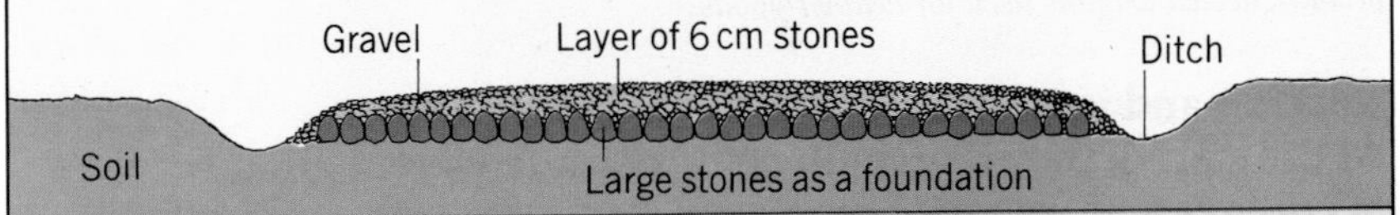

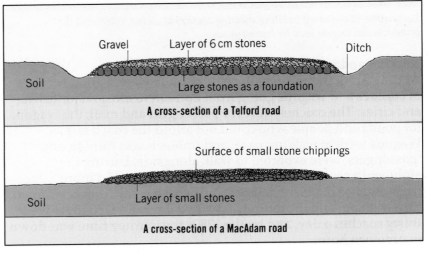

A cross-section of a Telford road

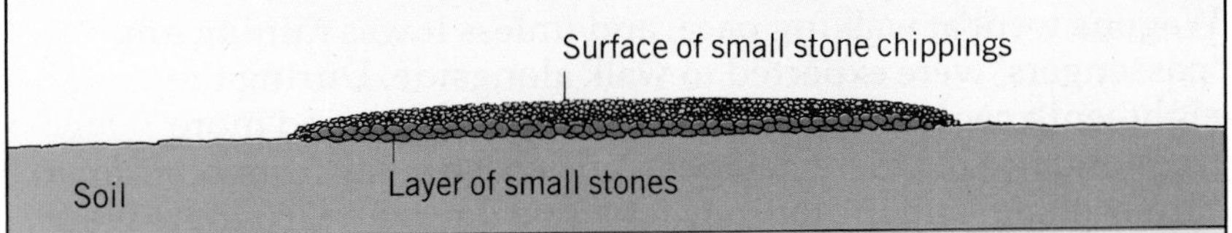

A cross-section of a MacAdam road

SOURCE D

Early ninteenth-century painting showing coaches at an inn, riders and the broad-wheeled wagons used for heavier goods.

Coaches and wagons

At the start of the eighteenth century there were regular services of **coaches** and **wagons** going from London to most major towns and cities. The coaches were for passengers and mail, the wagons for goods and people who could not afford the coach fare. Wagons went at walking pace, and unless it was raining any 'passengers' were expected to walk alongside. During the eighteenth century the coach services got faster and more frequent. In 1740 there had been one coach a day from London to Birmingham, and the journey took two days. By 1763 there were thirty coaches a day, and by the 1780s the journey time was down to nineteen hours.

SOURCE E

Coach journey time from London (average number of hours)

To	*1700*	*1750*	*1800*
Norwich	50	40	19
Bath	50	40	16
Edinburgh	256	150	60
Manchester	90	65	33

Falkus, 'Britain Transformed', 1987.

SOURCE F

'Mail Diligence commenced Monday 2 August

'The proprietors of the above carriage, having agreed to convey the mail to and from Bristol, in 16 hours, with a Guard for its protection, respectfuly inform the Public, that it is constructed to accommodate 4 inside passengers in the most convenient manner – that it will set off every Night at 8 o'clock, from the Swan-With-Two-Necks, Ledlane, London, and will arrive at the Three Tuns in Bath before Ten next morning, and at the Rummer Tavern, near the Exchange, Bristol, at Twelve.

'The Price to and From Bristol, Bath, and London, £1 8 shillings, no outsides allowed.

'Parcels will be forwarded agreeable to their direction, immediately on their arrival at London, the price of Porterage as well as the Carriage on the most reasonable terms.'

From an advertisement in the 'Bristol Journal', 2 October 1784.

The end of the turnpikes

The **turnpikes** reached their high point around 1830. From then on they began to lose customers to the railways. The little trusts could not maintain their roads cheaply, and some of the parliamentary grants which set up the trusts expired. Not all trusts tried to have them renewed. The trusts themselves were slow to see the problems they faced. There were few amalgamations, yet bigger trusts responsible for more roads would have been much more efficient. In 1839 the **Royal Commission on Roads** sent a questionnaire to all trusts, asking whether they felt railways were a threat. Out of the 1,107 replies only 226 thought that railways would harm their business.

Most trusts struggled on into the second half of the nineteenth century, but with growing debts or shrinking profits. In 1871 there were still 851; ten years later there were only 184; and ten years after that only two. The last one was wound up in 1895. Responsibility for roads went back to groups of parishes, then to the new **County Councils** (1888) and to local bodies called **Rural Sanitary Authorities** (1894).

SOURCE G

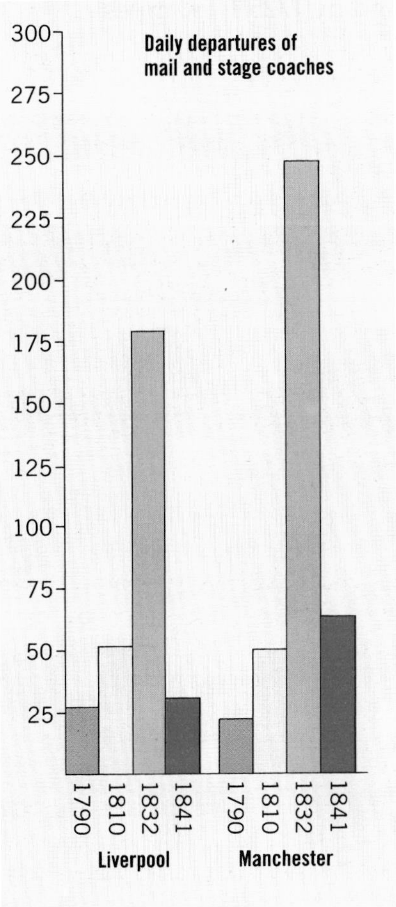

QUESTIONS

1 a What was wrong with the parish system of maintaining roads?
  b Are the men in Source B statute labourers like those described in Source A?

2 a Why did people set up turnpike trusts?
  b What was the average length of road looked after by a turnpike trust in 1838, and what was the average number of toll gates for each trust?
  c If only 1,000 miles of 'improved' road were built, were Metcalfe, Telford and McAdam really important?
  d Does Source C suggest that turnpikes were less important after 1770? Explain your answer.

3 Explain six things a historian might learn from Source D.

4 Is there any reason why the 'golden age of coaching' started soon after, and finished just before, the turnpike roads?

5.2 NAVIGABLE RIVERS AND EARLY CANALS

River transport

In 1700 water transport was vital to Britain's economy. Just the coal taken by sea from Newcastle to London weighed more than all of Britain's imports. The sea was Britain's most important **internal** trade route. Even on an island, however, the sea is not enough. Rivers were a vital extension of the sea as a trade route. For instance the Newcastle Colliers sailed down the east coast to the Thames Estuary and then up the Thames to London. The sea was the more important trade route of the two. The value of goods taken by sea was five times that of goods taken by river.

Not all rivers would have been suitable for transporting goods. Rivers could have **shallows** through which a boat could not pass, or weirs or low bridges. Other problems were long and winding routes and the possibility of flooding or freezing in winter and drying up in summer. Some of these problems could be overcome by **improving** the river (sometimes called making a **navigation**). Bridges could be re-built, locks added instead of weirs, and shallows dredged. New channels could even be cut to avoid some of the loops in a winding section. All this cost money and the work was usually paid for by a group of landowners and merchants in the area served by the river. They made a profit by charging tolls to boats which used their improved river. In the mid-seventeenth century there were 685 miles of navigable river in Britain; by 1700 there were 960, and by 1725 1,160 miles.

How a lock works

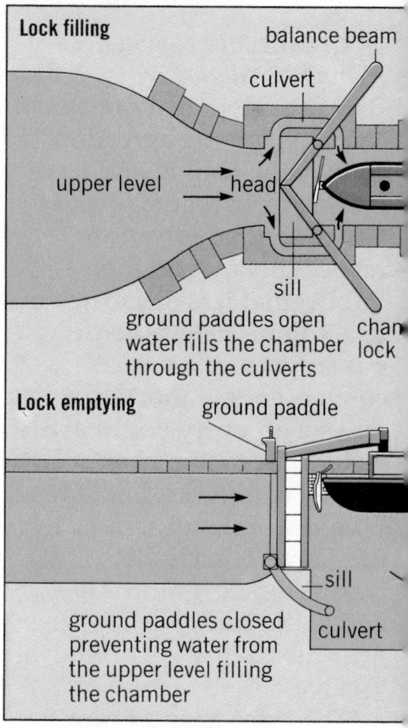

SOURCE A

▼ *The Barton Aqueduct on the Bridgewater Canal.*

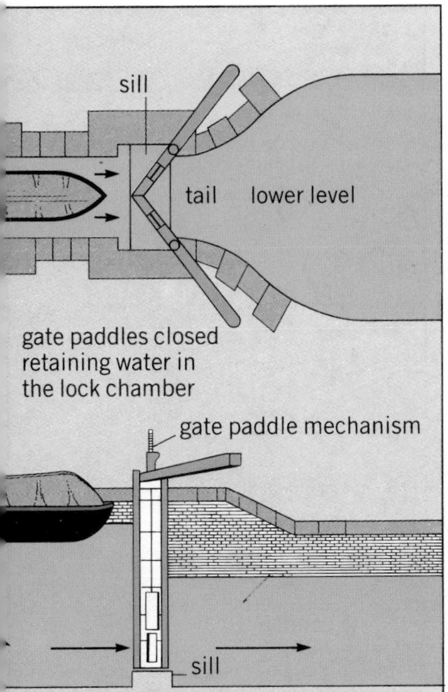

SOURCE B

'I have been viewing the Duke of Bridgewater's navigation. At Barton Bridge he has erected a navigable canal in the air, for it is as high as the tops of the trees. Whilst I was looking at it with a mixture of wonder and delight, four barges passed me in the space of about three minutes, two of them being chained together, and dragged by two horses who went along the towpath. All in these parts are in high praise of the navigation and contemplate the coming winter with a calm spirit, their pockets not being as much emptied as in the past.'

Part of a letter written by a traveller, 1763.

The rivers improved included the Mersey and the Irwell (Manchester), the Don (Sheffield) and the Aire and Calder (Leeds and Wakefield).

The early canals

Despite improvements rivers were not a solution to Britain's transport problems. Too many areas simply were not served by suitable rivers, including growing industrial areas like Birmingham and the Potteries. As it was so much better to take goods by water rather than road the answer was to dig **canals**, artificial rivers which linked important places together. Exeter had been linked to the sea by canal in 1699, but the idea was slow to catch on. The next canal, the **Sankey Brook Navigation**, was built between 1754 and 1757. The canal linked St. Helens to the River Mersey. The scheme had started as a plan to improve the Sankey Brook, but the surveyor realised the brook was not suitable, so for most of its length it was a purpose-built canal. The work was financed by local merchants, especially salt merchants, who formed a company with 120 shares. Building the canal resulted in cheaper coal in Liverpool and some new industry in St. Helens.

The Bridgewater Canal

A more significant canal was the Bridgewater Canal, built by the Duke of Bridgewater. It ran between his coal mines in Worsley to Manchester, a distance of eight miles. The canal was a great success. Bridgewater's coal had been too expensive to sell in Manchester because of transport costs, but after the canal was opened it sold for half the previous price. Bridgewater made vast profits – the canal had cost about £200,000 and the tolls were about £80,000 a year. Not only did the Bridgewater Canal suggest canals could be profitable, it also suggested they could overcome technical problems. The canal successfully crossed a marsh, and a river by the **Barton Aqueduct**. The canal's engineer, **James Brindley**, was to be a key figure in the expansion of the whole canal system.

Engineering problems

Aqueducts could be used to cross rivers and steep valleys: they could not solve the problem of gentler changes in height. Brindley's solution was the **contour canal**, which followed the contours of the ground and often took a winding route, avoiding big changes in height. Straighter canals needed another solution – **locks**. By dividing the canal into sections with locks and pounds (the stretches of canal between locks), engineers were able to take canals over ranges of hills like the Pennines. The locks allowed boats to pass between different levels of the canal. (See diagram.) However locks were not a complete solution. Every time they were used, water passed from the higher pound to the lower. The problem was, how to keep water in the highest pound of all. Sometimes reservoirs were made, sometimes steam engines were used to pump water back to the highest pound.

5.3 THE CANAL SYSTEM

CHANGE

Britain's canal system developed piecemeal. Local companies were formed and canals dug wherever people felt they could make a profit. There was some logic to the system however. Brindley saw the importance of **the Cross**, canals which linked the Thames, Severn, Mersey, and Trent and crossed at Birmingham. Betwen 1766 and 1777 he built the **Grand Trunk Canal**, which linked the Trent and Mersey. The Cross was finally completed when the Oxford Canal linked the Thames with the Grand Trunk in 1790. As the system developed so did differences between the canals. The width of the canal and, more importantly, the width and length of the locks varied. **Narrow canals** could take boats measuring 21 metres by 2 metres, while **wide canals** could take boats of 18 metres by 3 metres.

SOURCE A

Canal barge loading coal from wagons on a horse-drawn railway.

Canal mania

As canals were profitable more and more people were willing to invest in them. But profitable canals could only be built where there would be enough traffic to pay the tolls. Between 1791 and 1794 canal mania struck. Parliament authorised the building of forty canals. For many there was simply not enough traffic to make a profit, or even repay the original investment.

The effects of the canal system

By 1820 the canal-building age was largely over. Canals had provided a great boost to industry, with their ability to transport bulky goods cheaply and relatively quickly. They also had a great effect on civil engineering. Bridges, cuttings and tunnels were all used in a way that the railways would be able to copy. The **navvies**, the itinerant labourers who actually did the work, were a recognizable group of labourers with particular skills: they went on to build the railways. Finally, the canals provided a model for the organization of railways. Large amounts of capital were needed which was repaid with the revenue earned through tolls. After the Bridgewater Canal they were all owned and built by **Joint Stock Companies**.

The decline of the canal system

From the 1830s the canal system began to decline. It failed to compete with the railways, and many canals were actually bought up by railway companies. The canal companies did not invest their profits back into improving the system. With wider canals, transporting more for the same cost, they might have succeeded. However, this did not happen. The canals continued to carry goods until the 1960s, although the amount carried shrank rapidly after the First World War. In 1919 22 million tons of goods were carried, by 1938 it was only 13 million tons. Lorries were being built which could carry as much as a canal boat, but five times faster.

EXERCISE

1 Compare the map of the canal system with map 2 on page 16. How did the canal system alter the transport network?

2 Study Source A. After 1830 locomotives usually provided the power on railways. By the mid-nineteenth century railways, not canals, dominated the transport of goods. Successful photographs were being taken by 1844. Does this help you date this photograph? Give reasons for your answer.

3 a How would you have expected a table similar to Source B to have looked 50 years *before*? Give reasons for your answer.

b How would you have expected a table similar to Source B to have looked 50 years *later*? Give reasons for your answer.

4 a Did the development of the canal system help to change Britain? If so, how?

b Would you expect the decline of the canal system to undo these changes? Explain your answer.

SOURCE B

Names of Canals.	Price per Share.			Div. per Annum.		
	£	s.		£	s.	d.
Ashby-de-la-Zouch	80	0	0	4	0	0
Ashton and Oldham	100	0	0	5	0	0
Barnsley	220	0	0	10	0	0
Basingstoke	5	0	0			
Ditto Bonds	-		-	-		-
Birmingham (⅛th sh.)	250	0	0	12	10	0
Birmingham and Liverpool Junction	60	0	dis.			
Bolton and Bury	106	0	0	6	0	0
Brecknock and Abergavenny	105	0	0	6	0	0
Bridgewater and Taunton	55	0	0			
Calder and Hebble	490	0	0			
Carlisle						
Chelmer and Blackwater	106	0	0	5	0	0
Chesterfield	170	0	0	8	0	0
Coventry	795	0	0	44	0	0
Crinan	2	0	0			
Cromford	420	0	0	19	0	0
Croydon	1	17	6			
Ditto Bonds	50	0	0	5	0	0
Derby	130	0	0	6	0	0
Dudley	52	0	0	2	15	0
Ellesmere and Chester	72	0	0	3	15	0
Erewash	700	0	0	70	0	0
Forth and Clyde	600	0	0	27	0	0
Glamorganshire	290	0	0	13	12	8
Gloucester and Berkeley O. S.	14	0	0			
Ditto Optional Loan						
Grand Junction	243½	241½		13	0	0
Grand Surrey	40	0	0	-		-
Ditto Loan	97	0	0	5	0	0
Grand Union	21	0	0	1	0	0
Grand Western	8	0	0			
Grantham	195	0	0	10	0	0
Hereford and Gloucester						
Huddersfield	15	10	0	0	10	0
Ivel and Ouse Beds	115	10	0	5	0	0
Kennet and Avon	25	10	0	1	5	0
Kensington	10	0	0			
Lancaster	18	0	0	1	0	0
Leeds and Liverpool	395	0	0	20	0	0
Ditto (New)	-		-	16	0	0
Leicester	218	0	0	17	0	0
Ditto	-		-	13	10	0
Leicester and Northampton	74	0	0	4	0	0
Loughborough	2100	0	0	180	0	0
Macclesfield	60	0	0			
Melton Mowbray	200	0	0	9	0	0
Mersey and Irwell	600	0	0	40	0	0
Monkland	90	0	0			
Monmouthshire	225	0	0	12	0	0
Montgomeryshire	80	0	0	4	0	0
North Walsham and Dilham	10	0	0	-		-
Neath	300	0	0	18	0	0
Nottingham	250	0	0	12	0	0
Nutbrook	-		-	6	2	0
Oakham	32	0	0	2	0	0
Oxford	500	0	0	32	0	0
Peak Forest	65	0	0	3	0	0
Portsmouth and Arundel	10	0	0			
Regent's	18	0	0	0	13	6
Rochdale	70	0	0	4	0	0
Shrewsbury	250	0	0	11	0	0
Shropshire	140	0	0	8	0	0
Somerset Coal	160	0	0	10	10	0
Ditto Lock Fund	13	0	0	5	10	p. ct.
Stafford and Worcester	710	0	0	36	0	0
Stourbridge	220	0	0	11	0	0
Stratford-on-Avon	35	0	0	1	5	0
Ditto Bonds						
Stroudwater	480	0	0	23	0	0
Swansea	200	0	0	15	0	0
Tavistock	105	0	0			
Thames and Medway	4	0	0			
Ditto New						
Ditto 1st Loan	-		-	2	10	0
Ditto 2d Loan	-		-	2	0	0
Ditto 3d Loan	-		-	5	0	0
Ditto 4th Loan	-		-	5	0	0
Thames and Severn, New	30	0	0	1	10	0
Ditto Original	25	0	0	1	10	0
Trent and Mersey (¼)	620	0	0	37	10	0
Warwick and Birmingham	240	0	0	12	0	0
Warwick and Napton	210	0	0	12	0	0
Wey and Arun	32	0	0	-		-
Wilts and Berks	5	0	0	0	4	0
Wisbeach	40	0	0	-		-
Worcester and Birmingham	87	10	0	3	0	0
Wyrley and Essington	115	0	0	6	0	0

Share prices and dividends (profits paid to shareholders) of canal companies, 1832.

5.4 THE FIRST RAILWAY?

CHANGE

It is hard to say when the first railway was built. The ideas behind our modern railways came together gradually over a number of years. In this unit you are asked to look for the **turning point** when the railway age began.

Wagonways were particularly associated with coal mining in the North East, although the first was built in Nottingham in 1604. Early wagonways had wooden rails and trucks were dragged along them by horse. Later some used **stationary engines**, steam engines which wound up ropes or wires attached to the trains. Iron rails were first used in Coalbrookdale in 1767 and the first public wagonway (one that could be used by anyone who paid the toll) was opened in Surrey in 1804.

A **locomotive**, a steam enging on wheels which moved with the train it pulled, was first built by **Richard Trevithick** in 1804. His locomotive worked, but it was so heavy it broke the rails. Another, the *Catch-me-who-can*, which he demonstrated in London in 1808, again broke a rail. The ideas was taken up by engineers working in the North East, encouraged by an increase in the price of horse fodder caused by the Napoleonic wars. In 1813 **William Hedley** built *Puffing Billy*, for the Wylam Colliery waggonway. The next year **George Stephenson** made his first locomotive and by 1823 there were 20 locomotives working on the wagonways of the North East.

Three railway companies

The **Stockton and Darlington Railway** (1825) used horses to pull passenger coaches and locomotives to pull freight (especially coal). It also used stationary engines for some of the steeper hills. The railway did not have a timetable and anybody could run their own coaches on the line if they paid a toll.

SOURCE C

The opening of the Stockton and Darlington Railway, 27 September 1825.

SOURCE A

SURREY
Iron Railway.

The COMMITTEE of the SURREY IRON RAILWAY COMPANY,

HEREBY, GIVE NOTICE,. That the BASON at *Wandsworth*, and the Railway therefrom up to *Croydon* and *Carshalton*, is now open for the Use of the Public, on Payment of the following Tolls, viz.

For all Coals entering into or going out of their Bason at Wandsworth,	*per Chaldron,*	3d.
For all other Goods entering into or going out of their Bason at Wandsworth - -	*per Ton,*	3d.

For all GOODS carried on the said RAILWAY, as follows, viz.

For Dung, - -	*per Ton, per Mile,*	1d.
For Lime, and all Manures, (except Dung,) Lime-stone, Chalk, Clay, Breeze, Ashes, Sand, Bricks, Stone, Flints, and Fuller's Earth,	*per Ton, per Mile,*	2d.
For Coals, - -	*per Chald. per Mile,*	3d.
And, For all other Goods, -	*per Ton, per Mile,*	3d.

By ORDER of the COMMITTEE.

W. B. LUTTLY,
Clerk of the Company.

Wandsworth, June 1, 1804.

SOURCE B

A collier with a wagonway in the background, from a book published in 1814.

The **Canterbury and Whitstable Railway** (1830) used both stationary engines and a locomotive. The route included a tunnel and embankments. There was a timetable and the company only allowed its own trains to run on the line. Both passengers and freight were carried.

The **Liverpool and Manchester Railway** (1830) used locomotives for the whole journey, after a trial organized at **Rainhill** in 1829 showed that locomotives could successfully pull trains uphill. The route included a viaduct, cuttings, and embankments. Only the company's trains ran on the line, there was a timetable, and passengers and freight were carried.

SOURCE D

The opening of the Canterbury and Whitstable Railway, 3 May 1830.

SOURCE E

The opening of the Liverpool and Manchester Railway, 15 September 1830.

EXERCISE

1 What claims do each of the following have to be the first railway:
 a the wagonways?
 b the Surrey Iron Railway?
 c the Stockton and Darlington Railway?
 d the Canterbury and Whitstable Railway?
 e the Liverpool and Manchester Railway?

2 What similarities and differences are there between Sources C, D, and E?

3 What features does a modern railway have?

4 Pick a turning point when the modern railway age began and justify your choice.

5.5 BUILDING RAILWAYS AND TRAIN TRAVEL

EVIDENCE

Railway Engineering

In order to build the railways a group of gifted engineers had to overcome great problems. Railways needed to avoid steep hills, because locomotive engines could not pull heavy trains up them. They also needed to avoid sharp corners, because the trains could not corner at speed. Even when surveyors had picked the best available route there were still problems. Cuttings, viaducts and embankments were used to keep the track level. Where they were not enough, tunnels were dug. These were all huge construction jobs, and the work was done by navvies, labourers who moved around the country from line to line.

The job was done by the strength of the navvies who, it was assumed, could shift an average of ten tons of earth a day with no more than a pick, shovel, and wheelbarrow. Gunpowder was sometimes used to blast through rock. The navvies lived in camps near the workings, and had a reputation for hard living and hard drinking. They were well paid by the standards of the time, 5 shillings a day for skilled workers and 3 shillings a day for unskilled. However the conditions they lived in were poor, often isolated from towns and shops as the lines passed through the countryside. They were paid by the month, and could buy food and drink at **Tommy Shops**, owned by the company. These shops charged high prices and the bills were stopped out of the men's wages when they were next paid. Pay day often resulted in a great drinking and fighting bout, called **going on the randy**.

SOURCE A

The Sankey Viaduct on the Liverpool and Manchester Railway.

SOURCE B

'Navvies are generally the terror of the surrounding country. Their ferocious behaviour can only be equalled by the brutality of their language. Woe befall any woman, with the slightest share of modesty, whose ears they can assail. From being long known to each other, they in general act together, and defy any local police force.

'Consequently crimes of the most atrocious character are common, and robbery, without an attempt at concealment, has been common wherever they have been in large numbers.'

Peter Lecount, one of Stephenson's assistant engineers on the London and Birmingham Railway.

EXERCISE

1 a Does Source C support the view of navvies given in Source B?
  b 'Source C is a drawing so it must be less reliable than Source B.' Do you agree?
  c What other evidence do you think a historian would need to check the view of navvies given in Source B?

2 What do you think a historian can learn from Source A?

3 Do you think Source D is a reliable source? Give reasons for your answer.

4 a What differences are there between Sources E and F?
  b What do these two sources add to your understanding of early-nineteenth century Britain?

SOURCE C

A Navvy with all his equipment 'going on the tramp' (looking for work).

5 Do the sources in this unit support the statement in the text that: 'In order to build the railways a group of gifted engineers had to overcome great problems'?

6 Do the sources in this unit prove the statement in the text that: 'The job was done by the strength of the navvies who . . . could shift an average of ten tons of earth a day with no more than a pick, shovel, and wheelbarrow.'

Train Travel

The railways increased travelling. Because they were cheaper and faster than any previous system, more people travelled – some for business, but many for pleasure on excursions. Train travel reflected the class structure of society, with very different conditions in first-class carriages to those in third-class.

SOURCE D

The Tring cutting on the London and Birmingham Railway, 1837.

SOURCE E

First-class travel, 1831.

SOURCE F

Third-class travel in the 1840s.

5.6 DEVELOPMENT OF RAILWAYS

Opposition to railways

The coming of the railways was not universally welcomed. Clearly there were sections of society who would lose out if railways were a success. When the Bill for the Liverpool and Manchester Railway first went to Parliament it was rejected. Not surprisingly the owners of the Bridgewater Canal, which was the main link between Liverpool and Manchester, were the most outspoken opponents of the scheme. They were joined in this opposition by trustees of turnpike roads and people employed in the coaching trade between the two cities. Early railway Bills always faced opposition from such interest groups.

Other opposition was based on different motives. Some felt that travel at the speed of the locomotives would be dangerous, either because of the crashes that might happen or because the human body could not cope with the stress of travel at such a speed. Country gentlemen and some town councils did not want their peace to be disturbed by the railway. Some people thought crops would be set on fire by the sparks from the engines, others that the cows would be so frightened that their milk would curdle. Another group feared railways because of the social effects they might have. They feared radical, immoral or irreligious ideas might be spread amongst the poor by cheap and easy travel. This group won some victories, the Canterbury and Whitstable Railway agreed to stop its Sunday trains, but usually the objections were overcome.

QUESTIONS

1 Do you think the author of Source A agreed with the arguments against railways? Give reasons for your answer.

2 a Make a list of all the arguments against railways. Divide them into the arguments of those who had something to lose, and other arguments.
  b Do you think those connected with the coach and canal systems only used arguments about their own position?

3 Why do you think Parliament allowed something as important as the railway system to grow unplanned?

4 'As Britain's railway system was unplanned it cannot have had efficient routes.' Do you agree?

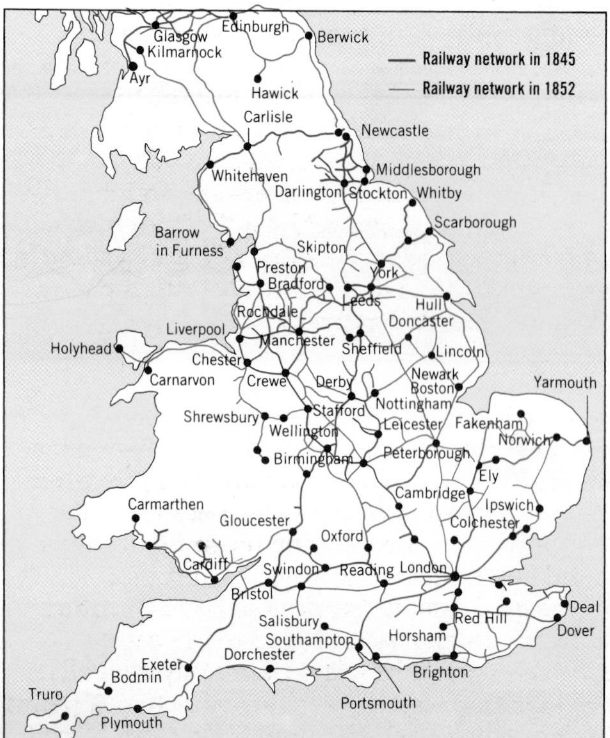

Railway network in 1852.

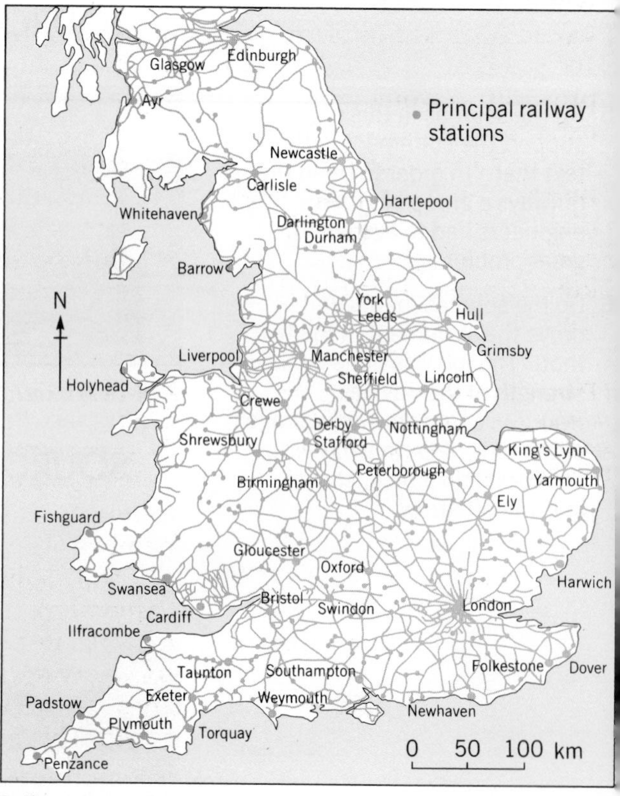

Railway network in 1921.

SOURCE A

'What was to be done with all those who had advanced money in turnpike roads? What was to become of the coach makers and harness makers, coach masters, coach men, inn keepers, horse breeders and horse dealers? The beauty and comfort of gentlemen's estates would be destroyed by it. Was the House aware of the smoke and noise, the hiss and whirl which locomotive engines, passing at the rate of ten or twelve miles an hour, would occasion? Neither the cattle ploughing in the fields or grazing in the meadows could behold them without dismay. Lease-holders and tenants, agriculturalists, graziers and dairy-men would all be in arms. Iron would be raised in price 100 per cent; or, more probably, it would be exhausted altogether. It would be the greatest nuisance, the most complete disturbance of quiet and comfort in all parts of the kingdom, that man could invent.'

J Francis, an early historian of the railway system writing in 1851, summarises the case made against railways in Parliament.

Railway mania

Most railway building happened in three great bursts, between 1835–7, 1845–7, and the mid 1860s. So many railways were planned in the second of these that historians have called this period **'railway mania'**. Investors had been encouraged by the 10 per cent dividends paid out by the Liverpool and Manchester Railway. All lines had to have their own Act of Parliament, which made setting them up an even more expensive business. During railway mania some six hundred planned lines did not get as far as an Act. Parliament did pass Acts for the building of 9,000 miles of line, but by 1858 only 5,000 miles of those lines had actually been built. Many of the lines proposed at this time competed with one another – five different London to Brighton lines were planned. Some covered routes that would never be very profitable anyway. The collapse of many schemes during the railway mania period put some investors off. The large number of railways being built at the same time pushed up the construction costs of all railways. The railway system survived, however, and the confidence of investors returned.

Britain was unusual in the nineteenth century in allowing railways to grow unplanned. Several problems resulted:

- There were too many different companies – 104 in 1844. This made through journeys a problem, but one largely solved by the setting up of a **clearing house** where the companies sorted out through journeys. The amalgamation of railway companies, led by Hudson in the 1840s, helped too.
- Two lines sometimes competed over the same route.
- Two different **gauges** were adopted. Most companies followed Stephenson who had used 4 feet 8 inches for the Stockton, Liverpool and Canterbury lines. Brunel, the engineer of the **Great Western Railway** (London to Bristol) thought 7 feet was safer and gave a faster and more comfortable ride. This meant all passengers and freight on a through journey which included the Great Western had to shift carriages. Parliament stopped other companies adopting the wider gauge and by the 1890s the Great Western had re-laid all its track in the standard gauge.

Parliamentary legislation

Gladstone, President of the Board of Trade in the Liberal Government, wanted to bring the railways under parliamentary control in the 1840s. The Board of Trade examined all proposed routes, to stop wasteful competition, but failed because of the number of applications for new lines during the railway mania period. Gladstone did get the **1844 Railways Act** through Parliament. It gave the government the right to buy any future railway after it had been run for 25 years. It also said each company must run at least one third-class train a day over all its lines, stopping at all stations, with fares of not more than 1 penny a mile. This was known as the **parliamentary train** and it forced the companies to run less profitable trains which were cheap enough for the working class to use.

5.7 THE EFFECT OF THE RAILWAYS

The railways have affected Britain in three ways. They affected the **economy** by providing a more efficient transport system, and, more directly, by becoming a **major industry** themselves. They also **changed the lives** of most people in nineteenth-century Britain in many different ways.

Railways as an industry

Building the railways affected the economy. Suddenly there was a new demand for iron, wood, bricks, mortar and labourers. This new demand was not constant. In 1847 at the height of railway mania 246,509 navvies were employed by railway companies. In 1852, when many of the companies formed during the height of railway mania had collapsed, there were only 36,000 navvies employed. The average number employed between the 1830s and the 1870s was probably about 60,000. The demand for iron fluctuated too. In 1848 the railways had taken 40 per cent of the iron made in Britain, yet in the 1850s and 1860s they took an average of 8 per cent. The demand for coal, which was linked to running trains rather than building lines, increased more steadily.

More important than the navvies were the permanent employees of the railways. Railway companies became one of the greatest employers in Britain, with a staggering growth during the second half of the century, as the following figures show:

	Permanent employees
1850	56,000
1856	100,000
1875	250,000
1890	350,000
1910	600,000

The effects of railways on the rest of the economy

The most obvious effects were on the other parts of the transport industry. Turnpike trusts and coaching were unable to compete wherever there was a railway running on the same route. Canals lasted a little longer. They carried more freight than the railways until 1852, and even after this date retained an advantage for bulky goods which did not need to travel fast. The railway companies, however, saw canal companies as a threat and often tried to take them over. Sometimes this was because they felt the canal could be drained and the route used by a railway. More often it was to stop competition. The Rochdale Canal, for example, was bought by a railway company and the tolls pushed so high few would use it. Because the Rochdale Canal was a vital link in the canal system this meant the canal link between Liverpool, Manchester, Leeds and Hull was hampered by a very expensive section of canal that could not be avoided. Industry was more likely therefore to send goods by rail.

Railways provided cheaper, faster and more reliable travel than

SOURCE A

LANCASHIRE & YORKSHIRE
RAILWAY.
SEA BATHING
FOR THE
WORKING CLASSES.
ON AND AFTER SUNDAY MORNING NEXT,
and on each succeeding Sunday until further notice, with a view of affording the benefit of
SEA
BATHING,
A Train will leave the following Stations for
FLEETWOOD AND BLACKPOOL.
FARES
THERE AND BACK THE SAME DAY.
A.M. Males. Females & Children.
Leave Manchester at 6 0 3s. 0d. 1s. 6d.
" Bolton at 6 30 2s. 6d. 1s. 3d.
" Chorley at 7 10 2s, 0d. 1s. 0d.
" Preston at 7 40 2s. 0d. 1s. 0d.
Arriving at Fleetwood at 9 a.m.
FROM SALFORD STATION.

Poster advertising excursions, 1850.

SOURCE B

'Now, who have specially benefited from this vast invention? The rich, whose horse and carriages carried them in comfort over the known world? The middle class to how stage coaches and mails were an accessible mode of conveyance? Or the poor, whom the cost of travelling condemned often to an almost vegetable existence? Clearly the latter. The railroad is the Magna Carta of their motive freedom. How few amongst the last generation ever stirred beyond their own village. How few among the present will die without visiting London? The number who left Manchester by cheap trips in one week of holiday time last year exceeded 202,000; against 150,000 in 1849, and 116,000 in 1848.'

'The Economist', 1851.

QUESTIONS

1 Make a table of all the different effects of the railways suggested in this unit. For each effect say whether you think it was something completely new in society, or something that was happening already which had been speeded up.

2 The coastal towns on the following map developed into seaside resorts. They did not all cater for the same type of customers. Some had mainly rowdy working-class trippers, others more respectable working-class holiday makers, and others specialised in middle-class visitors.

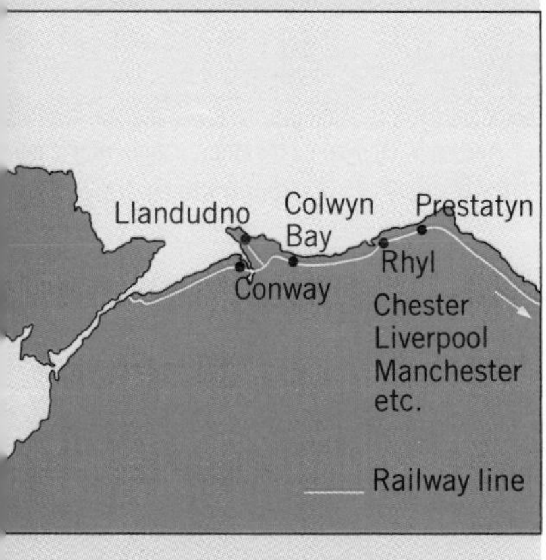

Look at the map and suggest which towns might have catered for which customers. Explain your answer.

3 Some historians think the railways made such important changes in Britain that they talk about the 'Railway Revolution'.

Do you think railways brought about a revolutionary change?

anything that had gone before. This was exactly what industry needed in order to grow. Because the transport problems were solved firms could produce more, getting the advantages of larger-scale production, and selling their goods over a wider area. The railways could, for example, get food into the towns and cities while it was still fresh. Farmers were able to open up new markets like the supply of fresh milk, which became much cheaper and therefore much more common in the towns. Fresh fish could be brought in from the coasts, and the fishing fleets found they could sell more fish. Animals could ride in trains to the market and the slaughterhouse instead of being driven along the roads. This may seem like a small advantage, and from the animals' point of view it was probably not one. The farmer, however, got more money because the animals had not lost weight on the drive.

Social effects

Some **new towns** grew up because of their position on the railway system. Crewe had been a village of some 203 people before the railway arrived, but within five years it had grown to 2,000 and in 1871 the poulation was 18,000. Swindon, Eastleigh and Wolverton all grew similarly because of the railways.

Cheaper transport meant more people could travel. In particular the working classes could **afford to travel**. Cheap Day Excursion trains were popular, and trips were arranged by the companies to the seaside, where new resorts grew up at the end of the railways. Excursions were also arranged for race meetings, religious revival meetings, and special events like the Great Exhibition.

It became possible for people to live further from their work, and suburbs began to develop, especially around London. The first underground railway was opened in 1863 and more lines both above and below the ground followed. The **commuter** was a new type of worker with a new life-style.

The railways also helped to break down the differences between the different parts of Britain, and make the country more **unified**, something which television, radio and the motor car have continued in the twentieth century. It was possible for the first time to have **national newspapers**, and the new **penny post** introduced in 1840 would not have worked without the railways to provide the main transport. Local accents and building materials were less likely to survive as **communication** was easier. Even local time was abolished. Before the railways London had been eleven minutes ahead of Bristol, because it was further east. The railways could not run complicated timetables with many different time zones, so the whole country adopted Greenwich Mean Time in 1852. Trade Unions and political groups found it easier to organize because travel was easier. They could send speakers to different part of the country quickly and cheaply. National chains of shops, which today dominate the high streets of most towns, could only start developing after the railway network was established.

5.8 FROM SAIL TO STEAM

From wooden to iron ships

Eighteenth-century ships were wooden. 'Iron Mad' Wilkinson had made an iron barge which floated, but there was a lot of opposition to using the idea for sea-going ships. People worried that the compass would be affected by an iron ship, or that the cargo would be contaminated, particularly if it was food. However there were good reasons for changing to iron. In Britain supplies of suitable wood were running out, and timber had to be imported from the Baltic. More seriously, wooden ships over 100 metres long were not safe because their wooden framework disintegrated in heavy seas.

The success of one ship had a great effect in the change from wood to iron. Isambard Kingdom Brunel had built a successful wooden ship, the *Great Western*, in 1838. His next ship, the *Great Britain*, launched in 1843, was made with iron. Strangely, it was an accident which showed the strength of the ship. It ran aground off Ireland in 1846 and was only re-floated 11 months later. A wooden ship would have broken up, but the *Great Britain* only needed a small hole to be patched, the structure of the ship was sound. After this, ships with an iron framework covered with wooden planking became common.

No sooner had iron triumphed over wood than steel replaced iron. *The Servia*, built on the Clyde and launched in 1881, was the first ocean-going steel ship. With space for 1,250 passengers it was a success. Steel was lighter and stronger than iron and became the preferred shipbuilding material.

Steam ships

Steam was originally used to power river and canal boats. The first was the *Charlotte Dundas* (1804); after 1812 *The Comet* was a successful steam ferry crossing the Clyde from Greenock to Glasgow. However, steam was not thought suitable for an ocean-going ship. So much coal would be needed that there would be no room for passengers or cargo, and steam ships had a nasty habit of breaking down. This would be no great problem in the middle of the River Clyde, but less acceptable in the middle of the Atlantic. Brunel was again the key figure. His first ship, *The Great Western*, was powered by paddle wheels driven by a steam engine. Although wooden, the ship was so large there was enough room for coal as well as passengers. It was the second ship to cross the Atlantic by steam some hours after *The Sirus*. However the *Sirus* had run out of coal and started to burn the cargo. The *Great Western* arrived with plenty to spare. It began a successful service between New York and Bristol (where it linked with Brunel's Great Western Railway). Brunel's second ship, the *Great Britain* was powered by a propeller rather than paddle wheels, which was better able to cope with rough seas.

SOURCE A

SOURCE B

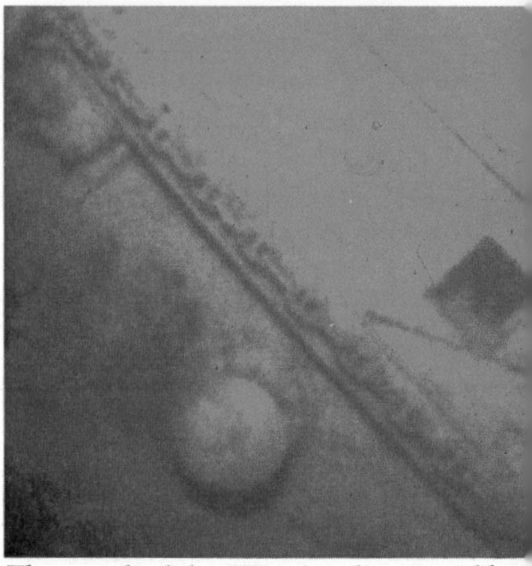

The wreck of the 'Titanic', discovered by remote controlled submarine in 1985.

SOURCE C

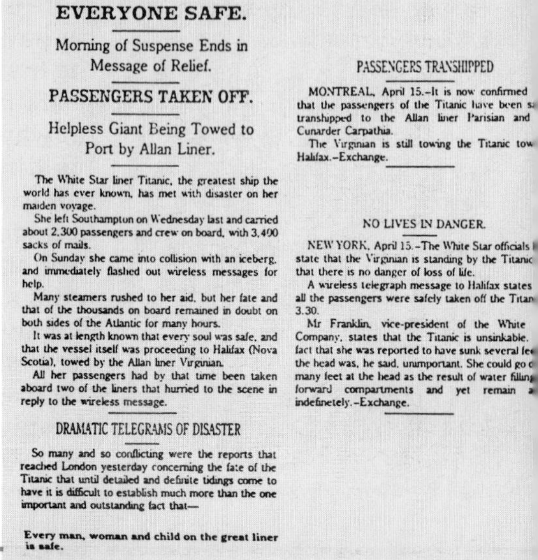

April 16, 1912 THE DAILY MIRROR

EVERY ONE ON BOARD WORLD'S GREATEST LINER SAF
AFTER COLLISION WITH ICEBERG IN ATLANTIC OCEAN.

TITANIC'S WIRELESS SIGNAL BRINGS VESSELS TO SCENE.

46,000-Ton Ship, with 2,300 Abroad, in Peril.

EVERYONE SAFE.

Morning of Suspense Ends in Message of Relief.

PASSENGERS TAKEN OFF.

Helpless Giant Being Towed to Port by Allan Liner.

The White Star liner Titanic, the greatest ship the world has ever known, has met with disaster on her maiden voyage.

She left Southampton on Wednesday last and carried about 2,300 passengers and crew on board, with 3,400 sacks of mails.

On Sunday she came into collision with an iceberg, and immediately flashed out wireless messages for help.

Many steamers rushed to her aid, but her fate and that of the thousands on board remained in doubt on both sides of the Atlantic for many hours.

It was at length known that every soul was safe, and that the vessel itself was proceeding to Halifax (Nova Scotia), towed by the Allan liner Virginian.

All her passengers had by that time been taken aboard two of the liners that hurried to the scene in reply to the wireless message.

DRAMATIC TELEGRAMS OF DISASTER

So many and so conflicting were the reports that reached London yesterday concerning the fate of the Titanic that until detailed and definite tidings come to have it is difficult to establish much more than the one important and outstanding fact that—

Every man, woman and child on the great liner is safe.

PASSENGERS TRANSHIPPED

MONTREAL, April 15.–It is now confirmed that the passengers of the Titanic have been s transhipped to the Allan liner Parisian and Cunarder Carpathia.

The Virginian is still towing the Titanic tow Halifax.–Exchange.

NO LIVES IN DANGER.

NEW YORK, April 15.–The White Star officials state that the Virginian is standing by the Titanic that there is no danger of loss of life.

A wireless telegraph message to Halifax states all the passengers were safely taken off the Titan 3.30.

Mr Franklin, vice-president of the White Company, states that the Titanic is unsinkable. fact that she was reported to have sunk several fee the head was, he said, unimportant. She could go many feet at the head as the result of water filling forward compartments and yet remain a indefinetely.–Exchange.

'Daily Mirror', 16 April 1912.

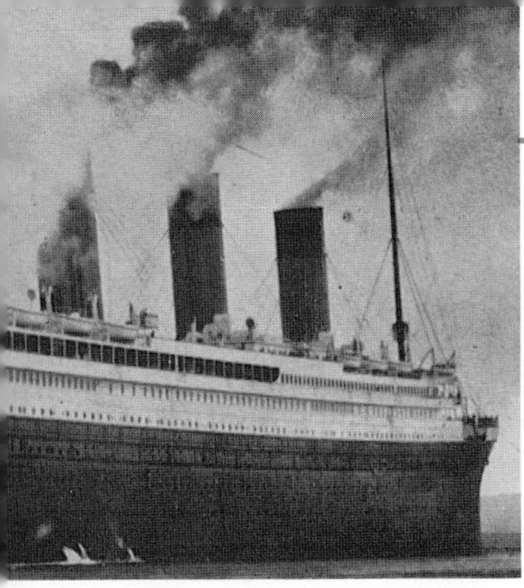

The SS 'Titanic', launched in 1913. The 'Titanic' sank on its first voyage with the loss of 1,500 lives.

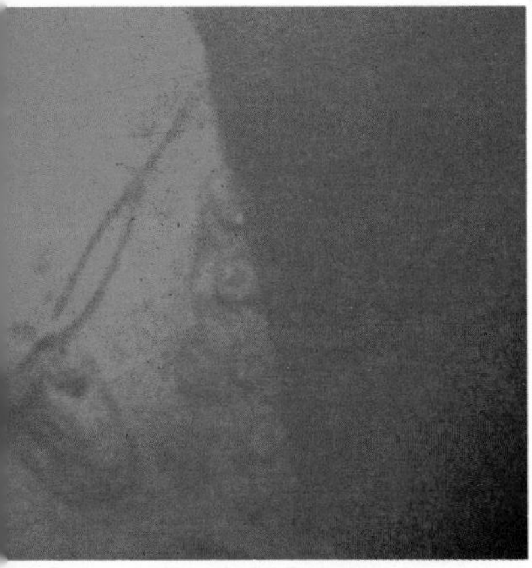

Later developments improved the power that engines gave ships. More efficient steam engines meant less coal had to be carried. The development of **coaling stations** on main routes helped, as ships no longer had to carry enough coal for the whole voyage. Steam turbines were successful, making steam ships faster than before, and oil- and diesel-powered engines were developed at the end of the nineteenth century.

Sail in competition with steam

Sailing ships continued to be a vital part of the merchant fleet of most countries until the First World War. The **Clippers**, sailing ships designed for speed, were faster than the steam ships of the 1850s and 1860s, and could carry more cargo. The improvements in engines and the development of coaling stations helped steam ships to be more competitive. The opening of the **Suez Canal** in 1867 was decisive. The canal offered a short cut to and from the Far East, via the Mediterranean. It was not suitable for sailing ships, which had to be towed through, so they used the longer route around the Cape.

Parliament and shipping

Parliament allowed the shipping industry to develop by itself. Supervision concentrated on safety. The **Merchant Shipping Act 1859** set minimum conditions for the crews and gave the Board of Trade the power to insist officers were trained. The **Merchant Shipping Act 1876** insisted all ships had a **Plimsoll Line** painted on the side. This was to stop overloading. However it was not until 1890 that the place where the line was to be painted was decided by government inspectors and not the owners.

Shipping and the economy

Britain's export trade grew during the nineteenth century. A good merchant navy to trade with the rest of the world was as important to this as a good transport system was at home. One part of the economy, farming, probably suffered. British farmers could not compete with the cheap grain from America and meat brought in refrigerated ships from Australia and New Zealand. Shipbuilding became a great industry, boosting demand for iron and steel, which in turn boosted the demand for coal. By the end of the century Britain was the largest ship-owning nation, with half the world's cargo being transported in British ships.

Passenger liners

The only way to travel from continent to continent was by sea. Companies like the P and O line and Cunard grew up providing a service that was regular, safe, fast, and increasingly luxurious. The great liners cut the time for an Atlantic crossing down to four days and the companies competed with bigger, faster, and more luxurious ships. Despite the well known example of the *Titanic*, which sank on its first voyage in 1912, safety standards on the great liners were high. They dominated passenger transport until replaced by the growth of airlines after the Second World War.

QUESTIONS

1 *Chance* often plays a part in history. Pick an example of how chance affected the development of shipping. Give reasons for your answer.

2 Ships changed more in the nineteenth century than they had since the Romans.
 a Why do you think this happened?
 b Despite all the changes of the nineteenth century there was also *continuity*. Pick one example of continuity and say why you think things did not change in this case.

3 Source C is a Primary Source. Does this mean it is reliable?

4 a Is Source B a Primary of a Secondary source?
 b What do you think historians might learn from it?

5.9 TRAMS, BUSES, CARS AND LORRIES

Public transport

Horse-drawn buses were common in British cities by the mid-nineteenth century. On many routes they were replaced by **trams** which ran on rails sunk below the level of the street. Trams could be horse-drawn, but after 1885 they were usually electric. They were cheap and popular. By 1914 there were 2,500 miles of tramline and 3,500 million journeys were made each year.

Trams were challenged by **trolley buses**, which took their power from overhead lines but which ran on the road rather than rails, and **motor buses** with petrol or diesel engines. The motor buses triumphed: they could run anywhere. After the First World War thousands were sold off by the army, and many men who had learned how to drive and maintain them bought them and started their own bus service.

There was **unregulated** competition. Many buses ran only at the busy times and without a proper timetable. There were accidents as rival buses raced to be the first to queues, and many buses were not properly maintained. To stop this, competition was **regulated** by the **Road Traffic Act** of 1930.

Buses became less profitable after the Second World War as more people had their own cars. In many areas bus services were **subsidized** by local councils. Mrs Thatcher's Conservative Government believed this was not the way to run the bus service and it was **deregulated** by the **Transport Act** of 1986. Smaller firms could compete with the big companies on any route. It was felt this would keep the less profitable routes open as well as the most profitable ones.

Private transport

The private car was not common before the First World War. As cars became cheaper, car ownership became more common. A speed limit of 20 miles per hour was set up in 1904, enforced by speed traps. The **Automobile Association** (AA) developed a system to beat this. Its men (who used bicycles not cars) would wait before a speed trap. Normally, they would salute any car with an AA badge as it passed, if they did not salute it meant there was a speed trap ahead.

Regulation of traffic was needed as the amount of traffic grew. The first traffic lights started in the late 1920s; third-party insurance was made compulsory in 1930; Belisha beacons and zebra crossings were introduced in 1934, as was the Driving Test, and the speed limit in built-up areas was fixed at 30 miles per hour in 1935. Since the Second World War this regulation has continued, largely to increase safety. Front seat-belts are now compulsory, as are crash helmets on motor-bikes, and there have been a series of laws preventing people from drinking alcohol and driving.

Since 1945 car ownership has become more and more common. The road system has expanded dramatically, the **motorways** being the most obvious example. In 1988 the government began talking about the possibility of letting private companies build stretches of motorway and finance them by tolls.

SOURCE A

Horse-drawn bus, London, 1911.

SOURCE B

Horse-drawn tram, London, 1885.

SOURCE C

Electric tram, London, 1903.

Road haulage

In Britain today, more freight is carried by road than by rail or canal. Like motor buses, the road haulage industry grew rapidly after the First World War. Again, ex-army lorries were sold off, and many were bought by ex-soldiers. Once again a period of unrestricted competition was followed by a period of regulation in the **Road Traffic Act** of 1933. After the Second World War the industry continued to grow, however, following the pattern of private cars rather than the decline of buses. By 1970 83 per cent of Britain's freight was carried by road. Large freight lorries were a common sight, often unpopular with those whose houses they thundered past, but a vital part of the distribution system of the country.

Some effects of the triumph of the internal combustion engine and road transport.

Traffic jams and 'rush hours'.

New jobs in many different industries.

Ribbon suburbs stretching out of towns along main roads.

More personal freedom through car ownership.

Health hazards such as lead pollution from car exhausts.

Development of out-of-town hypermarket shopping.

Noise pollution.

More efficient transport for industry, therefore more jobs and lower prices.

Much hospital time taken up with victims of road accidents.

SOURCE D

Motor bus, London, 1919.

EXERCISE

1 Study Sources A, B and C.
- **a** In what ways is the bus in Source A similar to the long-distance coaches (see Source D page 84)?
- **b** Why do you think trams were cheaper than horse-drawn buses?
- **c** In what ways are the trams different from modern buses? Give reasons for these differences if you can.
- **d** In what ways is the 1919 bus different from modern buses?

2 Do Sources A to D show continuity or change? Give reasons for your answer.

3 'History often repeats itself' is a common saying, though not usually of historians. Does the history of transport in this unit suggest this saying is true?

4
- **a** Pick any four effects of the changes given in the table. Explain how they have been caused by changes in the transport system.
- **b** Produce four effects of the changes in the transport system that are not in the list given here. Explain how changes in transport have caused each one.
- **c** Would you agree that without our modern transport system we could not have our modern society?
- **d** Does this mean that changes in the transport system have been the most important cause of the way our modern society has developed?

5.10 THE DECLINE OF THE OLD TRANSPORT SYSTEM

The railways before 1945

The First World War put a great strain on the railway system. In 1914 there were 123 different companies running Britain's railways. If the railways were to be able to cope with the demands put on them by the war they would need better organization than this. The **Railway Executive Committee** was set up by the government to run the whole system. It was a great success and the railways moved the vast quantities of men and equipment needed by the war. After the war many felt the railways should stay under government control to keep the advantages of central planning. However, the government depended on the votes of Conservative MPs to stay in power and it decided on a compromise. The **Railway Act 1921** returned the railways to private companies, but set up 4 large companies rather than the 123 companies there had been before.

The railways did not compete well with other forms of transport between the wars. By law they had to accept any freight that was offered to them, and publish their charges for all freight. Road haulage companies could choose to take only profitable freight and make sure their prices were lower than the railways' published ones. Also the railways grew up with the old declining industries, and the new industries of the 1920s and 1930s were usually sited near main roads rather than railway lines.

The railways were better able to compete for passenger traffic. The Southern Railway electrified many lines, which improved commuter services, and the other companies concentrated on faster locomotives, which suited their longer runs. The **Mallard** set a new world speed record for steam locomotives in 1936 – 126 miles per hour. There was little money invested in rolling stock, however, and little on track improvement outside the south.

During the Second World War the railways were again controlled by central government. This time they only just managed to cope with the increased demands. In 1945 the railways were in a poor state. There had not been enough investment in the system before the war. During the war only essential repairs had been made, and the system had been a target for German bombing. There was very little opposition to the Labour Government's nationalization in 1947.

The railways after nationalization

The **Transport Act of 1947** nationalized canals, docks, most of the road-haulage industry, as well as the railways. The aim of the Act was to produce a co-ordinated national transport system. By 1952 it was beginning to succeed. There had not been much money for new investment, but a policy of **cross subsidy** had been used. Profits from road haulage were used to improve the railway system. By 1952 more freight was being carried by fewer locomotives and freight wagons, and with fewer people employed. In 1954 the Conservative Government de-nationalized the road haulage industry and cross subsidy stopped. From 1956 the railways were running at a loss.

The 'Mallard', 1936. ▶

QUESTIONS

1 What effect did the First and Second World Wars have on the railway system?

2 Is it right to say that the railways were rationalized rather than nationalized after the First World War?

3 Was it *inevitable* that the railways would be unable to compete with road haulage for freight between the wars?

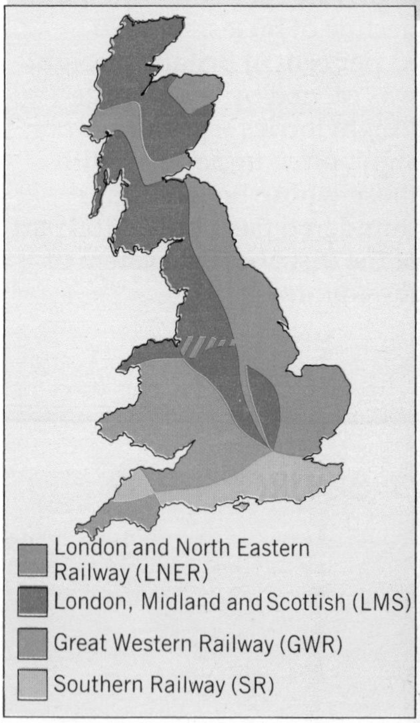

The areas of the four railway companies.

SOURCE B

4 Which photograph, Source B or Source C, best sums up the railways between the wars? Give reasons for your answer.

5 a Describe how the policy of cross subsidy worked.
  b Do you think it was a good idea?

6 'More canal boats have been built since 1963 than in the rest of the century'. Do you think this statement is likely to be true? Give reasons for your answer.

SOURCE A

Photograph from a canal holiday brochure, 1988.

Worried by the losses, the Conservative Government recruited a top manager from industry. The **Beeching Report** published in 1963 radically changed the railway system. Beeching insisted that the nineteenth century system was not right for the twentieth. He wanted to concentrate on mainline services which accounted for most of the revenue, and specialized freight. The smaller lines, which ran at a loss, would be closed. Inter-city services would be improved. Beeching's plan was largely followed. Only 6,000 miles of track (rather than the 9,000 he recommended) were closed, but mainline services were improved with the introduction of **Intercity 125** trains. In a return to the situation before 1852, revenue from carrying passengers was more than revenue from freight. More investment is still needed to improve the railway network and in 1988 the Conservative Government began to discuss **privatizing** British Rail.

Shipping

The British merchant navy began to decline in world importance before 1914. In 1900 over 50 per cent of the world's freight was carried in British ships; by 1914 it was 43 per cent; and by 1938 only 26 per cent. British shipping lines were slow to use diesel engines, and slow to build oil tankers, the two growth areas in shipping between the wars. Since 1945 shipping has been revolutionized by the **container** system. Goods are packed into containers at the factory, the containers are taken to ports by lorry and loaded straight onto specially-built ships. These container ships are much larger than previous cargo ships and different docking systems are needed. Most of Britain's traditional ports have not been suitable and new container docks such as Tilbury and Harwich have dominated the trade. Goods for Europe are now much more likely to go by lorry all the way, using a **roll-on roll-off** ferry to cross the Channel. Channel ferry ports like Dover have expanded greatly to meet the new demand.

The canal system

The amount of freight carried by canals has dwindled throughout this century. By the late 1950s there was very little. A very hard winter in 1963, which closed the canals for nearly three months, killed off the rest. Since then the canal system has developed a new lease of life as a leisure resource. Canals have become popular as places to spend a holiday, with boat-hire firms springing up in most areas.

SOURCE C

▼ *Goods train, 1930s.*

5.11 AIR TRAVEL

Lighter or heavier than air?

The first lighter than air manned flight was by the Montgolfier brothers in Paris in 1783. After 1900 the **airship** was developed. Much larger than a balloon it was kept in the air by gas and used engines to drive itself forward. Germany developed the **Zeppelin** airship and used it to bomb some British towns during the First World War. The airship could be very large, and give passenger accommodation as luxurious as any liner, however there was some danger. The gas which kept the airship afloat was explosive.

The first flight of a heavier than air machine was the Wright brothers' *Kitty Hawk* in 1903. By 1909 aeroplanes had developed enough for Louis Blériot to fly the Channel. The First World War caused a great deal of development as both sides found aeroplanes were ideal for spying on, and attacking, the enemy.

After 1918 both airships and aeroplanes were used to start passenger services. Airships concentrated on the luxury market but never overcame the safety problems of inflammable gas. British airship development stopped when the R101, then the world's biggest airship, crashed in France on its first flight to India, killing forty-four people. Germany persisted with the idea and an even bigger airship, The *Hindenburg*, began a transatlantic service from Frankfurt to New York. On its eleventh journey, however, on 6 May 1937, the *Hindenburg* exploded while mooring at New York, killing thirty-three people. All development of airships stopped.

Aeroplanes had first been thought to be less safe than airships. If their engines brokedown they crashed, whereas if an airship's engine broke down it could still float. A bigger problem was the size of the plane. The earliest passenger planes were converted bombers and could only carry four passengers. It was hard to run these at a profit. Soon bigger planes were built and the British government felt it was important that Britain should develop a good passenger airservice to improve communication with the Empire. In 1924 Imperial Airways was started, with a yearly grant from the government to help it make a profit. It ran regular services to Europe, Australasia, and India. A second large British airline, British Airways, merged with Imperial in 1938 to make BOAC (now called British Airways). Because airports were not developing as fast as airlines the main long-distance services were usually in large and luxurious flying boats.

The Second World War

During the War there was again rapid development in aircraft building. Indeed, without high-quality fighter planes such as the Spitfire the war may have had a different outcome. More significant for later passenger transport, however, was the development of the bomber. Bombers got larger every year of the war, and after 1945 some of these larger planes were converted into much larger airliners. Two other developments vital to modern air travel were produced by wartime research, **radar** and the **jet engine**.

SOURCE **A**

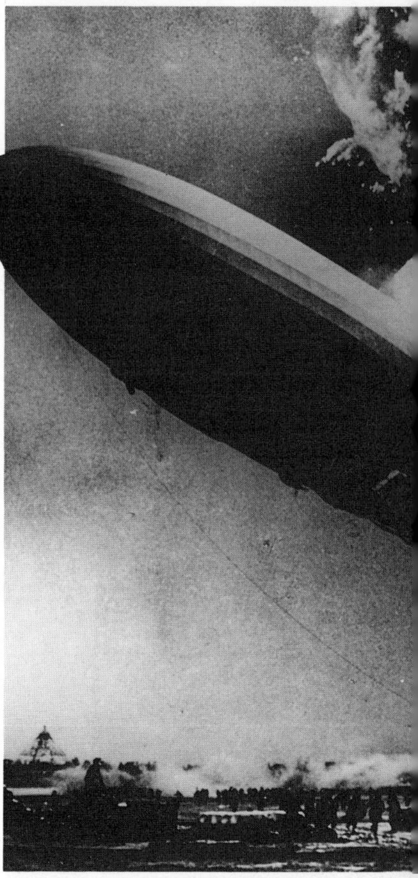

The 'Hindenburg' explodes while mooring, New York, 1937.

SOURCE **B**

1930s poster.

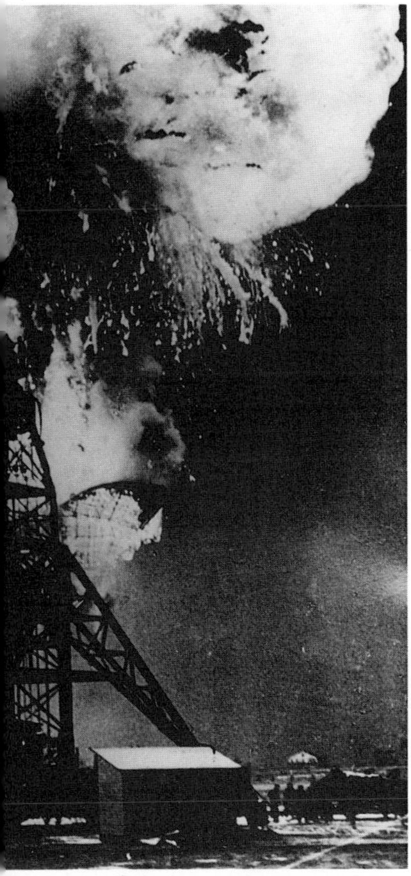

SOURCE C

Nannies and their charges watch an Empire flying boat land at Rochester on the River Medway, 1937.

Air travel since the Second World War

Airlines now dominate long-distance travel. The much larger planes, powered by jet engines since the 1960s, have been fast, relatively cheap, and much more convenient than sea travel. Patterns of travel have changed completely. Once, only business people and the rich regularly travelled around the world. Now package holidays have changed many people's expectations. In the same way as the development of rail transport opened up seaside resorts around Britain's coasts to people from the inland towns, cheap air travel has opened up the possibility of holidays from Greece to Florida at much the same relative cost.

The growth of air travel has not been without its cost. Planes are noisy, especially on take-off, and many people have found that airports do not make good neighbours. At the same time, we need more airports. There have been battles between the planners and people who live in the area chosen for development who fear it will be ruined. The development of new aircraft has become a very costly business. The British and French governments combined to build *Concorde*. While it was a technical success as the fastest-ever passenger aeroplane, it has not been a commercial success. It can cross the Atlantic in 3½ hours, but noise and air pollution have made it unpopular with many airports. Only 16 were made.

QUESTIONS

1. What effect did the First World War have on the development of aeroplanes?
2. Why do you think airships were not used for spying on and attacking the trenches on the Western Front?
3. Very occasionally modern airliners crash. When they do more people are killed than were killed in the R101 or *Hindenburg* disasters. Why have aeroplanes not been abandoned as unsafe in the way that airships were?
4. What changes between 1937 and now might a historian use Source C to show?

5.12 OTHER METHODS OF COMMUNICATION

Improvements in the old systems

So far this section of the book, which is called 'communications', has concentrated on ways of getting people and things from one place to another. This is not the only sort of communication; we also need to move about ideas, opinions and information. Many ways of moving these things about had been developed before. A postal service for letters and parcels; newspapers; stories in the form of novels or plays; and speeches and lectures. New technology, and improvements in the transport system, have meant these things can be done differently and better.

The **Post Office** had existed for hundreds of years before the modern system began in 1840. Under the old system the cost of letters was worked out by weight *and* distance, and the charges, which were paid by the person who received the letter, were high. Rowland Hill's new system, adopted in 1840, changed this. Charges were low – one old penny a letter and paid by the sender, however far it was going. Stamps were introduced to prove the sender had paid. This meant the delivery postman did not have to wait to be paid for each letter delivered. Our modern postal system has developed these ideas – we have two classes of mail and letters are usually sorted by machine not by hand.

Newspapers first appeared in the seventeenth century, when they were published weekly. By the late-eighteenth century local papers were published in many towns which carried national news, often copied from the London papers. Newspapers were expensive, however with a special tax on sales. Moreover the fact that many people could not read, meant they were usually seen only by the rich. A number of changes helped the mass-circulation national newspapers to develop. The railway network meant papers could be taken from London to the rest of the country overnight. The ending of stamp duty on newspapers in 1855 meant they could be cheaper. Forster's Education Act (1870) meant most people would leave school able to read. Finally the invention of the steam-powered printing press meant large numbers of papers could be printed quickly.

Lord Harmsworth was the first to see the possibility of cheap national papers, starting the halfpenny *Daily Mail* in 1896. It was a great success, and was soon followed by the *Daily Express* (1900), and the *Daily Mirror* (1903). Newspapers became so popular that their owners and editors were very important in influencing the ideas of large sections of the population. Since the *Daily Mail* they have relied on money from advertising to help pay for the paper – the cover price alone would not be enough. The more readers a newspaper has, the higher it charges for advertising space. This has led popular papers into circulation battles as they try to win readers from their rivals. These were particularly strong in the 1920s and 1930s, and again in the 1980s.

Since the late 1970s changes in technology have revolutionized the printing of newspapers. Skilled printers are no longer needed to set each page in metal type; the journalists' stories are typed into, and typeset by, computers. The same computers can be used to layout each page.

SOURCE A

THE DAILY MAIL.

BOVRIL

H-O

'Daily Mail', 1896.

SOURCE B

The Daily Mirror.

PAQUIN

REDFERN
PARIS & LONDON

DEBENHAM & FREEBODY.
Special Sale
MANTLES and JACKETS,
Coats and Skirts

PETER ROBINSON'S, OXFORD STREET.

DEBENHAM & FREEBODY,

PETER ROBINSON, OXFORD-STREET.

PRECIOUS STONES. JEWELLERY.
TIFFANY & CO.,
LONDON, W.
PARIS. NEW YORK.
SILVERWARE. FAVRILE GLASS.

VICTORY'S
FURS.
ELEGANT
EXCLUSIVE
MODELS.
162, REGENT ST., W.

READ PAGE THREE FIRST.

'Daily Mirror', 1903.

QUESTIONS

1 a What differences are there between Sources A and D?
  b What differences are there between Sources B and C?
  c How many of these differences do you think are due to technical improvements? Explain your answer.
  d What other reasons might there be to explain these differences?

SOURCE C

'Daily Mirror', 1988.

SOURCE D

The 'Sun', 1988.

e Do you agree that the difference between Sources A and D shows that today's education is not as successful as education was then? Explain your answer.

2 What difference do you think it would make if there were no
a telephones?
b television?

New methods of communication

In 1837 the first **telegraph** message was sent and in 1840 **Morse Code** was invented, a much better system for sending messages along telegraph wires. The telegraph was first used by railways but business was quick to spot its potential. It gave instant communication, although the messages had to be spelled out one letter at a time. Telegraph lines were laid across the Channel (1850) and the Atlantic (1866). The system was taken over by the Post Office in 1869 and phased out in the 1980s.

The **telephone** was a development of this system, sending human voices rather than code along lines. First demonstrated in 1876, the idea caught on quickly. Telephone systems were set up by local companies in some British towns in the 1880s. In 1912 these companies were nationalized and the service was made part of the Post Office. Now telephone messages are just as likely to travel part of their journey by radio wave, bounced off satellites orbiting the earth.

Radio sent messages by radio waves not wires, which meant it was potentially much more useful than the telegraph. The first practical demonstration was by **Marconi** in 1899, and the system developed quickly. Sending messages to and from ships was an early use. In 1910 Dr. Crippen, a murderer, was caught when a radio message was sent to the ship on which he was attempting to escape to the United States; the *Titanic* radioed for help when sinking in 1912. Radio was also important as a means of mass communication. In Britain the BBC began broadcasting in 1922, financed by a licence fee paid by all owners of radios rather than by adverts. Most households had a radio by 1939 and it was the key method of communication during the war. In the 1960s the BBC monopoly was challenged by 'pirate' radio stations. In response the BBC reorganized its own services, adding Radio 1 and setting up local radio stations run by the BBC and independent companies.

Television was first demonstrated by Logie Baird in 1925. The first public broadcast service began in 1936, but it was closed down during the war. In 1946 the service re-started, one channel run by the BBC. One ITV channel was added in 1955, a second BBC channel in 1964, and a second ITV channel in 1982. The growth of television ended the short boom of the **cinema**. London's first show was in 1896 and after the First World War mass audiences were normal and every town had at least one cinema. Together cinema, radio, and television have been a way of getting stories and news across to people. This is not new, but the speed with which they are brought to people and the numbers of people that are reached have increased massively.

Information Technology (IT) can be seen as a new type of communication. Computers 'talking' to each other across the world allow communication to be more **interactive** – the users can get just the things they want by issuing precise instructions. We do not know yet whether IT will re-shape our world in the way railways did, or turn out to be a change which has very little effect.

6.1 POPULATION GROWTH, 1700–1880

By the eighteenth century the **population** of Britain was growing rapidly. Yet despite the scale of the increase, historians still argue about what caused it.

We have plenty of information about the **size of the population**. We know that there were about 5.5 million people in England and Wales in 1695. Gregory King analysed the hearth-tax returns for that year. Details of the tax returns can be used to work out the number of households, and this gives us an estimate of the total population. We also know the size of the population in 1801, which was 9.2 million for England and Wales and 10.7 million for Britain. This was the year of the first modern national census. Since then a census of the population has been held every ten years, except during the Second World War (see Source A).

We therefore know a lot about the **rate** of population increase. By the end of the the eighteenth century the increase was more than 10 per cent per decade. At times in the nineteenth century the population was rising by 15 per cent every decade. The twentieth century has averaged a 4 per cent increase per decade. The growth rates between about 1780 and 1880 show the fastest population increase in the whole of British history.

We also know that this increase **varied from area to area**. The fastest areas of growth were in Lancashire and the north-west, Yorkshire and the north-east, southern Scotland, South Wales and the Midlands (see the map on page 112). These were the main industrial areas of the country. The national rate of population increase between 1801 and 1811 was 13.5 per cent; but the increase in Lancashire was 23 per cent.

Historians argue about the **causes** of the increase. There are only three possible ways for the population to increase: the number of births can increase; the number of deaths can decrease; or the number of immigrants compared to emigrants can increase. We know that in Britain after 1700 the number of immigrants was similar to the number of emigrants and was never great enough to effect national population totals. So in Britain the population increase must have been caused by an increase in the **birth rate** (usually expressed as the number of births per thousand in the population) or by a fall in the **death rate** (the number of deaths per thousand in the population) or by a combination of both.

But there are no accurate figures. Official records of births and deaths began only in 1837. Before this date we have to rely on records of baptisms and burials kept by Church of England clergy in each parish. Extracts from these records were collected in London and called the **Parish Register Abstracts**. Unfortunately, these can be misleading.

For the years before 1780 the Abstracts were collected for only one year in every ten. If any of those years are not typical (if, for example, they were years of epidemics, food shortage or high unemployment), then they could give a very misleading impression. Also, the figures record Anglian (Church of England) baptism, not births; and Anglican burials, not deaths.

SOURCE A

The population of Britain (taken from national census figures)

	Population total (in millions)	*Rate of increase (% per decade)*
1695	5.5*	
1801	9.2*	
1801	10.5	
		14%
1811	12.0	
		17.5%
1821	14.1	
		15.5%
1831	16.3	
		14%
1841	18.5	
		12.5%
1851	20.8	
		11%
1861	23.1	
		13%
1871	26.1	
		14%
1881	29.7	
		11%
1891	33.1	
		12%
1901	37.0	
		10%
1911	40.8	
		4.5%
1921	42.8	
		4.5%
1931	44.8	
		3.8%**
1941	46.5**	
		5%**
1951	48.9	
		5%
1961	51.3	
		5%
1971	54.0	
		0.5%
1981	54.3	

* Totals for England and Wales only; all other totals include Scotland.

** Estimate

QUESTIONS

1 Describe how the Parish Register Abstracts (PRA) were collected.

2 Why are the PRA figures misleading records of birth and death rates in eighteenth-century England?

3 Comment on the following statements:
   a No one involved in the recording of the PRA figures was trying to mislead anybody. They cannot be biased. Therefore the PRA figures are reliable.
   b The PRA figures are inaccurate, therefore they are useless.

They omit all Catholics and Nonconformists and anyone given a private or pauper burial outside the parish churchyard. We also need to worry about whether the figures were recorded consistently. Once the population began to increase quickly, many clergy couldn't cope with all the needs of their parish, and the gap between recorded baptisms and burials and actual births and deaths grew. The **inaccuracy** of the figures was greatest in the areas where the population was rising fastest.

As a result, most historians distrust any simple picture of the birth and death rates based purely upon the Parish Register Abstracts. These almost certainly **underestimate** the number of births and deaths. Historians therefore look at other sources of information to compare with the picture presented by the Abstracts figures. They look at the changes they *know* were taking place in society at the time and work out how these would have affected birth and death rates. This way it is possible to build up **hypotheses**, or theories, about why the population increased. Pages 110–11 examine these theories.

SOURCE B

A satirical cartoon by George Cruickshank called 'Taking the Census', 1851.

6.2 WHY DID THE POPULATION INCREASE?

A fall in the death rate?

Medical treatment improved during the eighteenth and nineteenth centuries. **New hospitals** were built in large towns, particularly in London, where Guy's Hospital was opened in 1724. Voluntary organizations founded 150 hospitals, including many 'lying-in' or maternity hospitals, by 1825. But the impact of these scattered hospitals on the mass of the public must have been small, particularly since the key medical improvements of these centuries, such as antiseptics, anaesthetics, most vaccines and better nursing, were introduced only after 1850 (see pages 148–51). Many historians have even said that the eighteenth-century hospitals were full of infection and may have even *increased* death rates among the sick. There is some evidence that more babies were surviving childbirth, however.

Smallpox was the only disease to be seriously affected by medical progress. **Inoculation** was first tried in Britain in 1721, and **vaccination** was introduced by Jenner in 1796 (see page 150). But although deaths from smallpox fell, this cannot explain the huge increase in population that occurred. If general death rates stayed high, most of the people saved from smallpox would die soon after of other diseases. People were also very suspicious of inoculation – it sometimes caused the death of the receiver. Vaccination was not free or readily available to all; and many people were worried by the deliberate infection with cowpox which it involved (see the cartoon on page 12). Eventually, in 1853, the government introduced a compulsory programme of vaccination for children.

Epidemics of bubonic plague, scarlet fever and other such diseases which had held back population increase in previous centuries did not occur in the eighteenth century. This was probably due to a natural decline in the epidemics and not to medical progress. In any case, these epidemics declined throughout Europe without causing population growth on the same scale as Britain's.

Better living conditions may have reduced death rates. Improvements in **agriculture** and **transport** produced a bigger and more reliable supply of cheap food. Industry now provided cheap **cotton** for clothes, which could be washed more regularly than the woollen clothes people relied on before. Bed linen was healthier for the same reason. Better-quality **housing**, built of brick and tile, with piped water and drains, were healthier. However, some historians doubt whether living conditions in the industrial towns were much improved. Piped water and drains came to few houses before 1850; cheap cotton would have had little impact when water supplies were so scarce. Better **nutrition** is more convincing perhaps, but there were plenty of periods of hardship caused by food shortages (such as in 1810–12 and 1828–32) or high unemployment (such as in 1815–22), when diet suffered.

SOURCE A

From a drawing by Hogarth of a London street in 1738. What impressions are given here about living conditions, sewage-disposal arrangements and medical treatment in the eighteenth century?

ACTIVITY

Population growth in the eighteenth and nineteenth centuries:

- was unusually rapid;
- started to speed up after 1750;
- slowed down towards the end of the nineteenth century;
- was especially marked in industrial areas.

In this unit there are a number of theories which might explain this.

A rise in the birth rate?

Married couples usually try to avoid having children if the circumstances are not right – if their jobs are insecure or if they can't afford enough food, for example. This keeps the birth rate low. **Contraception** was very inefficient in the early eighteenth century, so it was difficult for parents to limit the number of children they had, but circumstances made it necessary. Some historians think that, as the lives of people improved, there was less need to restrict the number of children in families, and the birth rate went up.

For example, as industry expanded, **employment** became more reliable. It was safer for people to have large families. In addition, many of the jobs created in the Industrial Revolution were for children. **Child labour** became very common in factories. If children could work early, they could soon earn their keep. Couples did not have to worry so much about the cost of feeding large families, and so the birth rate may have risen.

The **Poor Law** may also have helped bring about larger families. In 1795 the Speenhamland System was introduced (see page 142). This gave financial help to the poorest families. A large family could get more money than a small family could. Parents did not have more children in order to claim more money, but the fact that they could get financial help may have meant that people did not try so hard to limit the size of their

Other **social changes** may have reduced the **age of marriage**. In 1700 the average age of marriage was 27. By 1800, in industrial areas, it was about 20. In other areas it was about 24. The growth of **unskilled jobs** in factories, for example, meant that fewer men started **apprenticeships**, and the old practice of workers 'living in' with their employer declined. This meant that men became independent, started to earn their full wages and could marry earlier. If, because of this, women married earlier too, then women would have had more **child-bearing years** in their marriages. With contraception so inefficient, this would tend to increase the size of families.

Although the national records of births and deaths are unreliable, some **local studies** have supported these birth-rate theories. One historian, Professor Wrigley, analysed the records in the parish of Colyton and was able to build up complete **family histories** of many people there. Another historian studied the aristocracy, for whom there are better records. Both historians found that in the families they studied there was a distinct increase in the birth rate. But can we treat these families as typical of Britain in the 1700s and 1800s?

What attracts many people to the birth-rate theories is that the extra children born in one generation become parents in the next generation and have children of their own. This can create a population increase which gets faster and faster. A fall in **infant mortality** can have the same effect.

For each one:

- **a** Describe the theory.
- **b** What are the strong points of the theory?
- **c** What are the weaknesses of the theory?

(Remember to match each theory against the features above.)
Finally, decide on *your* explanation for the rise in population after 1700. You may decide to use parts of several theories.

6.3 THE EFFECTS OF POPULATION GROWTH, 1700–1880

The rate of population increase varied around the country. Thus the **distribution** of the population changed. Traditionally, most people had lived in the south-east. But although London's population rose very rapidly, the other areas of fastest increase were the industrial areas of the north-east, the north-west, southern Scotland, South Wales and the Midlands. No counties in England and Wales declined in population.

Towns also grew more quickly than country areas, so the percentage of people living in them increased. We call this process **urbanization**. Many of our biggest modern towns became prominent at this time (see Source A). Whereas 25 per cent of the population lived in towns of more than 10,000 people in 1801, by 1851 the figure was 50 per cent, and by 1901 it was 75 per cent.

SOURCE A

The growth of population in towns

Year	*Manchester – Lancashire*
1801	75,000
1841	25,000
1881	500,000

Year	*Birmingham – Midlands*
1801	70,000
1841	200,000
1881	550,000

Taken from national census figures.

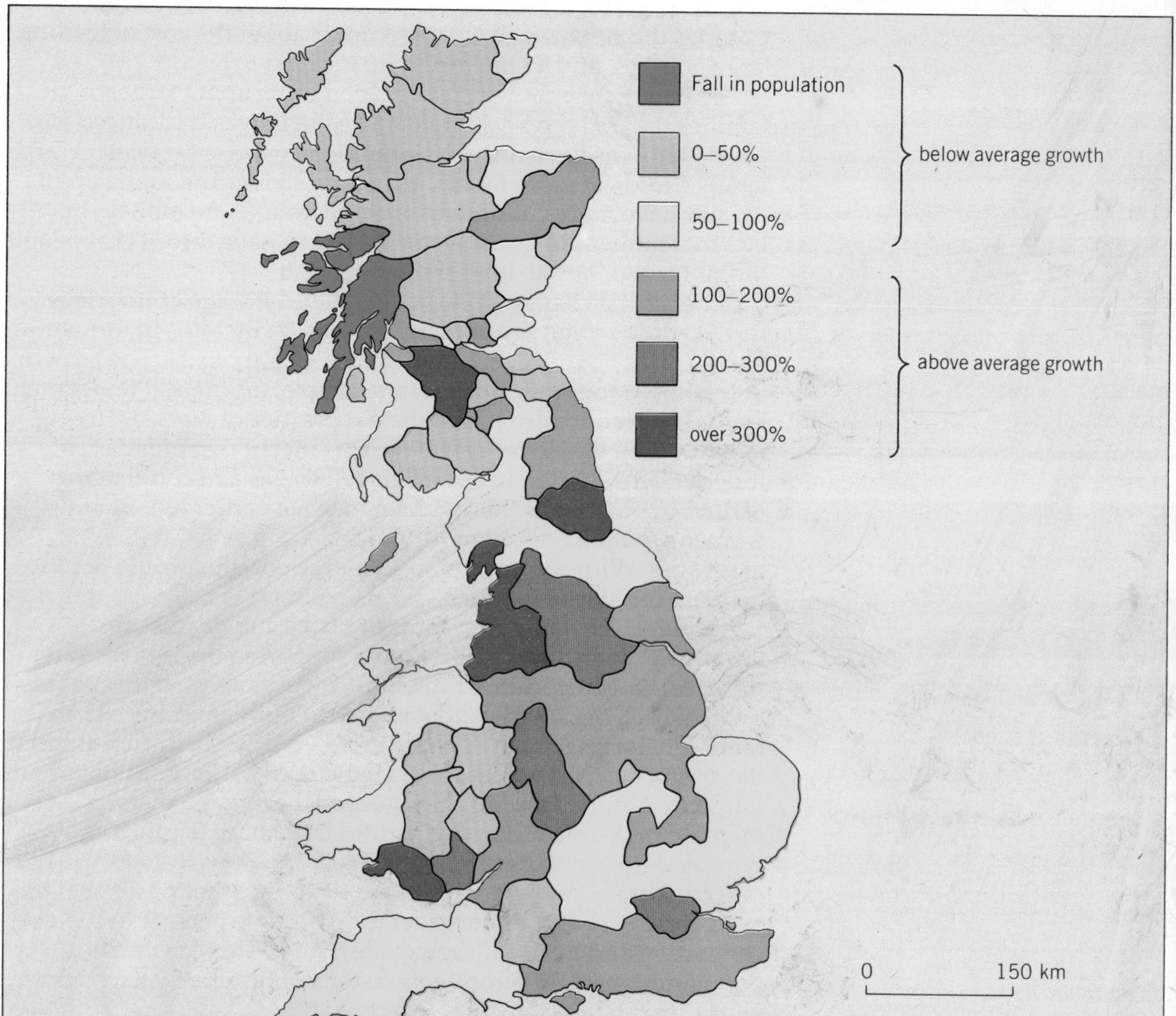

Regional population increase, 1801–71.

There are three reasons why towns and industrial areas grew more quickly than other areas. Firstly, they gained people by **immigration from abroad**. Although immigration was not great enough to affect national figures, because immigrants tended to congregate together, there were marked *local* effects. By 1851, for example, 10 per cent of the population of Manchester and 15 per cent of Liverpool were of Irish origin. Secondly, people moved into the towns and industrial areas through **migration from the surrounding countryside** where agricultural changes limited the number of jobs available. Thirdly, the **natural rate of growth** in the towns and industrial areas was greater. Whatever was causing the national population increase worked more powerfully in these areas. It may be that the hospitals and doctors were concentrated there; or that living conditions improved most there; or that most jobs were in these areas and therefore family size grew fastest there. The high percentage of immigrants would have meant more young people and thus more births than the national average.

This rapid growth of towns caused severe **social problems**. There were severe shortages of housing, water, sewerage and refuse disposal (see pages 124–5). The number of schools, churches and hospitals became inadequate. Overcrowding and poor sanitation brought disease – the first cholera outbreaks began in the 1830s. These social problems among large numbers of people concentrated in the towns caused **political unrest**. The urban poor were dissatisfied with their living conditions, and all kinds of political activity began to take place among the urban masses. The early nineteenth century is marked by mass political movements like **trade unions** and **Chartism** (pages 130–41).

But the rise in population had good effects on industry and agriculture. More people meant more **demand** for food, clothes and household goods. It was partly this demand that led to the prosperity of the farms and the cotton, coal, iron and pottery industries. Just as important, more people meant a plentiful supply of cheap **labour** for the farms and factories.

Another effect of population increase was on **transport**. The huge volume of food and other goods which had to be transported to the towns was one reason for the growth of the turnpike trusts, the canals and the railways. The railway owners also benefited from the huge volume of passenger traffic which went by rail after 1830.

Therefore, by helping agriculture, industry and transport, the growth in the population was an important **cause** of the Industrial Revolution. But the changes in population were also an **effect** of the Industrial Revolution. The changes in industry encouraged larger families. The extra food produced by new farming methods allowed the population to grow without starving. Improved transport helped to get this food to the towns cheaply. So the connection between population increase and industrialization was not a simple one-way process. Population increase was just one aspect of the complex changes we call the Industrial Revolution.

QUESTIONS

1 Listed below are some of the changes linked to urbanization in the nineteenth century. Which ones are *causes* and which ones are *effects* of urbanization? Explain your answer in each case.
   - **a** Immigration from abroad.
   - **b** Migration from the countryside.
   - **c** High birth rate in the towns.
   - **d** Shortage of housing.
   - **e** Political unrest.

2 The high birth rate in the towns could be seen as both a cause and an effect of urbanization. Why? Explain your answer.

3 **a** List as many ways as you can by which changes in industry, farming and transport caused the population to increase between 1700 and 1880. (Pages 110–11 will help you.)
   - **b** List as many ways as you can in which the population increase caused changes in industry, farming and transport.

4 Which of the following statements do you prefer? Explain your answer in each case.
   - **a** Population increase was a cause of the Industrial Revolution.
   - **b** Population increase was an effect of the Industrial Revolution.
   - **c** Population increase and the Industrial Revolution were interrelated; they depended on each other and they fed each other.

6.4 POPULATION CHANGES SINCE 1880

The **rate** of population increase has slowed down considerably since 1880. Between 1800 and 1880 the birth rate was much higher than the death rate. Many more people were being born than were dying, and so the population increased rapidly. After 1880, however, the **birth rate** fell sharply. Fewer babies were born; the population increase slowed. It would have slowed even more, but the **death rate** also fell after 1880 as people began to live longer. However, since 1920 the death rate has fallen only slightly. Britain now has a low death rate and a low birth rate, and the rate of population change is therefore very small.

These changes have affected the **age structure** of the population. In the nineteenth century the proportions of the population consisting of people under 14 and over 65 stayed about the same. This meant that the proportion of workers compared to dependent members of society was stable. However, in the twentieth century the size of the group aged over 65 has become much larger. By 1980 there were five times as many people in Britain over 65 as there had been in 1901. There were ten times as many people over 85. This has had serious effects on the cost of old-age pensions, the National Health Service and other social services. The proportion of children in the population has fallen.

The **geographical distribution** of the population has also been affected. The decline of the old industries like coal and textiles caused high unemployment in areas such as the north-east and South Wales, particularly between the wars and in the 1980s. This caused lower birth rates there, and less migration into those areas. The new industries which have grown up in the twentieth century have been based elsewhere. The car industry, for example, grew in the Midlands and the south-east. Population growth in London and the south-east between 1921 and 1932 was 14 per cent; in the Midlands it was 7 per cent. Over the same period, population growth in Lancashire was only 2.5 per cent; in Wales the population *fell* by 5 per cent.

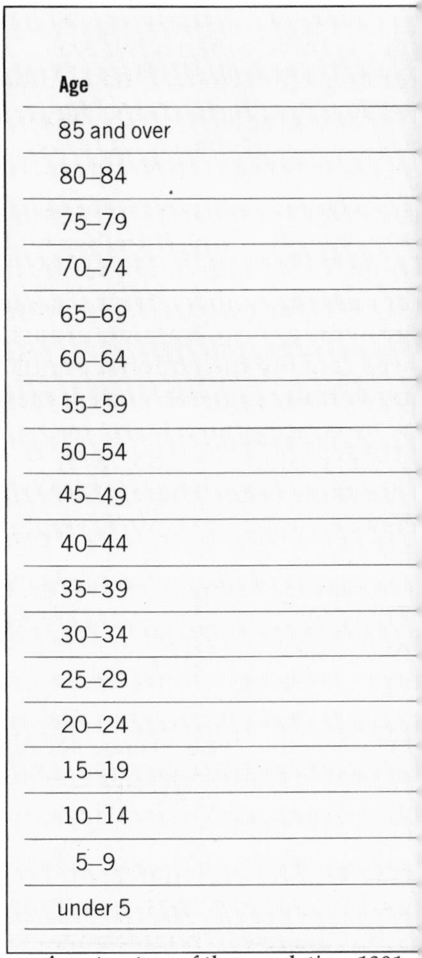

▲ *Age structure of the population, 1901 and 1980.*

Birth and death rates for England and Wales, 1841–1980. ▼

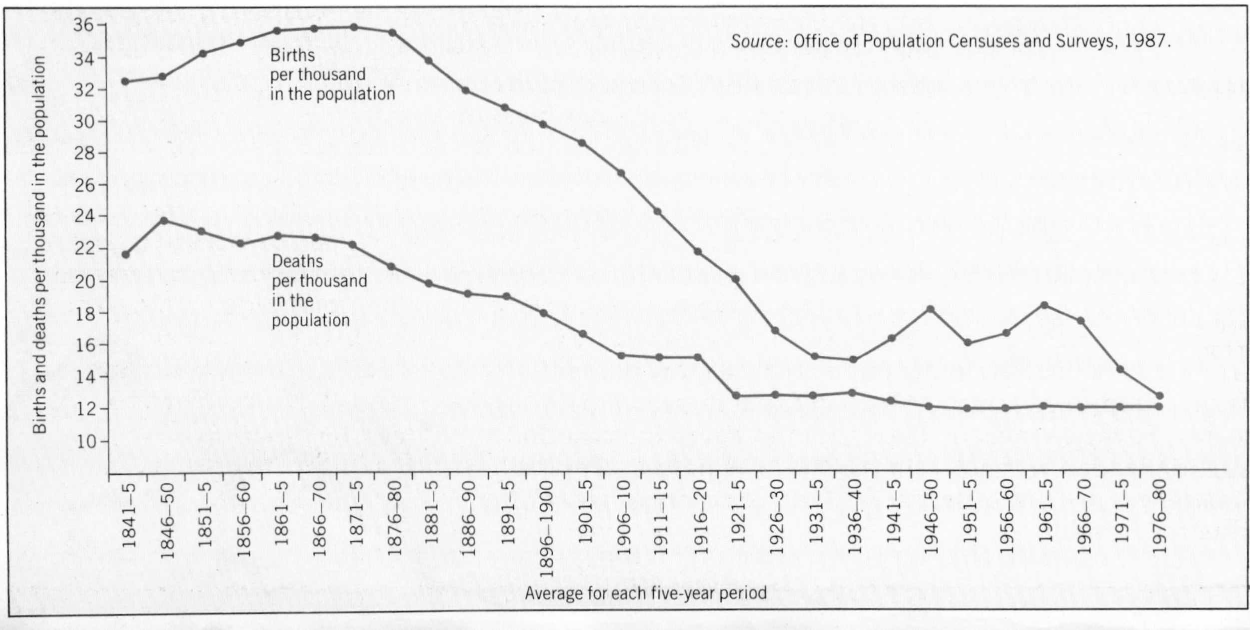

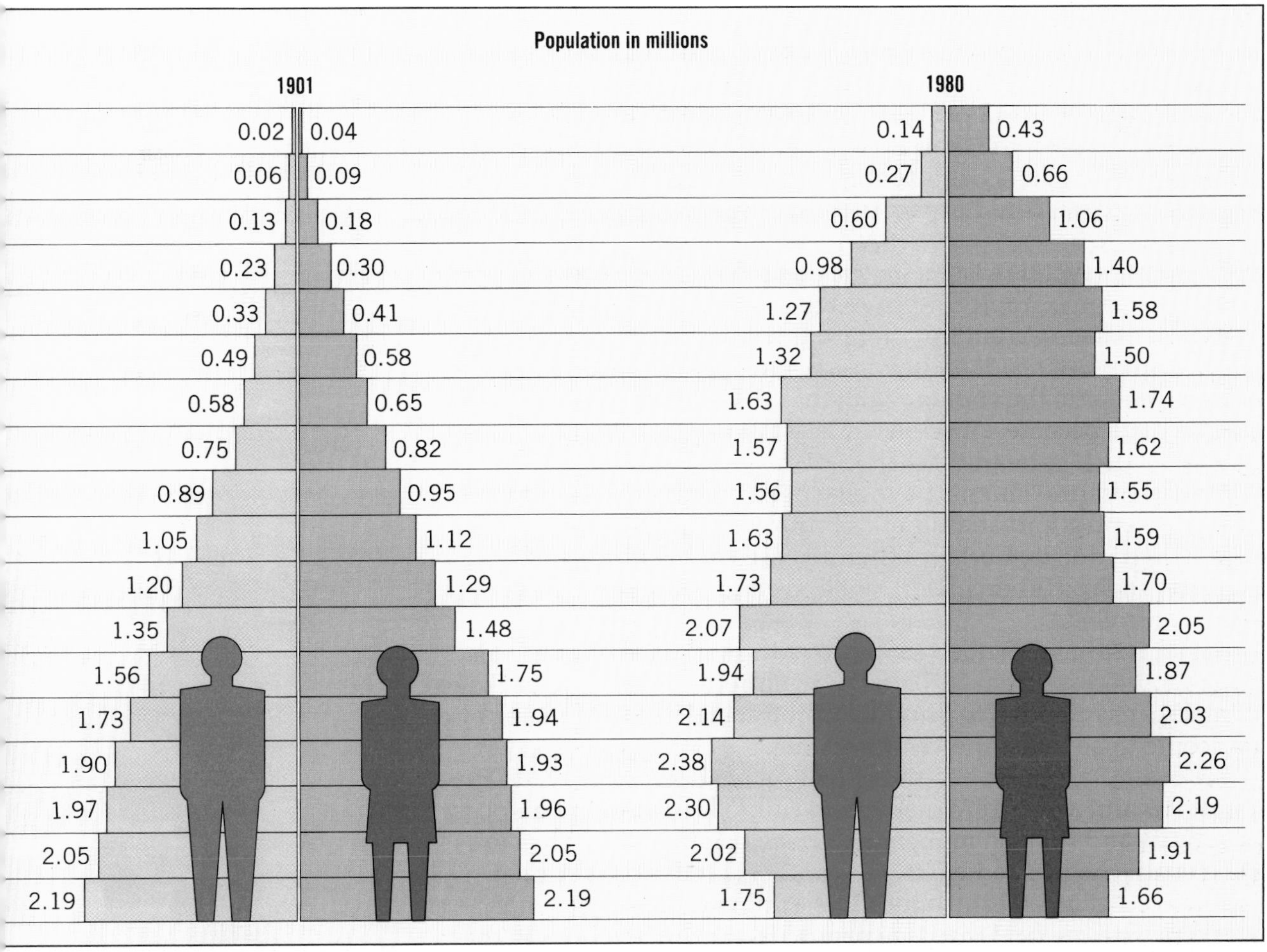

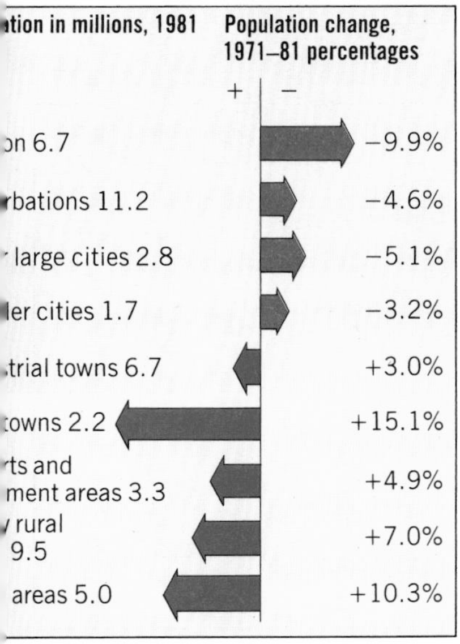

The changing pattern of urbanization, 1971–81.

Urbanization has also changed in character. The proportion of people living in towns continues to grow, though more slowly. In 1861, 50 per cent of the population of Britain lived in towns; by 1901 the proportion was 75 per cent; by 1961 it was 80 per cent. But the character of town growth is changing. The old industrial town centres are being cleared of old housing. Many town centres are increasingly dominated by businesses and shops, reducing their population. Manchester's population, for example, fell from 999,000 in 1931 to 850,000 in 1951. New urban growth has come elsewhere. Sprawling **suburbs** have been built around the edges of towns, sometimes causing urban areas to merge creating **conurbations**. 'New towns' like Harlow, Crawley and Milton Keynes have been built. Better road and rail transport have allowed people to travel longer distances to work. The decline of arable farming in agriculture has made rural land cheaper to buy for housing development. Retirement areas are also growing as the population ages. The conurbation of Bournemouth, Christchurch and Poole, for example, had a population of 150,000 in 1931 and 300,000 by 1981.

6.5 THE FALL IN THE BIRTH AND DEATH RATE SINCE 1880

The fall in the death rate since 1880

The **death rate** stood consistently at about 20 deaths per 1,000 in the population between 1800 and 1870. From 1870, however, it fell rapidly to about 12 per 1,000 by 1930. The fall in **infant mortality** has been the most striking of all (see table). But **life expectancy** for adults has also improved by a third since 1900. Men in the 1980s could expect to live to an average age of 70, women to 76.

There are several reasons for the decline in the death rate. **Better diet**, for example, improved the nation's health. The **standard of living** went up; there was a marked improvement, for example, as a result of the mass of cheaper imported food which came into the country from the 1870s. More recently people have become conscious of **healthy eating** to reduce problems such as heart disease.

Medical improvements have also been striking. From about 1870 antiseptics and anaesthetics improved surgery. X-rays were discovered in 1895. Certain **killer diseases** of the nineteenth century, such as tuberculosis, smallpox and diphtheria, have been controlled.

Social reforms intended to improve the standard of living also began to increase from 1870. In the twentieth century the package of measures intended to provide for the social needs of the public has come to be called the **Welfare State**.

For example, **public health facilities** have been improved. The Public Health Act of 1875 made local councils control the disposal of sewage and rubbish in their areas (see pages 152–3). Measures such as this helped reduce cholera and typhoid. The National Insurance Act of 1911 introduced **health insurance** to provide workers with medical care (see pages 154–5), and eventually the **National Health Service** was introduced in 1946.

Unemployment insurance and **old-age pensions** are additional features of the Welfare State which have been introduced. These have provided people with secure incomes during times of hardship.

Better housing also followed government legislation. Torres's act of 1868 allowed councils to improve existing housing, for example by installing sewerage. The Artisans Dwellings Act of 1875 allowed councils to clear slums and build new housing for the poor. The Town Planning Act of 1909 allowed councils to buy up new land and have housing built. They could also control the layout and size of new homes to ensure that they were healthy to live in.

Infant mortality (number of deaths per 1,000 in the first year of life) in England and Wales, 1900–60

Year	*Number*
1900	154
1910	105
1920	80
1930	64
1940	57
1950	30
1960	25

SOURCE **A**

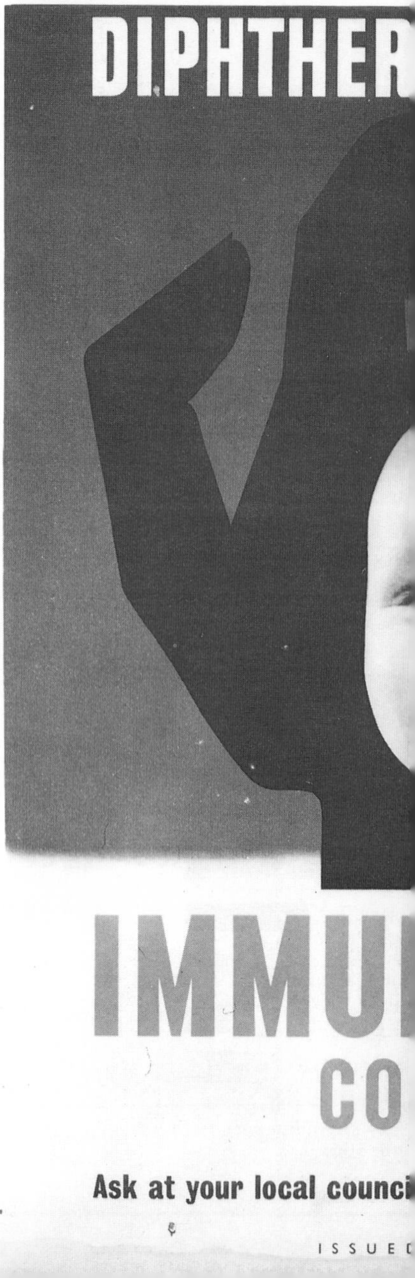

Government funds have helped to put medical advances to good use. This is a wartime poster from 1943 encouraging people to immunize their children against diphtheria.

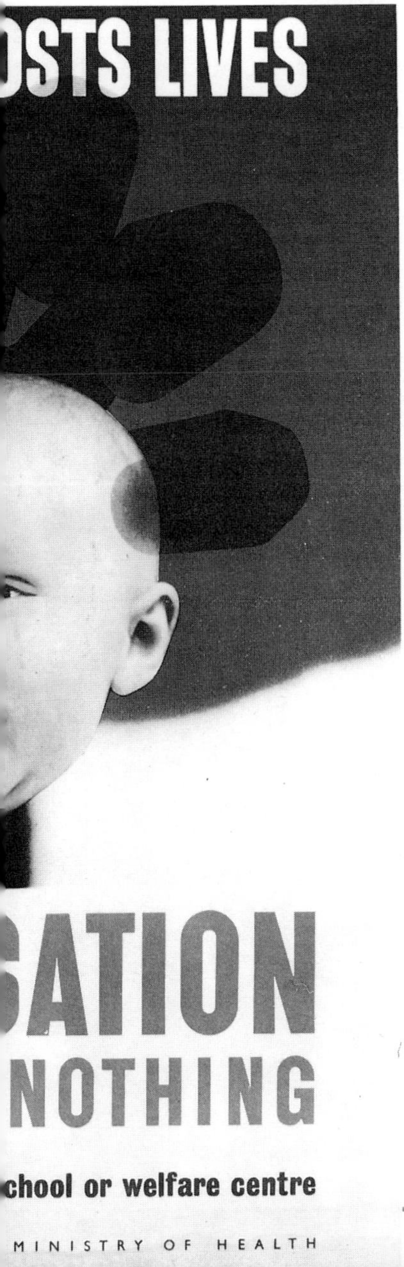
OSTS LIVES
ATION
NOTHING
chool or welfare centre
MINISTRY OF HEALTH

The fall in the birth rate since 1880

In 1880 the **birth rate** stood at 35 births per 1,000 of the population. By 1940 this had fallen to only 15 per 1,000. There was a 'baby boom' between about 1945 and 1965. This arose out of the optimism caused by the end of the war and the return to prosperity in the 1950s. Also, reunited couples had more children, and the age of marriage went down. But this was only temporary. The birth rate continued its downward path from the 1960s.

The fall in the birth rate was made possible by two factors. One was a rise in the **age of marriage**; the number of the 20–24-year-old age group who were married fell by a third between 1881 and 1911. Later marriage tends to lead to fewer children. The other factor was the development of effective **contraception**. This has, for the first time, given people the ability to *plan* the number of children they want. But why have they been planning smaller families? Would couples *always* have fewer children, given the choice, or have there been special reasons?

The decline of **child labour** is one factor. By the 1870s factory reforms were becoming effective at keeping young children from being put to work. The Education Act of 1870 introduced **compulsory schooling** for young children (see page 179), and this was not always free. So children were much more expensive to bring up. Later, the provision of **college and university education** encouraged many young people to marry later.

The **attitudes of women** have also changed. Women increasingly choose to remain unmarried, or not to have children, to go to college before marriage, or to have a small family and a paid job outside the home. This has raised the age of marriage and reduced the size of families.

The traditional preference for large families has also disappeared. The trend is now for **smaller families**. The average Victorian family had six children; the average family now has two. High infant mortality used to encourage people to have many children, because it was difficult to predict how many would survive. The need for security in their old age may have encouraged many parents to have large families. The Welfare State has reduced this need. Large families are also very expensive. Most people now prefer to have fewer children and keep some of their money for other things, such as better housing, cars and holidays. Other parents have the opposite problem – not enough money; the high unemployment of the 1930s and 1980s tended to postpone marriages and the decision to have children.

Emigration has also become more frequent in the twentieth century (see pages 118–9). This has mainly involved younger adults and has reduced the number of couples of child-bearing age. The death of hundreds of thousand of young men in the armed forces during the **two world wars** had the same effect.

6.6 EMIGRATION AND IMMIGRATION SINCE 1800

EMPATHY

In the **eighteenth century** emigration and immigration were relatively small and balanced each other out. In the **nineteenth century** emigration overtook immigration. Between 1815 and 1931, 20 million people emigrated from Great Britain.

Emigration

There were 'push' and 'pull' causes for **emigration. Hardships** at home sometimes 'pushed' people abroad. The best example of this is the Irish famine which began in 1845 and drove one million Irish to emigrate by 1850. But all over Britain periods of high unemployment, high food prices or the overcrowding caused by rapid population growth sometimes combined to push emigration up. The Corn Laws drove some people abroad (see the cartoon on page 30). During the great depression in the 1880s, 200,000 people per year were emigrating.

But not everyone who emigrated was forced to go abroad. Sometimes **ambition** 'pulled' people abroad. The discovery of gold in California and Australia in 1849, in the Transvaal in the 1880s and in the Klondike in the 1890s promised huge fortunes. The fertile and cheap land attracted many aspiring farmers to Australia, and the booming industries of the east coast of the USA promised rich prospects for hard-working people.

There was no shortage of **encouragement** for emigrants. Poor Law guardians helped paupers emigrate; trade unions had emigration funds for their members. The government was keen to populate colonies like Australia and New Zealand with Britons. Railways and steam shipping made long-distance travelling quicker, safer and cheaper than ever before.

In the **twentieth century** emigration slowed between 1931 and 1951 because of a worldwide depression which reduced the demand for labour. But after 1951 emigration resumed at over one million per decade, mainly to North America and Australia.

Immigration

Immigration also increased in the nineteenth and twentieth centuries, but not as dramatically. Most immigrants to Great Britain have come from **Ireland**, many of them fleeing the great famine of 1845. Many others have come from **Europe**, especially when large numbers of Jews, Germans, Poles, Italians and Russians began to flee from harsh governments in Europe between 1920 and 1950.

The most recent immigration has been since the 1950s from the **New Commonwealth**. The revival of the economy after the war created more jobs; Britain needed more workers. There were no restrictions on immigration for Commonwealth citizens, and between 1954 and 1962 one million immigrants arrived, many of them from India, Pakistan and the West Indies. Some people were concerned at the scale of this influx, and in 1962 legislation was passed to limit immigration from the Commonwealth countries. Since then restrictions have been tightened progressively, so that since 1962 the number of immigrants to Britain has usually been smaller than the number of emigrants.

SOURCE A

FREE EMIGRATION TO SOUTH AUSTRALIA
'Her Majesty's Colonial Land and Emigration Commissioners grant free passage to this healthy and prosperous colony to agricultural labourers, shepherds, male and female domestic and farm servants, miners and mechanics of good character. The demand for labour in the colony is urgent, with remuneration ensuring the comfort of every man and his family.'

Advertisment in the 'Northampton Herald', 1846.

SOURCE B

'Punch' cartoon, 1848.

EXERCISE

1 Emigration was generally approved of in the nineteenth century. Why might the idea of emigrating have appealed to:
  a a Manchester factory worker?
  b a Kent farm labourer?

  Why might their decision to emigrate be applauded by:

  c a local ratepayer?
  d a government minister?

2 **a** What did people in Britain feel about the large numbers of New Commonwealth immigrants who came to the country in the 1950s?
  b How do you think the New Commonwealth immigrants felt about how people in Britain received them?

Britain has always been an island of **mixed races**. Celts, Saxons, Angles, Jutes, Vikings and Normans were all thoroughly mixed together to form the British people of 1700 whose story this book tells. Nevertheless all the racial groups among the immigrants mentioned in this unit have suffered an uneasy welcome. First the Irish, then the Jews and since then the New Commonwealth immigrants all suffered initial **hostility**. But non-white skins and non-Western languages and cultures made the problems of mixing into the community harder. The first New Commonwealth immigrants tended to settle in low-cost housing areas in big towns. Thus although nationally only one in fifty of the population were immigrants by the 1980s, in Birmingham they were one in sixteen, and almost all West Indian or Asian. **Racial tensions** emerged. There were fears that there wouldn't be enough jobs and housing to go round. What would be the effect on schools? Immigrants complained of **discrimination**. Racial unrest sometimes erupted into street violence. But prejudice and discrimination have declined gradually since the 1950s, and British society has been enriched rather than damaged by its newest members.

HERE;

OR, EMIGRATION A REMEDY.

SOURCE C

THE BOYS FROM JAMAICA

They were born in Jamaica. Do you recognise the uniform?

● People are human beings even though they come in different colours. The main reason for race riots is plain IGNORANCE of this simple truth.

This is the first of a series which Keith Waterhouse is writing to give people the facts about the coloured people. Today—meet the Jamaicans:

Smiling Percival Bennett works on a co-operative farm in Jamaica.

1 WHERE THEY COME FROM..

HALF the 200,000 coloured people in Britain come from the West Indies, a sunny chain of islands in the Caribbean, between North and South America.

About 70,000 of those are from Surrey, Middlesex and Cornwall—the three counties of Jamaica, British for 300 years.

By the cheapest route, it costs £75 for them to come to Britain—on a British passport.

Jamaicans have been leaving home to look for work since 1884. They helped to build the Panama Canal.

They emigrated to the U.S.A., to Cuba, to South America. After the war, they began to come here.

2 WHAT THEY DO AT HOME..

JAMAICA makes the sunshine things. Sugar. Bananas. Coffee. Cocoa. Rum. Tobacco.

About half its workers are in these jobs. And about half its produce comes to Britain.

Jamaica exports £49,000,000 of goods a year. Yet unemployment is still one of its big problems.

To keep in world markets, the country that desperately needs to create labour is obliged to import labour-saving machinery from Britain.

Jamaicans come here for jobs—but Jamaica helps to keep Britain in jobs. We make their machinery. And we provide 40 per cent. of their imports.

3 WHY THEY ARE HERE..

JAMAICA is the big-money island where jobs are few and pay is poor. The £30,000,000 bauxite industry employs fewer than 5,000 people. The luxury tourist business, earning £10,000,000 a year, has jobs for only 5,700.

One out of every five Jamaican workers is permanently out of a job. And there is big seasonal unemployment among those who do have a job. Pay is as low as this: An unskilled hand in the cigar business earns £2 11s. 6d. for a fifty-three-hour week. A van driver gets £4 15s. A grade one railway fireman gets £5 10s.

Unemployment pay does not exist. The Jamaicans come here for work.

WHEN WAR CAME...

● During the war, 10,000 Jamaicans came voluntarily to this country to fight for Britain.

● Eight thousand of them went into the Armed Forces, and 2,000 into munitions work.

FACTS

● **ARE THEY WASTERS?** In three years, Jamaicans in Britain have sent home £10,000,000 in postal orders to their dependants

● **ARE THEY CRIMINALS?** No Jamaican can leave the island without police clearance. Those with criminal records are not allowed to come.

● **ARE THEY HEATHENS?** Three out of every five Jamaicans are members of a Christian church or group. In Britain, the churches they attend are packed.

● **ARE THEY STEALING OUR WOMEN?** After the war, all the Jamaicans who came here were men. Nowadays, half of them are wives and children—coming to rejoin their husbands.

● **ARE THEY STEALING OUR HOUSES?** Many Jamaicans here live in decrepit houses which white people would not take. Some have done renovations themselves.

● **ARE THEY STEALING OUR JOBS?** Jamaicans today are in steel, coal, Lancashire cotton and public transport. Colour bar or no, there are still few jobs that employers will give to coloured people if they can get white workers instead.

Twenty-two per cent. of the Jamaicans coming to Britain were in white-collar jobs in the West Indies.

But only four per cent. can get office jobs here. Most become transport workers.

And that—according to West Indian welfare workers—accounts for the good manners of Jamaican bus conductors.

FACTS

★ This man is Sobert Clarke. He fought for the Commonwealth. Now he's eager to work for the Commonwealth.

TOMORROW: Meet the West Africans...

Extract from an article in the 'Daily Mirror', 1958.

7.1 LAISSEZ-FAIRE

Mercantilism is the name given to most people's ideas about the economy in 1700. Mercantilists believed that the government should interfere in the economy to make the country strong. The government would make it expensive to import everything except raw materials, and cheap to export everything except raw materials. This would mean that most manufactured goods would be made in the country, creating lots of wealth. The government made this happen by imposing high duties on most imports and exported raw materials.

This system was criticized by **Adam Smith** in his book *The Wealth of Nations*, published in 1776. Smith insisted that governments should not interfere. He said the economy would do better if people could compete freely. The actions of the government made things worse. The idea that government should not interfere was called ***laissez-faire***. It became the most important economic idea of the first half of the nineteenth century, and was applied to more than trade. Many people argued that the government should not interfere in anything, because its actions would always make things worse. This was used as an argument against government action to enforce safety standards in mines or to improve living conditions in towns.

SOURCE A

'Every individual is continually exerting himself to find out the most advantageous employment for whatever capital he can command. It is his own advantage, indeed, and not that of society, which he has in view. But the study of his own advantage naturally, or rather necessarily, leads him to prefer that employment which is most advantageous to the society.'

Adam Smith, 'The Wealth of Nations', 1776.

SOURCE B

'What are the duties of the Government? Generally speaking, to maintain the frame of society; and for this end to restrain violence and crime, – to protect person and property, – to enact and administer the laws needful for the maintenance of peace, order, and justice, – to sanction public works, – to conduct relations with other countries.

'It is not the duty of Government to feed the people, to clothe them, to build houses for them, to direct their industry or their commerce, to superintend their families, to cultivate their mind, to shape their opinions, or to supply them with religious teachers, physicians, schoolmasters, books, and newspapers. These are things the people can and ought to do for themselves'.

Edward Baines, 'Letters to Lord John Russell on State Education,' 1846.

SOURCE C

'In one cul-de-sac in Leeds there are 34 houses and there dwell in these houses 340 persons,or ten to every house. The name of this place is Boot and Shoe Yard, from whence was removed, in the time of the cholera, 75 cartloads of manure which had been untouched for years. To build the largest number of cottages in the smallest place seems to have been the original view of the speculators. Thus neighbourhoods have grown up in which there is neither water nor toilets.'

From 'An Inquiry into the State and Condition of the Town of Leeds', 1842.

QUESTIONS

1. Would a mercantilist think the following were a good idea:
   - **a** a tax on importing wood from the Baltic?
   - **b** a tax on importing French furniture?
   - **c** a tax on exporting Boulton and Watt steam engines to France?
   - **d** a tax on exporting iron-ore to France?
2. What would a supporter of *laissez-faire* think about the taxes in question **1**?
3. Do you think Edward Baines would have approved of a government scheme to clean up places like those described in Source C?

CLASS

Britain had been a society with lots of divisions in it in 1700. Gregory King's description of the population of England in 1699 divided the country into many different **social groups** such as Lords, Gentlemen, Farmers, and Labouring People (see page 14). However, while people in the seventeenth century usually felt they belonged to one of these groups (they would have called it a **rank**), they did not usually see it as the most important group they belonged to, or the one they shared most with. In the sixteenth or seventeenth century a person might say they were a Labourer; also that they came from Kent or whatever county; that they might be attached to a particular wealthy and powerful family, through working for that family or a lesser family connected with it; and that they were English.

Our word **class** is like the 'rank' that Gregory King and other seventeenth-century people would recognize. It defines a group of people by their economic and social position. It is different in that we do not divide society up into as many classes as King used ranks. There is however a more important difference in the way many people now use the word. In the example of the Kentish person in the previous paragraph, that person would probably have thought they had most in common with other people from the same area, and then with other people connected with the same great family. The idea of all labourers or gentry having the same interests would have seemed strange. Class was not the group a person felt instinctively loyal to. Now people are much more likely to think of themselves as belonging to a class, and as having common interests with other people in that class. We are also more likely to decide what class someone belongs to by what job they do and how much they earn, rather than who their parents were.

A number of political thinkers, of whom the most famous is **Karl Marx**, thought that class could be used to explain many things that happened in society. Slowly during the late-eighteenth and nineteenth century **class consciousness** began to be more common. More people got used to thinking about groups like **the middle class** or **the working class**. More importantly they got used to feeling that they belonged to one of them.

SOURCE A

'Fundamental Principles
First – That labour is the source of all wealth; consequently the working classes have created all wealth.
Secondly – That the working classes, although the producers of wealth, instead of being the richest, are the poorest of the community; hence they cannot be receiving a just recompense for their labour.'

From the rules of the Ripponden Co-operative Society, 1832. Ripponden was a weaving village in the Pennines.

QUESTIONS

1 a How many classes or ranks did Gregory King divide the population of England into?
b How many of those classes would you use if you wanted to describe the population of England today?

2 Did the Ripponden Co-operative Society believe that class was important? Give reasons for your answer.

3 a Study Source A on page 130. This cartoon is about the differences between 'Capital' and 'Labour'. Is this the same as class?
b Do you think *Punch* was likely to be read by working class people?

7.3 CAPITALISM

Capitalism began to develop long before 1700, and it has continued to develop since. A simple example illustrates the main features of the system. **Capital** is the money needed to set up any business. In running a hot-dog stand capital would be needed to buy or rent the stand, and to buy the rolls, frankfurters, sauce, and some way of cooking the frankfurters. All this would be needed before any hot dogs could be sold and therefore before the hot dog stand could make any money. Under the capitalist system, the capital is provided by people who hope to make a profit. You can't have a hot-dog stand without capital and you can't have a hot-dog stand without **labour** – someone to run the stand and cook and sell the hot-dogs. Usually the person who provides the capital owns the business, and therefore takes more in **profit** than is paid to the worker. However, capitalists take risks: if hot-dogs go out of fashion all their capital may be lost.

Obviously most businesses are much bigger and more complicated than hot-dog stands. The bigger a business, the more capital has to be invested to start it up and keep it running, and the longer it takes for the capital to start making a profit. Capital can come from personal wealth, from banks, and from shares. For instance the Duke of Bridgewater was wealthy enough to provide all the capital needed for his canal by himself. Later (and longer) canals needed so much capital that they were built by companies. The companies raised capital by selling **shares**. Modern companies are usually **limited liability** companies. This means that each shareholder can only lose the money they paid for a share. Even if the company went bankrupt owing millions of pounds the owners (shareholders) could not be made to pay the debts from any other money they had.

People hope that companies will last for a long time, but those who invest in them may need to get their money back quickly. They can do this by selling their shares. This can be done through the **stock exchange** which plays an important part in any capitalist system. This does not give the company any more money, the investor keeps it all. Each year companies pay a **dividend** to their **shareholders**, a share of the company's profit if it made any. Obviously people are more likely to want shares in companies which pay high dividends, and these companies' shares have a high price on the stock exchange.

Many people believe that capitalism, or the **free market**, is the best way to make economic decisions in a country. Competition will mean that things will be made and sold at the cheapest price, and only those things wanted will be made. Companies which are inefficient, or which make things people don't want, will change or go out of business. New companies grow up which will supply what people want. The system works by rewarding people unequally. Those with rare skills or capital will get much more money than others. People will be motivated to work hard and excel because they want the things a lot of money will give them. In order to work the system needs **inequality**, with some people having a better life than others.

QUESTIONS

1 Why does a stock exchange make it more likely people will buy shares?

2 **a** Why might the price of a company's shares on the stock exchange go down?
b What would you expect the shareholders to do if the price of the company's shares went down?

3 Why might the capitalist system be an efficient way of deciding what should be produced in a country?

4 Why does a capitalist system need some people to be able to afford better things than other people?

SOCIALISM

Socialism means different things to different people. A general definition would include **public ownership** and **central planning**. Socialists believe that most industries should be owned and run by the state. Instead of competition, planners should decide what will be produced. Some socialists have been **revolutionaries**, believing that the only way to achieve socialism was by violent change. Others have been **gradualists**, who believed that the way to change was by slow and peaceful reform. The **Fabian Society**, founded in 1884, was the most influential group of gradualists. It collected and published information and arguments in favour of socialism. It was influential in setting up the Labour party which has supported gradualist rather than revolutionary socialism.

As socialists have not been in a position to start a new society they have looked for ways to change the system they found. **Nationalization** has been a key policy. This involved taking over an industry so that it was no longer owned and run by and for its shareholders, but owned by the whole country and run by the government on behalf of the people. Labour governments have been associated with nationalization, particularly the 1945 Labour government, which nationalized major industries like transport and coal.

Socialists have tried to get rid of inequalities in society. They believe that everyone has a right to decent conditions and that it is more important to raise general standards a little than allow a few to enjoy the highest standard of living. It was a socialist government which set up the National Health Service after the Second World War because it felt that all people should have access to the best medical treatment, whether or not they could pay for it.

Critics of socialism have suggested that planners cannot organize the economy effectively, that nationalized industries are inefficient, and that individual freedom is lost as central government becomes more powerful.

During the twentieth century Britain developed a **mixed economy**. There were elements of both capitalism and socialism in the economic system. Some services and industries have been nationalized, others have not. The political parties disagree about how the balance should be tilted one way or the other. In the 1970s and 1980s, however, both the Labour and Conservative parties have become more extreme. Mrs Thatcher's Conservative government, in power throughout the 1980s, has followed a policy of **privatization**. Industries which had been nationalized have been sold back to private shareholders. Even basic services like telephones, gas and the water and electricity industries are moving out of government control as the balance of the mixed economy is fundamentally changed.

QUESTIONS

1. Why do socialists believe nationalization is a good idea?
2. Why might socialism be an efficient way of deciding what should be produced in a country?
3. What is the difference between gradualist and revolutionary socialism?
4. How would you expect a socialist to feel about Britain's private hospitals and medical system?

8.1 LIVING CONDITIONS

Between 1801 and 1851 the population of Britain doubled from 10.5 million to 20.8 million. This was the fastest period of **population increase** in British history. But some areas – the north-west, north-east, Midlands and London, South Wales and southern Scotland – were growing even faster than average. These were mainly industrial areas, with several rapidly expanding towns (see Source A). It wasn't just the biggest towns which grew; they were usually surrounded by smaller satellite towns. Manchester's growth, for example, was mirrored by nearby Stockport, Oldham and Bolton. Small communities grew so fast that the proportion of people who lived in towns of 5,000 or more rose from 25 per cent in 1815 to 50 per cent by 1850.

Many of the towns grew too fast for proper planning, and serious **social problems** resulted for the people who lived there. We have plenty of evidence about this. The government held a series of public investigations and published the results in reports called the **Blue Books**.

Overcrowding was the key problem. The 1840 Report on the Health of Towns recorded 15,000 people in Manchester and 39,000 in Liverpool living in one room-cellars. One investigator reported: 'In a cellar in Liverpool, I found a mother and her daughters sleeping in a bed of straw in one corner. In the other corner, three sailors had their beds.' Housing was cramped into the centre of the towns, close to the factories, and people had to crowd in as best they could (see Source B). The three worst problems associated with this kind of substandard housing were water supply, sewage disposal and rubbish disposal.

A good **water supply** is essential for hygiene. We rely on it for drinking and for washing food, crockery, clothes and ourselves. In many towns, the homes of the poor didn't have taps. In Highgate, in London, water was purchased by the bucketful; at Hyde, near Manchester, people paid one shilling a week to water-carriers who brought water into the town on carts. Others used stand-pipes in the street. In 1846 a Royal Commission on the Health of Towns reported that, in Westminster, 'On the principal cleaning day, Sunday, the water is on for about 5 minutes, and it is on also for three days in the week for half an hour.' One witness to the investigation said: 'Many of the poor beg water – many steal it.' With water so difficult to obtain, many others used muddy ponds and dirty rivers, or went without.

Sewage disposal is also essential for healthy living. The homes of the poor had neither drains nor sewers. Dirty water was thrown into the street and sewage dropped into ash pits (see Sources C and D). Where there were sewage pipes, these were usually directed into the nearest river, which was also likely to be the source for the water supply. The main Battersea sewer emptied into the Thames just above the Chelsea water intake.

There was no proper system of **rubbish disposal** either. Rubbish piled up in the streets until scavengers or muck carts came along to remove it. In 1842 after an epidemic in Boot and Shoe Yard in Leeds, seventy-five cartloads of manure were removed that had been untouched for years.

SOURCE A

Official census figures showing population growth in the industrial towns.

	1801	*1851*
London	1,100,000	2,600,000
Birmingham	70,000	220,000
Leeds	53,000	170,000
Manchester	75,000	450,000
Sheffield	46,000	135,000

SOURCE B

'An individual who may have a couple of thousand pounds wishes to lay it out so as to pay him the best percentage in money; he will purchase a plot of ground, then what he thinks of is to place as many houses on this acre of ground as he possibly can, without reference to drainage or anything.'

Report on the Health of Towns, 1840.

SOURCE C

'Shepherd's Building consists of two rows of houses back to back. The privies are in the centre of each row, about a yard wide; over them is part of a sleeping room. The street between the two rows in the centre of which is the common gutter, or more properly sink, into which all sorts of refuse is thrown; it is a foot in depth and at the end is a pool of water, shallow and stagnant.'

Report on the Sanitary Conditions of the Labouring Population, 1842.

SOURCE D

'Dungheaps are found in several parts in the streets and privies are seen in many directions. Large swill tubs are placed in various places by pig farmers for collecting the rubbish from families. The chief sewerage in the back streets is open channels.'

James Smith, Report into the Sanitary Condition of Bradford, 1845.

SOURCE E

'Vomiting or diarrhoea come on; the eyes sink; the lips, face, neck, hands, thighs and the whole surface become a leaden blue, purple, black or deep brown; the pulse becomes weak. The skin is deadly cold, the tongue flabby and chilled like a piece of dead flesh. The patient struggles for breath.'

A contemporary observer describes the symptoms of cholera.

Other problems included the cost of soap, which was taxed until 1853, and lack of fresh air. The crowded courtyards trapped the factory smoke and the stench from open drains.

Disease thrived in such conditions. **Typhoid** was spread by infected water; **tuberculosis** or TB was carried by bacteria coughed into the air by infected people; **typhus** was a virus carried by lice. It is easy to see how living conditions in industrial towns encouraged such diseases. In 1831 a new killer disease arrived, **cholera**, spreading from India, across Russia and Europe. The first case of cholera in Britain was reported in December 1831 in Sunderland. An epidemic swept the country in 1832, and others followed in 1838, 1848 and 1854. One in ten who caught cholera died. In September 1849 almost 7,000 people died in London alone. Source E describes the symptoms of this terrible disease.

Average **life expectancy** in 1840 was only 41 years. One in every six children died before the age of 1; one in three died before the age of 5. But these statistics hide the true extent of the problem in the towns. Poor public health was a problem for everyone, but it was worst among the working people in the towns – as Source F shows.

SOURCE F

Average age of death among different classes in 1842

	Professional classes	*Labourers*
Rutland (rural area)	52	38
Leeds	44	19
Manchester	38	17

From a Report on the Sanitary Conditions of the Labouring Population, 1842.

QUESTIONS

1 Look at Sources A to F. What evidence can you find for the following in mid-nineteenth-century British towns?
  a Overcrowding.
  b Poor sewage disposal or drainage.
  c Poor water supply.
  d A high death rate.

2 Sources B, C and D come from official reports. Do you think they give a reliable picture of living conditions in mid-nineteenth-century Britain? Explain your answer.

3 Source G is an artist's impression. Do you think it gives a reliable picture of living conditions in mid-nineteenth-century Britain? Explain your answer.

SOURCE G

'A court for King Cholera', 'Punch' cartoon, 1852.

8.2 WORKING CONDITIONS – THE FACTORIES

New forms of power destroyed the domestic system. Water wheels and, later, steam engines could drive bigger, faster machines which produced goods much cheaper. They were much too expensive to install in every worker's cottage, but they could drive hundreds of machines in **factories**. The work no longer went to the workers; they had to come to the work.

Factories first became common in the **textile industry**. After 1770 they used Hargreaves's spinning jenny for cotton spinning and from about 1810 they used power looms for cotton weaving. By 1830 factories dominated the **woollens industry** too, and by 1850 most of the textile and **engineering** industries were factory based.

Working conditions in these factories were very different from today. We must remember the outlook and circumstances of people at the time when forming our opinions about them.

One problem was **long hours**. A twelve-hour day was common; an eighteen-hour day was not unknown (see Source A). However, people were used to long hours. Farmworkers commonly worked from dawn until dusk at harvest time. Even in the domestic system, families worked very long hours.

Low wages were another complaint, especially since factory workers in the towns could not add to their income by part-time farm work. But the factories were very profitable and often short of workers. Factory wages were usually higher than the wages of farm labourers or outworkers.

Factories were unpleasant and dangerous to work in. They were often **crowded** and **badly heated. Poor ventilation** made the air stuffy and polluted, causing industrial sickness. **Dangerous machinery** was rarely fenced in for safety; accidents were common, especially when workers became tired (see Sources B and C). Against this, we must remember that traditional farmwork also took place under unpleasant circumstances, and outworkers' cottages could be damp and draughty.

Factories also brought **new problems. Harsh discipline** was one. Factory owners set up very strict rules to organize their huge workforces. **Fines** were the most common punishment, but humiliation, dismissal and even corporal punishment were used. The **regularity** and **monotony** of the work were also a strain on the workers. The machines were relentless; they dictated when and how fast the work was done. Workers had to learn to be strictly **punctual** for the first time; they lacked the independence and security of the outworkers (see Source D).

Some of the greatest problems concerned **child labour**. This was not new, for children had worked with their families in the domestic system and the fields. Many families relied upon children earning their keep from an early age. It was natural for families to work in the first factories. On the spinning mule, for example, the father was often the machine operator, the mother the 'piecer' mending broken threads, and the children 'scavengers' who cleaned under the machines (see Source E). But problems developed. Factory owners found that children were ideal for most of their work since there was little skill required

SOURCE A

'My Hours in work at Mr Connell's mill are from a few minutes before half-past five in the morning till seven at night. Half an hour for breakfast. An hour for dinner. No baggin (tea).'

From a parliamentary report on child labour in textile factories, 1833.

SOURCE B

'The process of pointing (sharpening pins) can scarcely fail to affect the health of the operator; for although the brass dust flies away behind the stone into a wooden hood, a portion reaches the mouths and lungs of the grinder; yet he employs no precaution to avert any such injurious consequences.'

A visitor to a Birmingham metal works, reported in 'Chambers's Journal', 1844.

SOURCE C

Sheffield fork grinders in 1866.

SOURCE D

'The supervision of machinery is no activity to claim the operative's thinking powers. Thus it is not work, but tedium, the most deadening, wearing process conceivable. The operative is condemned to let his powers decay in this utter monotony; it is his mission to be bored every day and all day long from his eighth year. Moreover, he must not take a moment's rest; the engine moves unceasingly; if he tries to snatch one instant, there is the overseer at his back with the book of fines.'

'riedrich Engels, writing in the 1840s.

SOURCE E

Working on a power loom. Can you identify the machine operator, the piecer and the scavenger?

and they could be paid less, usually one-third of a man's wage. At first factory owners used orphans supplied cheaply by the Poor Law overseers. Later they employed children from local families. Supervisors resorted quickly to corporal punishment when large numbers of children were employed away from the care of their parents.

How could **employers** be so cruel? Some, like Robert Owen and Sir Robert Peel senior, were well known as good employers. They provided housing, schools and churches for their workers. But with no effective government control of working conditions there were as many bad employers as good ones. Yet even the bad employers weren't necessarily evil. The workers themselves rarely pressed for shorter hours or the reduction of child labour; they couldn't afford to. Many nineteenth-century churches taught that hard work was essential for a Christian life – empty hours led to laziness and sin. Factory owners had only a simple grasp of the economics of running their businesses. Most wrongly assumed that long hours were essential for making a profit, believing that their profit was all made in the last hours of the day. Shorter hours would mean bankruptcy.

Another problem was the size of the workforce. Many factories had hundreds of workers. The only experience of handling such large groups of workers was the army or the slave plantations. Both depended on strict discipline. Factory workers were difficult to manage. The first owners of cotton factories complained of workers who were often too dirty or drunk to work. Most workers couldn't read. Over half of the workforce might be children. In the domestic system, people were used to stopping work whenever they wanted, for a local fair or the races. In many areas no one worked on 'Saint Monday', making up for lost time by longer hours for the rest of the week. Some factory owners saw harsh discipline as the only way to solve these problems.

8.3 WORKING CONDITIONS – THE MINES

EMPATHY

Coal was essential to the Industrial Revolution. This meant employing more people in the coal industry and mining deeper. In 1840 the government set up a **Royal Commission of Inquiry into Children's Employment** in mines and factories. The section describing conditions in the mines horrified the nation when the report was published in 1842. Some of the problems were the familiar ones of long hours and low pay. But what particularly worried the public was the employment of very young children, the work being done by women and girls and the immorality exposed during mixed shifts. The extracts and illustrations on these pages are from this report.

SOURCE A

'Where there is distress or there are large families, they will go down as early as six or seven years old. Lads six years old can keep doors well enough and soon learn as well as old persons the ways of a pit. Parents could not keep their children if they were not allowed to go down a pit.'

A mine worker giving evidence to the Parliamentary Commission.

SOURCE B

A 'trapper' at work. Trappers were young children who operated the ventilation doors in the shafts. The report said: 'The little trapper of eight years of age lies quiet in bed; between two or three in the morning, his mother shakes him. He fills his tin bottle with coffee and takes a loaf of bread sets out for the pit. All his work is to open the door and then allow it to shut itself. He sits alone and has no one to talk to. He has no light. His hours are passed in total darkness.'

SOURCE C

A woman hauling coal. Betty Harris, 37, was a 'drawer' like this. She reported: 'I have a belt round my waist and a chain passing between my legs, and I go on my hands and feet. The road is very steep, and we have to hold by a rope. The pit is very wet. My clothes are wet through almost all day long. The belt and chain is worse when we are in the family way (pregnant).' ▶

EXERCISE

1 Look at the text and sources on pages 126–29 and describe the problems of the working people in the factories and mines.

2 a Which of these problems would *they* have considered cruel?

b Which would *you* consider cruel?

3 Do the working conditions in the factories and mines mean that the employers were cruel?

SOURCE D

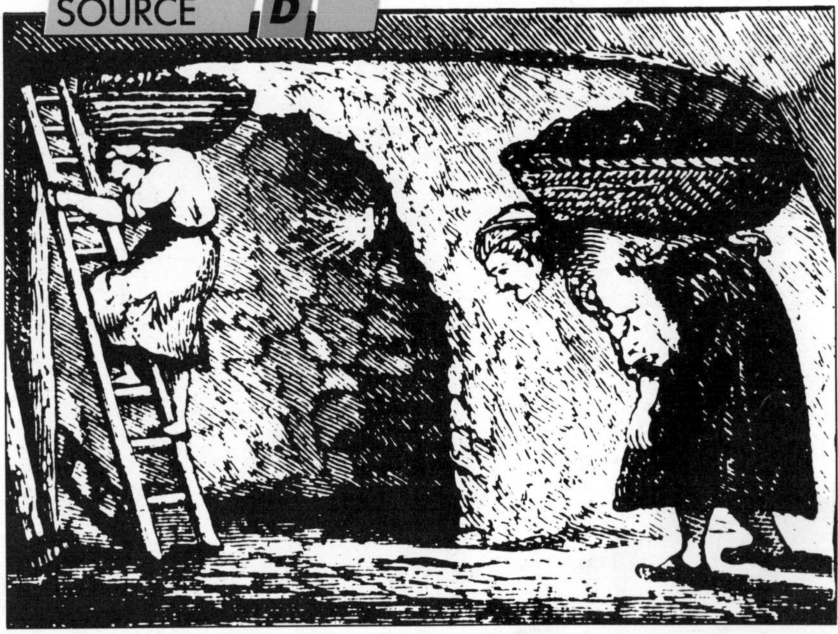

▲*Women carrying coal up to the surface. Agnes Kerr, 15, was a 'bearer' like this. The report described her as 'nine years old when she commenced carrying coal; makes 18 to 20 journeys a day; a journey is about 200 fathoms (approx. 400 metres); has to ascend many ladders; can carry 1½ cwt (about 75 kilos).' This was hot work. The report later commented: 'At Hopwood's pit at Barnsley, the girls as well as the boys work naked to the waist. And in the Flockton pits, though the girls are clothed, at least three-fourths of the men work stark naked.'*

8.4 WORKING-CLASS REACTIONS

Working people did not always just stand by and accept the kind of living and working conditions created during the Industrial Revolution. Eventually, **legislation** removed many of their grievances, but before then working people attempted their own remedies. They made up a very mixed group. They included skilled craft workers and unskilled labourers; workers in industry, farmworkers and domestic servants; Irish immigrants; male, female and child labourers; and the unemployed. They don't appear to have had much in common. But the Industrial Revolution created bonds between them.

Working-class consciousness
Before the Industrial Revolution, many workers lived in with their employers – as farm labourers or apprentices, for example. Many more were self-employed. Such arrangements blurred the divisions between employers and workers. But the Industrial Revolution brought bigger farms and factories; this meant fewer employers and more employees. The divisions between those who **owned** farms or factories or mines and those who **worked** in them became wider. Poor living conditions in the towns and harsh discipline in the factories made these divisions even more obvious. Source A shows how conscious people became of these social divisions.

This cartoon was published in 'Punch' i 1843 soon after the report on working conditions in mines. It sharply illustrate the hardships of the workers in contrast the wealth and luxury of the employers.

SOURCE A

CAPITAL AND LABOUR.

SOURCE B

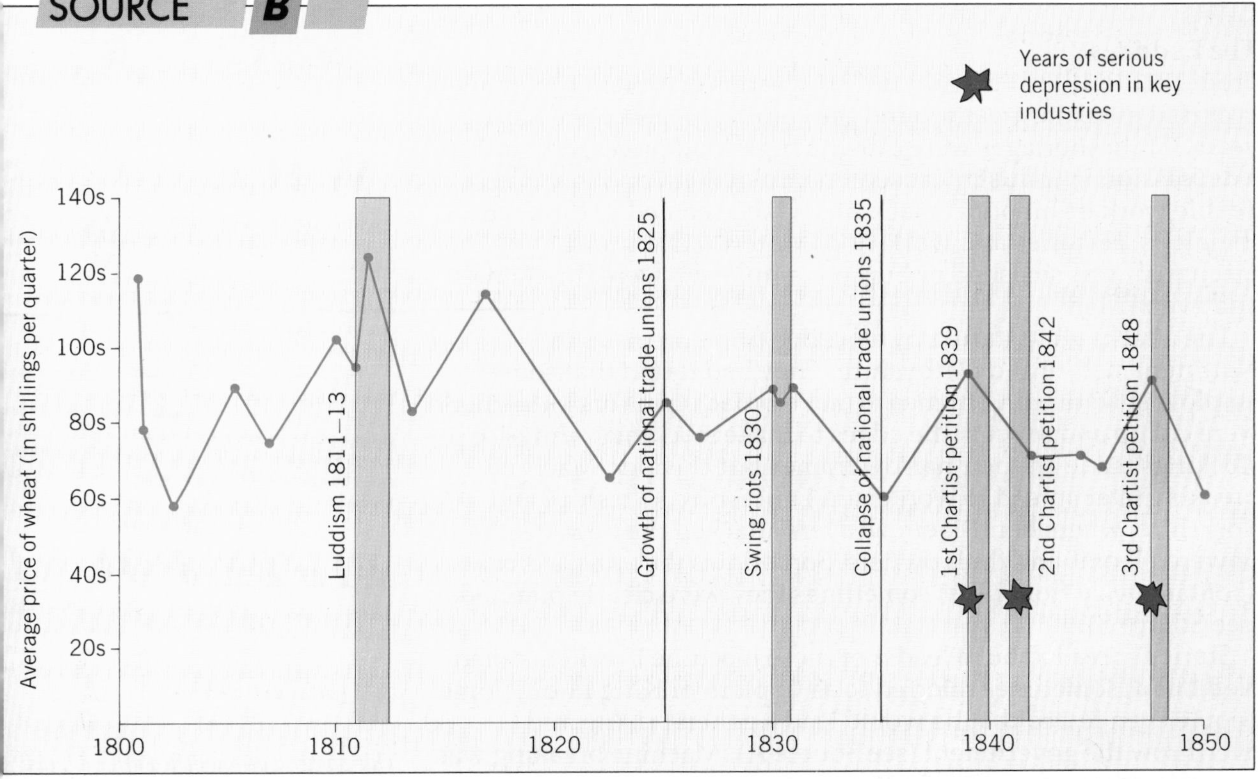

Working-class unrest and economic conditions.

As it became clearer that all workers shared some of the problems caused by the Industrial Revolution – social problems of living and working conditions – so this began to create a bond between workers in different trades and in different parts of the country. Their old loyalties to their village, parish, county or trade lingered on, but slowly a sense of working-class identity began to grow. Workers became more conscious of their shared problems and more willing to work together to do something about them. This sense of belonging to a separate class with separate problems is **working-class consciousness**. We can see it growing through the events described on pages 132–41.

Types of response

There were a number of different ways in which working people responded to the problems created by the Industrial Revolution.

Sometimes their actions were fairly spontaneous and violent, as with the **Luddites** or the **Swing Riots** (see pages 132–3).

Sometimes there were organized attempts to improve working or living conditions, as with the growth of **trade unions, friendly societies** and **co-operatives** (see pages 134–7).

The **Chartists** (pages 138–41) tried to influence Parliament to pass laws which would protect them against the worst effects of the industrial changes.

Working-class activity was always greatest when problems were at their worst. Source B plots grain prices (therefore food prices) and industrial depressions (therefore low wages and high unemployment) against the main events in working-class activity.

8.5 THE LUDDITES AND THE SWING RIOTS

The Luddites

From 1811 to 1813 and again in 1816 a series of violent incidents occurred in textile areas around the country. These were hard years. Grain shortages were causing high food prices, and in 1816 a depression in industry caused unemployment and low wages. **Textile workers** hit out at machines which seemed to threaten their jobs. Factories and workshops were attacked, and machinery was smashed or burned; employers were threatened and even killed.

The attacks were started by stocking-frame workers in Nottinghamshire and Derbyshire. They had found that some employers were using frames to make broad strips of cloth which were cut up and sewn at the edges to make stockings – inferior to stockings made on their narrow frames but cheaper. Machine breaking later spread to workers in Lancashire, Cheshire and Yorkshire, where hand-loom weavers attacked the new steam-powered looms and their owners. Sometimes the attacks arose spontaneously from riots; sometimes they were clearly planned (see Source B).

Stories spread about a leader of these machine breakers called **Ned Ludd**, sometimes referred to as Captain or King Ludd. Some people even feared that he would lead a general rising and overthrow the government (see Source A). Machine breaking was made a capital offence, and seventeen men were executed after

SOURCE B

December 23, 18

WHEREAS

A most violent Attack was made about 8 o'clock last N on the House of Mr. JOHN BRENTNALL, at L GRANGE, in the County of Derby, by Eight or more Per two of whom with their Faces blacked & armed with Pi entered the House, but in consequence of the spirited R ance of the Family, retired without effecting their villa purposes.

One of the Men about five feet nine inches high broad set, is supposed to have his Head, Face, and Neck injured in a struggle; and another Man about six feet is supposed to be wounded by a Bill Hook; the other who did not enter the House, as far as could be distingu from the darkness of the night, appeared to be above the mon size.

A REWARD OF

FIFTY POUN

Has been offered by his Royal Highness the Prince Reg the Conviction of EACH PERSON concerned in any Ou of the above nature, and a free Pardon in case the Person such information as may lead to the Conviction shall be to be prosecuted for the same.

This poster was published after a Luddite attack on a local employer.

SOURCE A

'Shirewood Camp

'Sir,

The first and most important part of my Duty is to inform you and I request you do the same to all your Colleagues in Office, also the Regent; that in consequence of the great sufferings of the Poor whose grievances seem not to be taken *into the least consideration by Government*, I shall be under the necessity of again calling into action (not to destroy more frames, but . . .) my brave Sons of Shirewood, who are determined and sworn to be true and faithful avengers of their country's wrongs. I have waited patiently to see if any measures were likely to be adopted by Parliament to alleviate distress in any shape whatever; but that hand of conciliation is shut and my long suffering country is left without a ray of hope. The Bill for Punishing with death has only to be viewed with contempt and opposed by measures equally strong; and the Gentlemen who framed it will have to repent the act: for if one man's life is sacrificed! blood for blood. Should you be called upon you cannot say I have not given you notice of it.

I have the honour to be

General Ludd.'

Letter sent by someone claiming to be General Ludd to Spencer Percival, the Prime Minister.

SOURCE C

SOURCE **D**

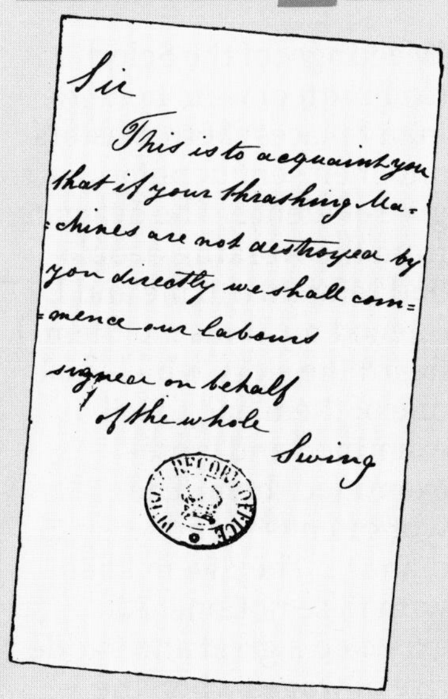

Sir

This is to acquaint you that if your thrashing Ma-chines are not destroyed by you directly we shall com-mence our labours

signed on behalf of the whole

Swing

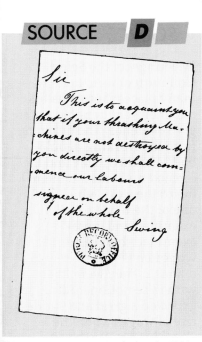

This letter was sent to a farmer in 1830 by someone claiming to be Captain Swing.

Luddite trials at York in 1812. Troops were moved into troubled areas. But Ned Ludd was almost certainly a mythical figure, and there was no national organization. Luddites came from a wide area, but the problems they faced were similar and they chose the same means of making their protest – machine breaking.

The Swing Riots

Machine breaking was also at the heart of rioting by farmworkers in the southern parts of England in 1830. Again there was talk of a leader, a **Captain Swing** (see Source D), though once more no such person existed.

British farming had been depressed since 1814 (see pages 32–3). Wages were low, and work was in short supply. Where new machinery was used instead of human labour it was bitterly resented. When the 1830 harvest failed, **riots** broke out among labourers in Kent and spread through Sussex, Hampshire, Berkshire and Wiltshire. There were over one hundred disturbances in each of these areas and eventually there were troubles in twenty-two counties. Rick burning and machine breaking were common. A total of 387 threshing machines were destroyed. Farmers were attacked as a protest against low wages, and clergymen and magistrates were threatened because of their involvement with tithes and the Poor Law. But there was only one death. Again the government reacted harshly. Nine rioters were hanged, 457 transported and over 400 imprisoned.

The meaning of the riots

Machine breaking was not unknown before the Industrial Revolution. In days before trade unions, machines were sometimes just a convenient target when workers wanted to hit out at their employers. So we must not see the machine breakers just as simple-minded folk opposed to new machinery. The years 1811–13 and 1830 were times of high food prices, lack of work and low wages. Luddism and the Swing Riots were a mixture of general unrest combined with opposition to the new machines which threatened people's jobs. This is why the machine breaking was often just one feature of widespread rioting.

Nor was machine breaking a very successful response to industrialization. Apart from slowing down the introduction of machines in some areas, the Luddites and Swing rioters achieved very little in the long run.

A contemporary artist's idea of a Luddite riot. Can you tell the artist's opinions about the Luddites from this picture?

8.6 WORKING-CLASS SELF-HELP

The Industrial Revolution made it harder for workers to survive hard times without help. The loss of the common lands, the reduction of part-time farmwork and the decline of the close master/worker relationships in small workshops all made workers' lives more insecure. There was more need for them to combine to help each other. At the same time, the growth of large towns and factories with thousands of workers made it easier for workers to set up their own self-help organizations.

Early trade unions

Some well-paid, skilled workers such as hatters, sailmakers and tailors already had **guilds** or **trade clubs**. They charged high subscriptions so that they could offer their members sick-pay, old-age pensions and funeral benefits. But these trade clubs were often limited to single trades in single towns and, with the exception of some based in London, they usually had less than 500 members.

After the French Revolution of 1789, when the Paris crowds overthrew their government, the authorities in Britain had became worried by workers' organizations. In 1799 and 1800, therefore, the **Combination Acts** were passed. These banned all 'combinations' or trade unions. They didn't destroy existing unions because they weren't strictly applied, and punishments were lenient. Many unions continued in secret. In Nottingham, for example, at least fifty unions existed, and fifteen strikes took place before the laws were repealed, but there were only five prosecutions. Even so, the development of new unions was held up.

It was 1824 before government fears relaxed enough to allow the **repeal of the Combination Acts**. This was largely the work of Francis Place, a London tailor, and Joseph Hume MP. They persuaded the government to set up a Select Committee to consider repeal. Place rehearsed workers who appeared as witnesses before the committee so that they made a good impression (see Source A). However, repeal in 1824 coincided with a period of prosperity in the economy, and a series of strikes broke out as unions pressed for increased wages. This alarmed many MPs, and in 1825 another law was passed which made it harder for unions to organize strikes (see Source B). Trade unions were now legal again, but their activities were restricted.

The period 1825–35 was an important one. Many workers became convinced that small unions could never succeed. Employers could too easily bring in workers from other areas. What was needed were **national unions** representing all of the workers in a trade. In 1929 John Doherty, the leader of the Lancashire cotton spinners, formed the Grand General Union of Spinners, and in 1831 other workers formed the Builders' Union. For even greater negotiating strength, the next step was to try to unite *all* unions in *all* trades into one single union. Doherty formed the **National Association for the Protection of Labour (NAPL)** in 1830. It had workers from textiles, mining and twenty other trades and its own newspaper, the *Voice of the People*.

SOURCE A

'Meetings (of the Select Committee) were held in many places; both masters and men sent deputations to give evidence. The delegates from the working people had reference to me and I opened my house to them. I heard the story which each one of them had to tell. I examined and cross-examined them. The workmen were not easy to manage. They were filled with false notions. All expected a great and sudden rise of wages when the Combination Laws were repealed.'

Francis Place.

SOURCE B

'No man shall threaten or obstruct another for the purpose of forcing that man to belong to any club or society. If any person shall force a workman to depart from his work or try to prevent any workman from accepting work, that person shall be forced to do hard labour for three months.'

The 1825 Act which made it difficult for unions to get full support for strikes or to prevent 'blackleg' replacement workers being used instead of strikers.

SOURCE C

'The design of the union is in the first instance to increase wages and to cut down the hours of labour. But the great and final object of it must be to set up a different order of things which will give the working classes more say in how the things they produce are used.'

Robert Owen, on the GNCTU.

SOURCE D

'We, the undersigned, do hereby declare that we are not members of a trade union; that we do not and will not pay towards the support of any such association.'

'The document' used in Derby in 1834.

SOURCE E

This hostile cartoon of a union meeting appeared in about 1830. The union leader addressing the motley crowd of workers is saying: 'Yes, gentlemen, these is my principles. No K..g, no L...ds, No Parsons, No Police, No Taxes...'

But all of the large unions created in this period failed. They were **too large** and **too radical**. This can be seen from the history of the most famous of them all, the **Grand National Consolidated Trades Union (GNCTU)**. The GNCTU was formed by **Robert Owen**, a constant figure in the history of working people at this time, whether through his work as a factory owner or as founder of co-operatives. In 1834 Owen persuaded many small unions to combine to form one union for all workers. By June 1934 it claimed to have 500,000 members.

Owen clearly hoped that the GNCTU's huge membership could be used as a threat to the economy and that this would give workers more control over the running of the country. A general strike of all workers was planned for 1834. But by 1835 the GNCTU had collapsed, like all the other national unions.

One reason for their collapse was that they were **too large**. Poor communications and low levels of literacy made local branches hard to control. It was difficult to co-ordinate action or to get everyone to agree to a common policy. Some unions refused to support workers in other trades. The clothiers, potters, spinners and builders never joined the GNCTU; they didn't think that other people's disputes were anything to do with them. Subscriptions were hard to collect, so finances were always weak. Worse still, some local secretaries disappeared with union funds (this caused the final collapse of the NAPL).

Another reason was that the unions were **too radical**. Because of the union's hopes to give workers much more influence, neither employers nor the government believed they could afford to stand by and watch them grow. In Derby in 1834 **employers** started to force their workers to sign 'the document' (Source D).

Fifteen hundred Derby workers who refused to sign 'the document' were locked out of work. Employers had the funds to close factories and wait for poverty to drive the workers back. Soon employers in other areas adopted the same tactics.

The **government** also reacted harshly. In 1833 forty farm labourers of Tolpuddle in Dorset, led by George Loveless, set up a local branch of the GNCTU. As was usual at the time, new members were sworn in at a special ceremony by making a secret oath of allegiance to the union (see Source F). Local magistrates had been warned about events and had asked the government in London for advice. They were told to arrest the leaders and to prosecute them for 'administering illegal oaths'. This 'offence' had been made a crime in 1797 after mutinies in the navy, although the law had not been intended to apply to trade union ceremonies. Now the authorities were scared by the political aims which seemed to lie behind Owen's schemes and were prepared to take desperate measures. In 1834 the six Tolpuddle leaders were found guilty and sentenced to seven years' transportation. The warning to other workers was clear (see Source G). Although a public outcry erupted at such unfair treatment, these **Tolpuddle Martyrs**, as they became known, were not returned to England until 1838.

The large trade unions collapsed by 1835, too large to be well organized and too radical for the government and employers to accept them. They were part of a growing sense of belonging among members of the working class; but working-class unity was not yet strong enough to sustain successful national unions.

However, there were successful working-class self-help organizations in the first half of the nineteenth century.

Friendly societies

Since there was no Welfare State in the eighteenth century, working people could not rely upon the government to help them through time of trouble. Sickness, family bereavement or unemployment forced people to fall back on savings or the support of friends and relatives. Only if they became destitute, totally unable to support themselves, did people usually get help from the Poor Law. In these circumstances, many workers joined **friendly societies**. They paid regular weekly sums into a central fund and, in return, they could draw out payments in times of hardship (see Source H).

Friendly societies varied in size from small village burial clubs to national organizations like the **Order of Foresters** and the **Manchester Unity of Oddfellows**, both of which were formed in 1833 and and had over 600,000 members by 1886. National membership figures rose from about 750,000 in 1801 to one million in 1850. Friendly societies were favoured by employers and the government because they encouraged responsible saving by the workers and kept down the demands upon the Poor Law. Parliament passed a **Friendly Societies Act** in 1793 to protect their funds from dishonest officials. But we must remember that the national membership figures quoted above represent only a fraction of all workers and that the people who were least able to afford payments to friendly societies were the poorest workers who needed them most.

SOURCE F

'I was blindfolded and taken into the main room. The President said: "Stranger in the dark, are you come here with a pure intention to support wages and protect the trade?"

'Suddenly the blindfold was taken away. The Inner Keeper was holding a sword at my heart. I had to swear an oath of loyalty on the Bible. To one side was a figure shrouded in white. The President pulled away the shroud to reveal a skeleton. He said that a rotting corpse was nothing to the real sting of death which is sin: the sin of betraying the society's secrets.'

The swearing-in ceremony of the Brushmakers' Society, described by Samuel Williams when he joined in 1790.

SOURCE G

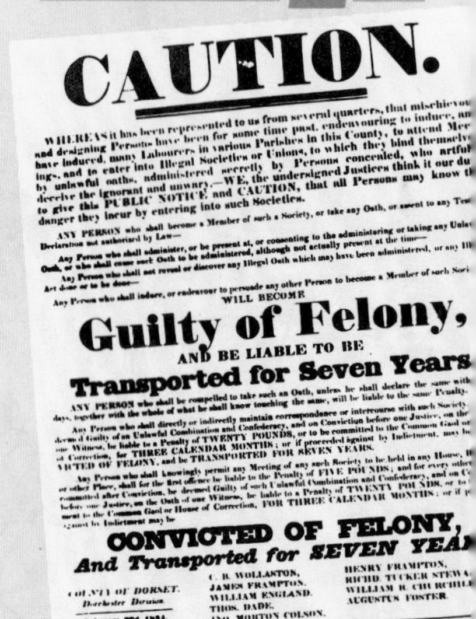
CAUTION.

WHEREAS it has been represented to us from several quarters, that mischievou
and designing Persons have been for some time past, endeavouring to induce, an
have induced, many Labourers in various Parishes in this County, to attend Mee
ings, and to enter into Illegal Societies or Unions, to which they bind themselv
by unlawful oaths, administered secretly by Persons concealed, who artful
deceive the ignorant and unwary.—WE, the undersigned Justices think it our du
to give this PUBLIC NOTICE and CAUTION, that all Persons may know th
danger they incur by entering into such Societies.

ANY PERSON who shall become a Member of such a Society, or take any Oath, or assent to any Tes
Declaration not authorized by Law—

Any Person who shall administer, or be present at, or consenting to the administering or taking any Unla
Oath, or who shall cause such Oath to be administered, although not actually present at the time—

Any Person who shall not reveal or discover any Illegal Oath which may have been administered, or any Ill
Act done or to be done—

Any Person who shall induce, or endeavour to persuade any other Person to become a Member of such Soci

WILL BECOME

Guilty of Felony,

AND BE LIABLE TO BE

Transported for Seven Years

CONVICTED OF FELONY,

And Transported for SEVEN YEA

COUNTY OF DORSET.
Dorchester Division.
February 22d, 1834.

C. B. WOLLASTON,
JAMES FRAMPTON,
WILLIAM ENGLAND,
THOS. DADE,
JNO. MORTON COLSON,

HENRY FRAMPTON,
RICHD. TUCKER STEWA
WILLIAM R. CHURCHILL
AUGUSTUS FOSTER

This poster appeared at about the time of the trial of the Tolpuddle Martyrs and was intended to discourage others from joining unions.

SOURCE H

Rules of the Friendly Society of Shoemakers
'*Subscription*: Entrance 2s 6d (12p). Monthly payment 1s 3d (6p). When the kitty is less than £20, the box to be declared shut and 1d (½p) extra to be paid to support the sick.

Benefits for the sick: When the kitty is over £20, 7s (35p) a week. When the kitty is less than £2, 4s (19p) per week.

For the retired and unemployed: A member after six weeks on the box to receive 4s (20p) per week for six months more. After that, if unable to work, to receive 2s 6d (12p) for life or until recovered.

At death: A member's funeral £7, his wife's £5.'

The shoemakers set up their society in 1780, to consist of eighty members.

Co-operatives
Robert Owen was a key figure in the co-operative movement. Co-operatives made no attempt to improve existing jobs or wages; they set out to start new enterprises as an alternative to the existing system. Owen's first idea was for **producer co-operatives**. He argued that workers should set up 'villages of co-operation' where nobody lived off profits of other people's work. The costs of land, housing, farming or manufacture would be shared, and work and profits would be shared. He started settlements along these lines at Queenwood in Hampshire and, in 1825, at New Harmony in North America. However, arguments among the settlers caused all of his experimental communes to fail.

Consumer co-operatives were tried next. In the late 1820s shops were started where goods were bought in bulk cheaply and then sold at low prices to working people. By 1832 there were almost 500 of these around the country. Yet all of them had failed by 1835. The system did not allow for the runnings costs involved. In the 1840s, however, consumer co-operatives were successfully revived in an amended form. Twenty-eight weavers invested one pound each to start a shop in Toad Lane, Rochdale. The **Rochdale Pioneers**, as they are now called, bought at wholesale prices, like other shops, and sold at retail prices, like other shops. But after paying running costs, all of the profits were then shared among the customers according to how much they had bought. Customers could either cash in their 'dividend' or leave it as savings, which could be used as capital for the shops. Committees of members ran the business and supervised the quality of goods sold. Their customers were not served adulterated foods, such as coffee mixed with soil or sugar mixed with chalk, which were common in Victorian England.

Again the idea caught on, and this time imitators of the Rochdale pioneers survived. There were 130 such consumer co-operative societies by 1850 and almost 1,000 by 1870, with 300,000 members. In 1863 local societies combined to form the **Co-operative Wholesale Society (CWS)** to make massive bulk purchases at very cheap prices on their behalf. In 1872 the CWS began producing some products itself, to cut out the manufacturers' profits completely.

The co-operative societies were a genuine success. They made wages stretch further and sold reliable goods. But to get their impact in perspective, we must remember that membership was only a fraction of the poor and that they had no impact on housing or working conditions. The biggest problem of all of the self-help schemes was that it was in the really hard times, when people most needed help, that self-help was least effective. At times of high unemployment and low wages, workers were least likely to support strike action. The danger of losing your job was too great. Many workers thought that the only certain way to improve living and working conditions was to fight for more **political power** so that the laws that governed their lives could be changed. These were the ideas behind **Chartism**.

8.7 CHARTISM

Many working people saw **Parliament** as their best hope of protection against the effects of the Industrial Revolution. But the Parliament of the 1830s seemed blind to their needs. In 1832 the Reform Act introduced a new system for electing Parliament. But the new voters were the middle and upper classes. The working classes were still denied the vote. The effect of this soon showed. Although a Factory Act was passed in 1833 to improve working conditions, it was completely ineffective. In 1834 a new law was passed to cope with the problem of poverty; but the new arrangements for looking after the poor pleased only the rich. The new system was cheap, and it treated the poor so harshly that it was hated, especially in the north of England. Working people began to campaign for a Parliament which would do more to solve their problems.

Chartist activities

William Lovett was the secretary of the **London Working Men's Association**. In 1836 he and Francis Place drew up a list of six demands which they wanted to give working people a share of political power. The demands were adopted by other working-class groups like Thomas Attwood's **Birmingham Political Union**. These groups met at a mass rally in Birmingham in 1838, and other rallies were held in Liverpool, Leeds, Glasgow and South Wales. The six demands became known as the **People's Charter** (see Source A) and its supporters as the **Chartists**.

In 1839 a **Chartist Convention** was held at Birmingham. Chartist delegates came from groups all over the country. Their aim was to get the Charter made law by Parliament, but they argued about how to do this. Lovett and Attwood favoured **'moral force'** – that is, persuading Parliament by peaceful means (see Source B). But another group, led by Feargus O'Connor, an Irish journalist, favoured **physical force**, using threats, strikes, violence and even revolution (see Source C).

Peaceful means were tried first. A **petition** demanding the Charter, signed by 1,250,000 people and two miles long was presented to Parliament in May **1839**. The House of Commons rejected it by 235 votes to 46. There was talk of calling a general strike in protest, but the convention could not agree and it broke up having achieved nothing.

Later in 1839 another group of Chartists tried to take matters into their own hands. John Frost and others in South Wales had been angered by the imprisonment of local Chartist leaders. They planned an attack on the town of Newport to release them. However, the authorities were ready for the **Newport Rising**. Magistrates had soldiers guarding their prisoners at the Westgate Hotel, and when Frost and about 1,000 Chartists stormed the hotel on the night of 3 November they were met with a volley of shots which left fourteen men dead. One hundred arrests were made; Frost and eight others were transported.

Chartist activity then died down until economic hardship revived demands for the Charter in 1842. The *Manchester Times* reported in July: 'Any man passing through the district will at

SOURCE A

The six points of the People's Charter

'1 A *vote* for every man 21 years of age, of sound mind and not undergoing punishment for crime.
2 *The ballot*. To protect the elector in the exercise of his vote (from intimidation by employers or landlords, for example).
3 *No property qualification* for Members of Parliament – thus enabling the constituencies to return the man of their choice, be he rich or poor.
4 *Payment of members*, thus enabling an honest tradesman, working man or other person to serve a constituency, when taken from his business to attend to the interests of the country.
5 *Equal constituencies*, securing the same amount of representation for the same number of electors – instead of allowing small constituencies to swamp the votes of larger ones.
6 *Annual Parliaments*, thus presenting the most effectual check to bribery and intimidation, since no purse could buy a constituency in each ensuing twelvemonth; and since members, when elected for a year only, would not be able to defy and betray their constituents as now.'

Summary of the People's Charter taken from a poster of the time. A seventh point, votes for women, was debated but rejected.

SOURCE B

'Let us, friends, seek to unite together the honest, moral, hard-working and thinking members of society. Let us draw into one group the influential and intelligent members of the working classes. Let us obtain a library of books which will inform us of our political and social rights. Let us collect information and statistics regarding the wages, habits and conditions of the labourer. Let us publish our views so that we create a moral, thinking, energetic force in politics. Then there will be a gradual improvement in the condition of the working classes without violence or unrest.'

Speech by William Lovett in 1836.

SOURCE C

'My desire is to use moral force as long as possible, but I would have you remember that it is better to die free men than live as slaves. Physical force is treason only when it fails; it is glorious freedom when it succeeds.'

Feargus O'Connor.

SOURCE D

The procession taking the 1842 petition to Parliament.

once perceive the deep and ravaging distress that prevails, laying industry prostrate, desolating families and spreading abroad discontent and misery.' A **second petition** gathered 3,317,000 signatures and was presented to Parliament in May **1842**, carried in bundles by fifty men at the head of a two-mile-long procession of workers (see Source D). The Commons rejected it by 287 votes to 49.

Once again disappointment caused unrest. Lancashire cotton spinners, on strike for higher wages, demanded that the Charter should be adopted before they would return to work. They called on other workers to join them and took the ingenious action of removing the boiler plugs from steam engines to disrupt work at factories where workers wouldn't join them. This **'plug plot'** encouraged Chartist leaders to call another convention at Manchester. O'Connor was by this time the undisputed leader of the Chartists. With his fiery oratory and his Leeds-based newspaper, the *Northern Star*, he had become the figurehead of the movement. There were calls for *all* workers to join a general strike to bring the economy to a halt. But few workers answered the call, and the authorities clamped down hard. About 1,500 men were arrested, and 79 were transported to Australia. By October the last strikers had been forced back to work. The depression lifted in 1843, and, as wages and employment improved, Chartism faded again.

In the mid-1840s O'Connor became keen on another scheme to solve working-class problems. In 1845 he formed the **National Land Company** to buy farmland for city workers to move to. The scheme was financed by selling shares to industrial workers and buying land with the proceeds. There was then a draw among shareholders to see who the first lucky settlers would be. In 1846 the first settlement began at **O'Connorville**, near Watford, and by 1848 there were five other settlements, including one called **Charterville** near Witney in Oxfordshire. However, the plots proved to be too small, and the townsfolk were poor farmers. The scheme was financially unsound and it eventually collapsed.

8.8 THE END OF CHARTISM

CAUSATION

Depression returned in the winter of **1847–8**, and unemployment rose. The Chartists organized a **third petition** and claimed over 5,700,000 signatures. A massive rally was called for 10 April 1848 at Kennington Common in London, with plans for the crowds to march to Parliament with the petition. O'Connor even published a constitution for a new British Republic, with himself as president. The government was alarmed. Queen Victoria was moved to the safety of the Isle of Wight, and the Duke of Wellington was given 100,000 soldiers and the task of defending the capital. He signed up a further 150,000 men as special constables and took over the railway and telegraph services. In the event, everyone had exaggerated the danger. Wellington refused to allow the march to Parliament. O'Connor agreed and took the petition to Westminster alone in a carriage, while the crowd dutifully dispersed. Upon inspection, the petition was found to contain less than 2 million signatures, many of them false. The House of Commons again rejected the petition, this time by 222 votes to 17. Apart from a few disturbances in London during that summer, Chartism died away.

Why did Chartism fail?

1 The most obvious reason for Chartism's failure was **parliamentary opposition**. MPs rejected the Charter on three occasions. Chartism never had the support of any large parliamentary party or faction.

2 **Government suppression**. The use of soldiers to defend Newport in 1839, the transportation of seventy-nine Chartists in 1842 and Wellington's massive use of strength in London in 1848 all show how the government, magistrates, army and courts used strong action to control Chartism.

3 Chartism arose out of social hardship. It flourished in times of depression. But after 1842 there was a marked improvement in the **standard of living** of the working class. Employment and wages rose as the economy entered a period of growth. Parliament also passed more useful legislation. There was a Mines Act in 1842 and a Factory Act in 1844 which improved working conditions. The repeal of the Corn Laws reduced the cost of living. There didn't seem the same need to reform Parliament to improve living conditions as there had in the 1830s.

4 **Alternative working-class movements** also drained Chartism of support. In the mid-1830s the GNCTU had collapsed, and the early co-operatives had failed. But the situation was different by the 1850s. The Rochdale Pioneers had shown that co-operatives could reduce the cost of living, and 'new model' trade unions began to restore workers' faith in the union movement.

5 The **leadership of the Chartists** was divided and ineffective. The split between the 'moral force' leaders like Lovett and Attwood and the supporters of physical force, such as Julian Harney, John Frost and Feargus O'Connor, discredited Chartism. Their disputes were openly fought at the conventions and in the pages of the *Northern Star*. As O'Connor gradually became the

SOURCE A

'The honourable member for Nottingham (Feargus O'Connor) stated that 5,706,000 names were attached to the petition. On the most careful examination this has been found to be 1,975,496. On many sheets the signatures are in one and the same handwriting. The committee also observed the names of famous people who can hardly be supposed to agree with the Charter's aims: among which occurs the name of Her Majesty as "Victoria Rex", April First, Cheeks the Marine, Robert Peel and the Duke of Wellington (several times!). The committee also noted a number of names which are clearly made up, such as "No Cheese", "Pug Nose", "Flat Nose"'.

Report of the House of Commons, 13 April 1848.

SOURCE B

SOURCE C

This 'Punch' cartoon is a comment on the 1848 petition. It shows what a strange gathering the Kennington Common meeting would have been if the names on the petition were true. Notice that the 'Duke of Wellington' appears several times.

leading personality, 'moral force' Chartists drifted out of the movement. One, Joseph Sturge, even started up a rival movement, the Complete Suffrage Association, in 1842. O'Connor was, even so, not an effective leader. He threatened violence but was not prepared to use it, as his confrontation with Wellington proved in 1848.

6 The **working people** of Britain were the backbone of Chartism. They supported the Charter in huge numbers at conventions, marches, demonstrations and strikes. Occasionally, some of them resorted to violence. But they were basically moderate. Once Parliament rejected the petitions, they accepted its decision.

Did Chartism really fail?

In some senses, Chartism was not a complete failure. All of the six points were eventually accepted into law except annual Parliaments. Many local Chartist leaders put their political experience to work in local government or trade union organizations. The publicity which Chartism gave to the situation of working people helped other efforts for reform, like the factory reform movement. But most importantly, Chartism strengthened the growing sense of working-class identity. It thus helped to create the climate for the successful growth of other working-class movements later, such as the Labour Party and the Trades Union Congress.

The 1848 Kennington Common meeting.

EXERCISE

Here is a list of reasons for the failure of Chartism:

- **a** Rejection by Parliament.
- **b** Opposition from the government, magistrates and courts.
- **c** Improvements in the standard of living.
- **d** Alternative working-class movements.
- **e** Poor leadership.
- **f** Moderate membership.

1. Are any of these *not* reasons for the failure of Chartism?
2. Are they all *equally important* reasons?
3. Could only *one* reason have caused the failure of Chartism *on its own*?
4. Why did Chartism fail?

9.1 THE OLD POOR LAW

We have seen in Part Eight that changes brought about by the Industrial Revolution caused various types of hardship for working people. The **Poor Law** was the means of dealing with the worst of these hardships. But the Poor Law was *not* for people who were just poor.

Poverty – that is, having too little for a comfortable life – was the constant situation for many working people in the nineteenth century. Few workers existed without being poor at some stage of their lives. Some people even considered poverty to be a necessary part of society; it was a spur to keep the people working hard.

Pauperism, however, was a different matter. Being a pauper meant being **destitute** – that is, so poor that you couldn't survive without help, too poor to feed yourself or your family. Pauperism was usually thought to be the pauper's own fault; laziness, foolishness or drunkenness were blamed. Governments tried to stop pauperism. Too many desperate paupers were thought to be dangerous to the stability of society.

In 1601 the final Act in a whole series of laws passed in the reign of Queen Elizabeth I set out the first national system for dealing with paupers. It was called the **Old Poor Law**. This made local magistrates responsible for appointing unpaid overseers of the poor to give help to paupers in their parish. But by 1800 that system had broken down. Magistrates had set up so many different schemes in various parts of the country that a confusing mixture local ways of dealing with paupers existed.

In some parts of Britain paupers were sent to work in a **workhouse** run by the overseer. Sometimes the workhouse was contracted out to business men who ran it for profit. In other places the **roundsman system** was used. This meant that paupers were sent round all the local employers in turn, who had to find them work. The employer paid them a fraction of a normal wage, and the overseer made up the rest. In other places an **allowance system** was used. This was first started in Berkshire in 1795. Because bread prices were rising so fast during the wars against France (see pages 28–9), even those farm labourers who had jobs were finding it hard to survive. The local magistrates met in the Pelican Inn in the village of Speenhamland and decided that to prevent starvation they should pay some workers an *allowance* on top of their wages. The amount of the allowance would depend upon the price of bread, the labourer's wage and the size of his family. This system became known as the **Speenhamland System** and it was adopted throughout most of the agricultural areas of southern England and the Midlands.

Reasons for reform

There were various reasons why this system was unacceptable by about 1830. Some people objected to the **working conditions** for paupers who were roundsmen or in the workhouses, especially those which were contracted out (see Source A). But the Speenhamland System caused the most criticism. It **demoralized** the paupers. They did a full week's work and still had to rely on

SOURCE A

'The workhouse was a scene of filth, misery and indecency. Imagine paupers who for weeks, months and years had breakfast, dinner and supper without knife, fork or plate. Imagine 600 persons badly looked after, crowded into rooms seldom or never ventilated, with their bedding swarming with vermin.

'Single and married, young and old, they all mixed together, without regard for decency. Imagine this and you will have some idea of what life is like in the workhouse.'

Conditions in one workhouse described in the 'Norwich Mercury', 1829.

SOURCE B

SOURCE C

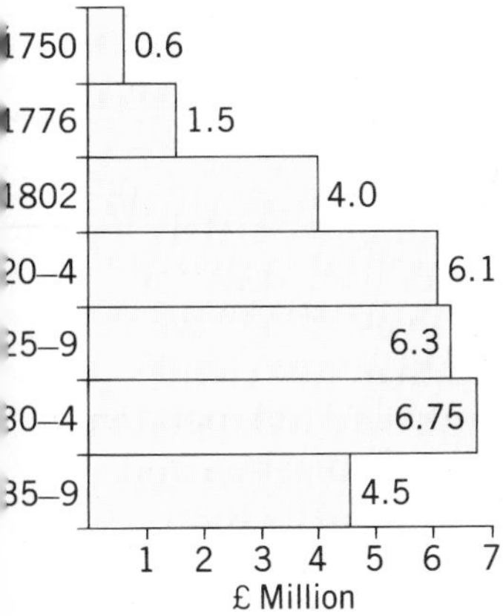

These figures show the average nount per year spent on poor relief

he cost of poor relief, 1733–1833.

hand-outs. Many people thought that this had helped to cause the Swing Riots in 1830. According to some, the Speenhamland System caused the **population** to grow too fast. By fixing relief to the size of a pauper's family, it encouraged him to have more children. It also encouraged **low wages**. Because the parish would always make wages up to a reasonable level, there was no need for farmers to increase wages. It encouraged **laziness**. Why should families search around for extra work to increase their wages, when the magistrates would give them an allowance anyway? It was also **expensive**, and cost was a big concern. Source B shows how the cost of providing poor relief grew at the start of the nineteenth century.

The cost of poor relief was paid by ratepayers; most ratepayers were middle class; the middle classes had just been given the vote in the Reform Act of 1832. It is no coincidence that in 1832 the government set up a **Royal Commission** to investigate the Poor Law.

The thinking behind the reform

The commissioners were very aware of all of the weaknesses of the Old Poor Law, mentioned above. But their attitudes and political ideas determined which weaknesses they reported on most and what changes they suggested. The two most prominent commissioners were **Nassau Senior**, an economist, and **Edwin Chadwick**, a journalist. They eventually wrote the report of the commission. They were **utilitarians** – that is, they thought that reforms should, above all, make society more efficient. They also believed that government should interfere in people's lives as little as possible; this is often called ***laissez-faire***, letting things work themselves out.

The report of the Royal Commission, therefore, attacked all the features of the Old Poor Law which were inefficient. For example, it highlighted the fact that the Speenhamland System was supposed to be curing poverty, but, by making workers lazy and encouraging low wages, it actually made poverty worse. The report also stressed the bad effects of the magistrates interfering too much in things which should be left up to individuals. For example, the report stressed the huge **cost** of the Speenhamland System, caused by the magistrates interfering in setting wage levels rather than leaving this for employers and their workers to sort out.

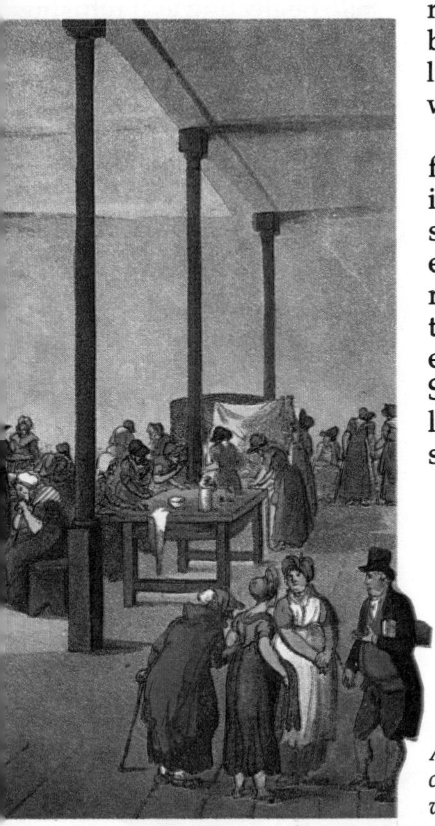

A London workhouse in 1809. Even though all of the women have been put to work, conditions don't look too bad. Rate payers would probably have felt that these paupers were being treated too well.

9.2 THE NEW POOR LAW

EMPATHY

The recommendations of the **Report on the Poor Law** were put into practice by the **Poor Law Amendment Act of 1834**. It set up a system of poor relief known as the **New Poor Law**.

The new system was to be under the **central control** of a **Poor Law Commission**, run by three commissioners and based at Somerset House in London. Edwin Chadwick became the secretary to the Poor Law Commission. This central authority supervised the work of 643 parish **unions**, or groups of parishes. Ratepayers voted in each union to elect a **board of guardians** to run the system locally. The guardians employed paid workhouse **overseers** to provide poor relief to paupers.

Poor relief was to be given in a **uniform** way. The commissioners wanted no local variations. Those paupers who could clearly not be blamed for their problems, for example the sick or disabled, were called the **impotent poor**, because they were powerless to help themselves. They were to be provided with **outdoor relief** – that is, money or food or clothes in their own homes; or special homes were to be provided to look after them. **Able-bodied paupers** were considered to blame for their condition. They were to be sent into **workhouses**; outdoor relief was to be gradually abolished for them. Furthermore, conditions in the workhouse were to be made **less eligible** (less desirable) than the worst conditions of ordinary labourers outside the workhouse.

Conditions in the workhouse

Workhouse **living conditions** were clean and well ordered, but they were also harsh. Families were always separated. Men, women and children had separate dormitories, dining areas, exercise yards and work areas. **Work** was compulsory; stone breaking and bone crushing were common for men, while women did the domestic work of the workhouse. Workhouse **uniforms** had to be worn at all times; smoking and alcohol were forbidden; and **punishments** for misbehaviour were harsh. The **diet** was intended to keep people alive but was deliberately kept uninteresting. One regime recommended by the commissioners allowed cooked meat and vegetables for dinner on two days, but only bread and cheese for the rest of the week. In addition, supper was always to consist of bread and cheese and breakfast always of bread and gruel. The **daily routine** was unchanging.

There was a chilling logic behind the system; its supporters considered it a triumph. Making the conditions in the workhouse worse than conditions outside meant that only those who were desperate would ask to come in. It was a true test between real pauperism and mere poverty. Also, the harsh conditions in the workhouse meant that paupers were punished for their mistakes and given an incentive to get back on their own feet. The workhouses even separated pauper husbands and wives to prevent more pauper children being conceived and born, and separated pauper children from the corrupting influence of their pauper parents.

SOURCE A

'Of the first eighty-seven labourers with families, to whom outdoor relief was refused, and to all of whom an order to the workhouse was given, not one half availed themselves of that offer, but immediately found means of providing for themselves. (They) were taught that they could honestly and independently support themselves and their families by their industry.'

Report by the Faringdon Poor Law Union, 1835.

SOURCE B

'*Twenty-nine women at the mill*, neglecting and refusing to work, dinner and supper milk stopped.

Owen Trainor, stealing onions, flogged.

James Acheson, going to town without permission, 6 hours in lock-up.

James Close, refractory conduct, 6 hours in lock-up.

F. Cambell and J. Burnes, absconding with Union clothes, flogged.

Mary Carroll, refusing to work and damaging clothes, 9 hours in lock-up.

Mary Carroll, persisting in refusing to work, 7 hours in lock-up.'

Punishment book, Newry workhouse, 1851–4.

SOURCE C

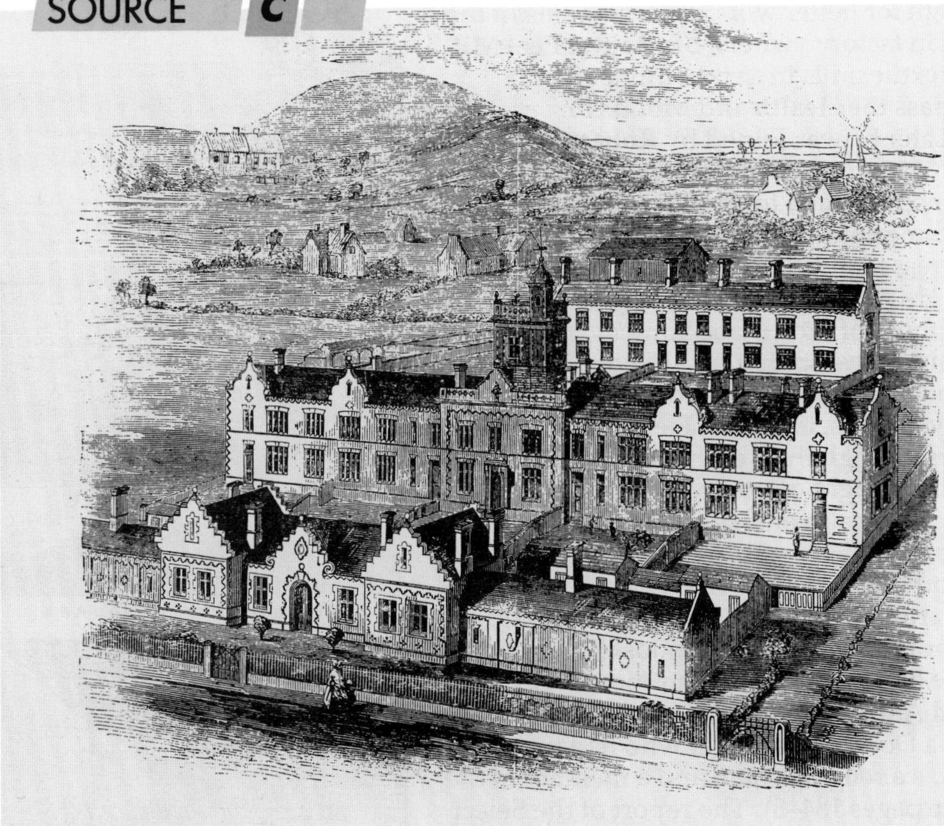

SCARBOROUGH NEW WORKHOUSE.

AMONG the improvements lately carried out in Scarborough is workhouse, which has recently been erected, situated in Dean-street, leading to the Cemetery. The group of buildings will accommodate from two hundred to three hundred inmates. The front range is for boardroom, offices, &c.; the entrance gateway forming a pleasing feature, being composed of moulded white bricks with a bold keystone over, which is a large shield with the Scarborough arms carved in high relief. The governor's apartments occupy a central position, and are so arranged that he possesses the fullest command of, and is in the closest approximation with, every ward of the establishment. These apartments are also crowned by a tower which furnishes a very efficient system of ventilation. The infirmary at the back is appropriately on the highest part of the ground (being nearly twenty feet higher than the front), and is thoroughly well lighted and ventilated; and, although the building, as a whole, is free from the expensive ornamental decoration that too often characterises similar establishments, it possesses, from the artistic mixture of brickwork, a most attractive and substantial appearance. The whole of the buildings are well supplied with water and lighted with gas; and these advantages, coupled with a capital system of drainage, make the sanitary regulations all that could be desired. The works have been erected from designs furnished by Messrs. George and Henry Styan, architects, York, under whose direction they have been successfully carried out.

An article in the 'Illustrated London News' about the new Scarborough workhouse.

EXERCISE

1 How do you think the Poor Law commissioners would have reacted when they received Source A? Explain your answer.

2 Do you think a member of the board of guardians of the Newry workhouse would have regarded the punishments in Source B as harsh? Explain your answer.

3 The building shown in Source C was obviously designed with great care. The article suggests people were proud of it. Yet people were treated harshly in workhouses. Why did the guardians act like this?

The effects of the New Poor Law

After 1834 the **cost** of poor relief was reduced. From an average of £6.75 million pounds per year in 1830–4, the cost went down to £4.5 millions for 1835–9. This was largely because the poor came to **fear** the workhouses. One northern newspaper reported in 1838 that 'Skins of old pauper women who died in the workhouse were used to provide chair covers for the commissioners or book bindings for parish records.' Such rumours were common; they were not true, but they were believed, and the commissioners were probably glad that they were.

By 1838 the south of England was organized into unions, and outdoor relief was abolished for the able bodied. But **opposition** to the new arrangements was stronger in the north. There were anti-Poor Law riots in Bradford in 1837 and in Dewsbury in 1838. The board of guardians in Huddersfield refused to operate the new system. The problem was that, in the industrial north, trade depressions could reduce wages and send up unemployment so that thousands were forced on to poor relief for no fault of their own. Local authorities realized this. There weren't even enough places in the workhouses. During the depression of 1839 there were 98,000 people in English workhouses, but a further 560,000 on outdoor relief. A compromise was reached whereby the guardians decided when outdoor relief was necessary for the able bodied, and the system continued, largely unchanged, for the rest of the nineteenth century.

9.3 FACTORY REFORM

The first people to campaign for better working conditions in the **factories** were humanitatian factory owners. **Sir Robert Peel MP** had made a fortune from textile mills in Lancashire before he persuaded Parliament to pass the **Health and Morals of Apprentices Act of 1802**. Later he was joined by **Robert Owen**, to push the **Factory Act of 1819** through Parliament.

After 1830 a variety of people joined forces in a concerted campaign to improve working conditions. **Richard Oastler**, a Yorkshire land agent, addressed public meetings and wrote letters to the newspapers. He claimed that working conditions in factories were worse than those of slaves (see Source A). A number of **'short-time committees'** sprang up all across the north of England to campaign for a working day of no more than ten hours. Sympathetic factory owners, like **John Fielden**, supported them, as did many workers, though their enthusiasm for shorter hours was restrained by the thought of lower pay. Even some landowners who resented the wealth of factory owners began to support the movement too.

Michael Sadler was a northern Tory MP and a friend of Oastler's. He persuaded Parliament to set up a Select Committee to investigate working conditions. When Sadler lost his seat in Parliament, his place at the head of the **'ten-hour movement'** was taken by another MP, **Lord Anthony Ashley Cooper** (Later **Earl of Shaftesbury**). Ashley was a Dorset landowner who had never visited the north, but he was a religious man and a member of the Evangelical movement (see pages 184–5). The report of the Select Committee deeply moved him. A private member's bill which Ashley introduced to reduce working hours failed, but the government did agree to set up a full-scale inquiry under a Royal Commission. When that commission reported, the government passed the **Factory Act of 1833**.

Now the pattern was set. Campaigns outside Parliament pressed governments into setting up inquiries, and their reports led to Acts of Parliament. Thus Shaftesbury's pressure led to Royal Commissions to investigate conditions in the mines (1840) and factories (1842) which led to the **Mines Act of 1842** and the **Factory Act of 1844**. When the limitations of each Act emerged, new laws were passed. The ten-hour day was not achieved until the **Factory Act of 1874**.

One key idea which slowed legislation down was ***laissez-faire*** – the idea that there were some areas of life in which the government should not interfere. Factories were private property; employment was seen as a private agreement between employers and workers. Many people believed that working conditions were therefore nothing to do with the government. But the first law passed of all the factory legislation was to protect pauper children. This seemed reasonable because they could not be expected to be able to protect themselves. Then other types of children were protected. Soon women were included. Spurred on by the findings of the official reports, people gradually got used to the idea that the government had a right to interfere in private factories to set reasonable working conditions.

SOURCE A

A CODRINGTON LABOURER.

A MORETON SLAVE.

This is a contemporary cartoon commenting on the lives of factory workers in Britain. Richard Oastler spoke of 'Yorkshire slavery', claiming that British workers were worse off than slaves. Parliament had acted to help slaves in British colonies, yet they seemed unwilling to help badly-paid workers in Britain.

The laws passed after 1850 concentrated upon extending protection to workers outside the textile mills and mines. The **Factories and Workshops Act of 1867** and the **Factory Act of 1878** were the most important.

1802 ***Health and Morals of Apprentices Act***
This law applied only to **pauper children** sent from workhouses to be apprentices in **textile mills**. It said that they could not be employed younger than **9 years old** and could not work longer than **12 hours a day**. They could not be given night work and had to be clothed, given schooling and sent to church at least once a month by their employer. Their workplaces had to be properly ventilated and whitewashed annually.

The Act had little effect. It applied to a very small part of the workforce and was supposed to be enforced by local magistrates. But since these often knew, and sometimes were, the factory owners, their sympathies were usually not with the child workers.

1819 ***Factory Act***
This law extended the 1802 Act to **all children** in **cotton mills**. It meant no work for children under **9 years old** and set a **maximum 72-hour week** for children between **9 and 16**, with 1½ hours allowed daily for meal breaks.

This Act was also ineffective. It still relied upon magistrates to enforce the law.

1833 ***Althorp's Factory Act***
Named after the Whig Home Secretary who sponsored it, this Act was the first effective legislation. It applied to the **whole textile industry** except lace and silk making. It banned work for children **under 9** and set a **maximum 48-hour week** for **9–13-year-olds**, with an additional 2 hours' per day compulsory schooling. Children aged **13 to 16** could work no more than **69 hours per week**, and night work was banned for those under 18. Meal breaks of 1½ hours per day were compulsory for all children, and there were to be eight compulsory half-day holidays. Children were not to be expected to clean machinery still in motion.

Four **factory inspectors** were appointed to enforce this law. Four were not enough, particularly since there was no official registration of births before 1837, so it was difficult to know a child's true age. However, the principle of an independent factory inspectorate had been established and the inspectorate grew in efficiency over the years.

1842 ***Mines and Collieries Act***
This Act controlled working conditions only in the **mines**. It outlawed the employment underground of **women and children under 10 years of age**. It also said that winding gear should not be entrusted to children less than 15. Mines inspectors were appointed to enforce the law.

1844 ***Graham's Factory Act***
Named after the Tory Home Secretary of the day, this Act also applied to the **whole of the textile industry** except silk and lace. It reduced the minimum age for child labour to **8 years**, and set a **maximum 6½-hour working day**, with ½ day schooling, for **8–13-year-olds. No women and no boys under 18** were to work more than **12 hours a day**. All dangerous machinery was to be fenced in.

1847 ***Fielden's Factory Act***
This law finally achieved a **maximum ten-hour working day** for **women and children under 18**. But employers still kept factories open from about 5.30 a.m. until 8.30 p.m. and worked the women and children in relays so that they could keep the men working the whole time.

1850 ***Grey's Factory Act***
The **maximum working day** for **women and children** was extended to **10½ hours** in exchange for an agreement that these must be **between 6.00 a.m. and 6.00 p.m.** This meant that factories could employ only men for these 12 hours which, with 1⅝ hours of meal breaks, meant **almost a 10-hour day** in the cotton industry.

1867 ***Factories and Workshops Act***
This Act applied all previous factory legislation to **all factories**. But it defined factories as places with over fifty workers, thus ignoring many small workshops where bad conditions continued.

1874 ***Factories and Workshops Act***
This Act finally achieved the **10-hour day** for all factory workers by setting a maximum **56½-hour week** (10 hours per day Monday to Friday and a 6½ hour half-day on Saturdays).

1878 ***Factory Act***
This Act redefined a factory as **any** workplace with machinery for manufacturing and thus brought **most workers** under the **protection of the law**. It also extended the work of factory inspectors to cover all factories and workshops.

9.4 PUBLIC HEALTH IMPROVEMENTS: MEDICAL PROGRESS

The appalling living conditions and high death rates of mid-nineteenth-century Britain were gradually improved. This was due partly to **medical progress**, the subject of the present unit, and partly to **public health reform** (pages 152–3).

SOURCE A

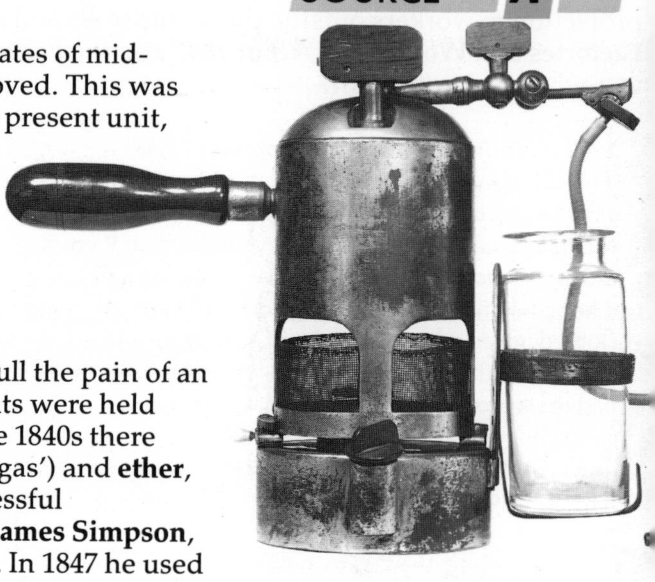

Joseph Lister's carbolic acid spray pump.

SOURCE B

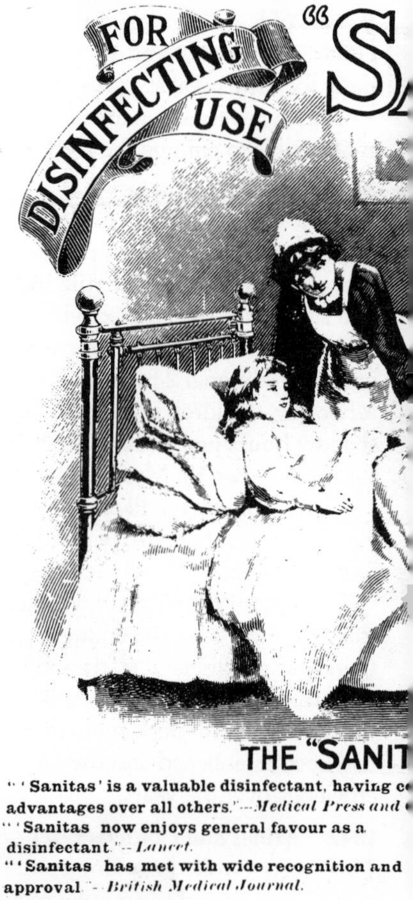
FOR DISINFECTING USE
"S
THE "SANIT
" 'Sanitas' is a valuable disinfectant, having c
advantages over all others."—*Medical Press and*
" 'Sanitas now enjoys general favour as a disinfectant."—*Lancet.*
" 'Sanitas has met with wide recognition and approval."—*British Medical Journal.*

Surgery

Before 1800 there were no **anaesthetics** used to dull the pain of an operation. Surgeons had to work fast, and patients were held down or made senseless with alcohol. During the 1840s there were experiments with **nitrous oxide** ('laughing gas') and **ether**, but both were difficult to control. The most successful development was the use of **choloroform** by **Dr James Simpson**, Professor of Midwifery at Edinburgh University. In 1847 he used chloroform to help women through childbirth, and it was adopted by surgeons for a range of operations. **Local anaesthetics**, based upon injections of cocaine, were developed from 1884.

However, some surgeons were inexperienced and made mistakes; this made others doubtful about the new drugs. A few maintained that patients ought to endure the pain, claiming that it was natural and that the moans of the patient could even help the doctor. Only after Queen Victoria used chloroform at the birth of her son, Prince Leopold, in 1853 did its use in childbirth become common.

Although anaesthetics allowed deeper and longer surgery, surgeons had not yet succeeded in overcoming **infection** of wounds. Most people survived the operations but died of blood poisoning afterwards. Until this could be resolved, anaesthetics, which encouraged more operations, were likely to cause only more deaths. **Antiseptics** were the answer. In 1865 **Joseph Lister**, Professor of Surgery at Glasgow University, read that the French scientist Louis Pasteur had discovered that tiny organisms or germs lived in the air and caused infection. Lister experimented with **carbolic acid** to keep these micro-organisms away from open wounds during surgery. First he used lint soaked in carbolic acid and place it over wounds. Later he devised a pump for spraying a cloud of carbolic into the air in operating rooms (see Source A). Others later followed his lead (see Source B). The survival rate of his patients rose from 55 per cent to 85 per cent.

Again, many surgeons were sceptical. Lister's methods slowed them down, and they believed that speed was essential to avoid infection. They credited general hospital improvements as the cause of his successes. It wasn't until the 1880s that his ideas became widespread.

By the 1890s the importance of combating germs was generally accepted. Surgeons began to adopt **aseptic** methods, which

SOURCE C

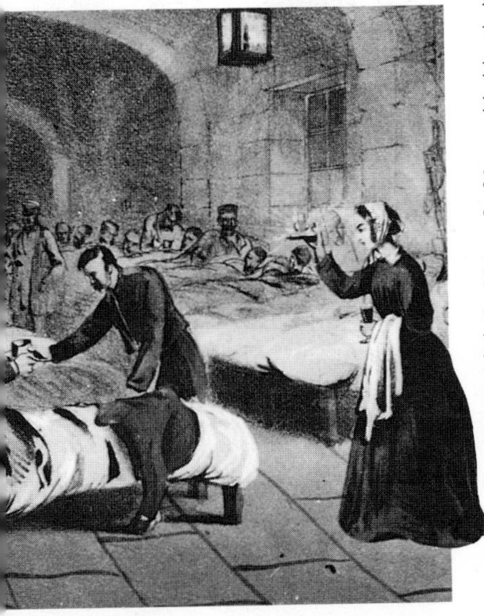

Florence Nightingale at the military hospital at Scutari.

entailed not killing off the germs in the operating theatres but keeping them out and operating in a **germ-free area**. Steam was used to sterilize surgical gowns, dressings and threads; instruments were made of metal and boiled; rubber gloves were introduced in 1890.

The discovery of **X-rays** in 1895 and of the four human blood groups in 1901, which enabled safe **blood transfusions**, also aided surgeons.

Standards of medical care

Changes in surgery were just part of a wider improvement in **hospital hygiene** – and the hospitals needed it. As late as 1861 Florence Nightingale (see Source C) stated that 90 per cent of patients entering London's hospitals died there. Hospital buildings were dirty and overcrowded. The bed linen at St George's Hospital was changed only every three weeks. Dressings and bandages were washed and then re-used. **Medical and nursing standards** were low. Few doctors were university trained; most had merely served apprenticeships, like carpenters or tailors, with practising doctors.

Useful improvements came only after 1850. In 1855 **Florence Nightingale** travelled to Scutari in the Crimea to run a hospital for the wounded in the Crimean War. She reduced death rates by improving standards of cleanliness and care. After she returned, she published a booklet about better nursing care called *Notes on Nursing*, the first of her many publications and articles. In 1860 she opened a nursing school in a wing of St Thomas's Hospital in London, and her teaching stressed clean wards and high personal standards. Student nurses at St Thomas's had to live in at the hospital, were not allowed boyfriends and were allowed to venture out only in pairs. Soon more nursing schools were opened. By 1901 there were 60,000 **trained nurses** in Britain. In 1902 the **Midwives Act** required midwives to have special training, and in 1919 minimum entry qualifications were established for nursing.

Standards among **doctors** improved too. The **General Medical Council** was established in 1858 to control entry into the medical profession. It kept a register of all qualified doctors and could discipline any doctors who broke its rules. By 1900 all new doctors were trained in medical schools.

An advertisement for Sanitas disinfectant spray.

SOURCE D

'At present nursing is the last resort of female adversity. Slatternly widows, runaway wives, servants out of place, women bankrupt of fame and fortune, from whatever cause fall back upon hospital nursing. When on a rare occasion a respectable young woman takes to it from choice, her friends most likely repudiate her.'

From a hospital report by the Medical Officer of Health for Glasgow, 1865.

SOURCE E

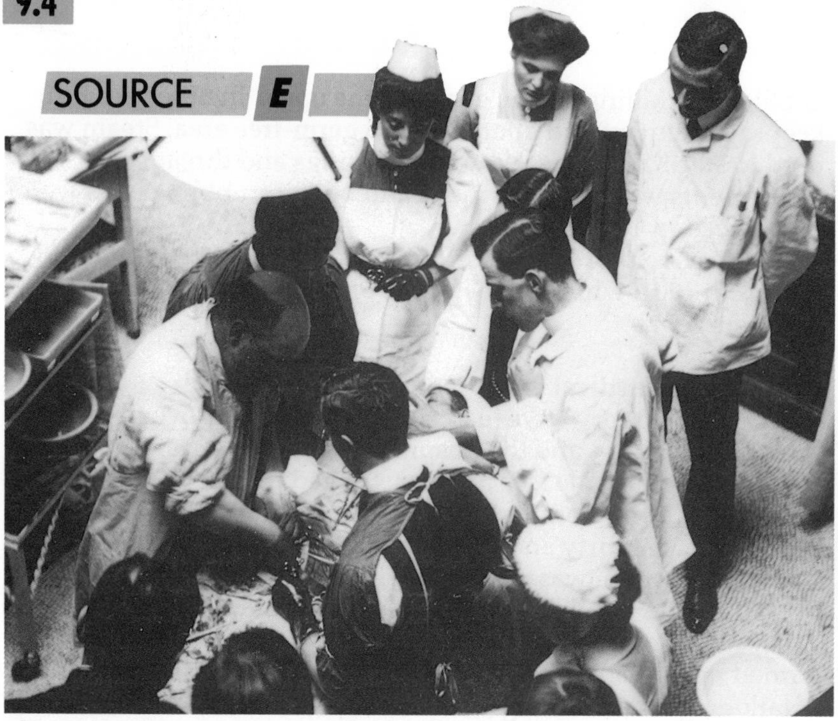

SOURCE F

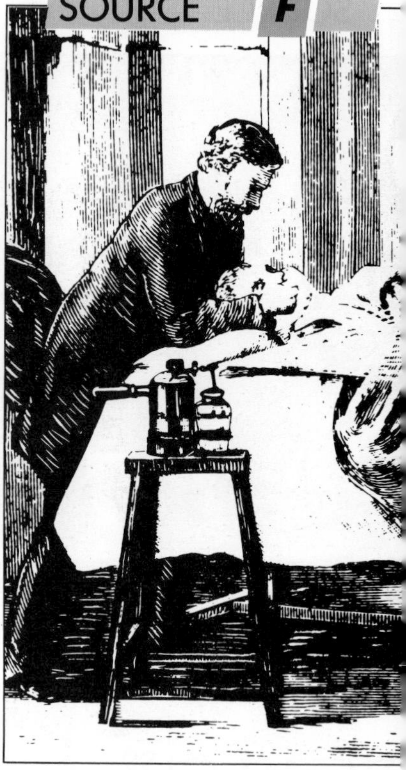

Infectious disease

The main killers of the nineteenth century were **infectious diseases** like cholera, tuberculosis, diptheria, typhoid, typhus, polio and scarlet fever. There was only slow medical progress against these.

Smallpox had been a major killer disease in the eighteenth century. People had known for a long time that anyone who survived a mild dose of the disease would never become infected again. It was common practice therefore to infect people deliberately with fluid taken from a patient suffering a mild attack of smallpox. Unfortunately, this often started a minor epidemic among people living nearby or, worse still, accidentally killed the person inoculated with the disease he or she was supposed to become protected from. However, **Edward Jenner**, a Gloucestershire doctor, decided to investigate the fact that people who had caught **cowpox**, a mild illness picked up by those who worked with cattle, rarely caught smallpox. Dairy maids, for example, were well known for their clear complexion, free from the pock-marks of smallpox. In 1796 Jenner therefore took some infected fluid from a girl with cowpox and used it to infect James Phipps, a healthy 8-year-old boy. Fifteen months later the boy was deliberately exposed to a smallpox victim but didn't catch the illness. Jenner had found a safe protection against smallpox. His process was called **vaccination**, after the Latin word *vacca*, meaning cow. There was some opposition to his discovery, but it soon became widely adopted, and deaths from smallpox declined.

Jenner had discovered his vaccine by chance. It eventually became possible to produce vaccines to prevent people catching many other human diseases, but nobody found a way to do this for almost a hundred years. The key work was done by two

SOURCE G

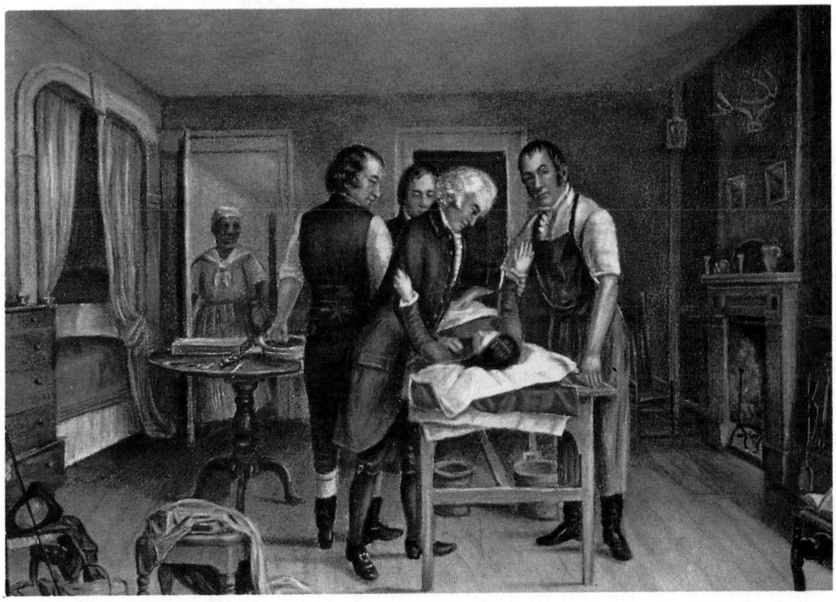

scientists, **Louis Pasteur** in France and **Robert Koch** in Germany. In the 1860s Pasteur found that micro-organisms in the air caused infection; he could show them under his microscope. In the 1870s Koch found out which germs caused blood poisoning and tuberculosis, two of the biggest causes of death. Having found the germs which *caused* disease, it was now necessary to find *vaccines* to protect people from catching them or *cures* to stop them killing an infected person.

Vaccines came only slowly. In 1885 Pasteur found a vaccine to protect people against **rabies**. Others were found to prevent **tuberculosis** in 1906 and **diphtheria** in 1913, but the development of vaccines was a slow process which belongs more to the twentieth century than to the nineteenth. **Cures** which killed the germs in the body even after a person had become infected came even more slowly. A cure for **diphtheria** was discovered by **Behring** in 1890, and in 1909 a team of scientists led by Paul Ehrlich discovered a chemical compound which they called Salvarsan 606 which cured **syphillis**. Other cures for infection, like sulphonamides and penicillin, were not developed until well into the twentieth century.

Doctors and scientists had made great progress in the nineteenth century. The quality of nursing and surgery had greatly reduced death rates in the hospitals; much more was known about infectious diseases, the scourge of Britain's industrial towns. However, the first victory over infectious diseases in Britain's industrial towns was won by the **public health reformers** who cleaned up the slums.

ACTIVITIES

1 Look at Sources E, F and G which show three operations.
   a Place them in chronological order.
   b Making detailed reference to the sources and the information given in the text in this unit, explain your answer.

2 Look at all of the illustrations in this unit.
   a Which one do you think gives the *most* accurate information for the historian?
   b Which one do you think gives the *least* accurate information?

3 What are the problems for historians in the use of:
   a photographs?
   b paintings?

9.5 PUBLIC HEALTH REFORM

Living conditions in Britain's mid-nineteenth-century industrial towns have been described on pages 124–5. The dirty, overcrowded housing, often lacking a clean water supply or sewers, was a breeding ground for infectious diseases. But governments were slow to tackle the problems of **public health**.

The cholera epidemic of 1831–2 prompted some action. The government set up a Central Board of Health in London which suggested ways to prevent the disease spreading. Local boards of health were set up in large towns to carry out their instructions. But as soon as the epidemic passed, these boards of health were disbanded.

It was **Edwin Chadwick** who did most to campaign for permanent public health reform. He was the secretary of the Poor Law Commission and he realized how much poverty was caused by sickness. He persuaded the Poor Law commissioners to set up a national inquiry, whose report was finally published in 1842 as *The Sanitary Conditions of the Labouring Population of Great Britain*. The report was widely read and had a major impact upon public opinion. It proved the connection between poor living conditions and high death rates and argued that the problem could no longer be left to local councils. They didn't have the power or funds for slum clearance. Local ratepayers were likely to think that new housing or new sewers were too expensive for the rates to bear. Local water companies argued against new schemes. Government action was needed (see Source A).

But the government responded only by setting up an even bigger inquiry, by the **Royal Commission on the Health of Towns** in 1842. Its reports in 1844 and 1845 confirmed all the earlier findings, and the **Health of Towns Association** was formed to put pressure on the government to act. Eventually it took another cholera epidemic in 1848 to stir Parliament to action. The **Public Health Act of 1848** was passed.

This Act set up a **Central Board of Health** for a period of five years. Its members included Lord Shaftesbury, Edwin Chadwick and his friend Dr Southwood Smith. The Central Board could work only through local boards which were set up if local councils wanted one, or if 10 per cent of the local people petitioned for one. If the death rate in a town was higher than 23 per 1,000, then the Central Board could insist on a local board being started. But even if a local board was set up, the Central Board could only 'inspect, audit and advise' it. The Central Board could not force changes on anyone. Two hundred boroughs did set up local boards, which affected about 2 million people, but the Central Board was unpopular. Its life was extended in 1853 for one year, but it was weakened in 1854 and abolished in 1858.

Progress was so slow and faltering because there was plenty of opposition to central government reforms. Many people believed in the *laissez-faire* approach – that people should be left alone to run their own lives and that the government should interfere as little as possible. Why should local ratepayers be forced by ministers in London to make expensive changes which would increase the rates? What business was it of theirs? Chadwick

SOURCE A

A cartoon from 'Punch' showing 'King Bumble', representing the town councils, inactive and deaf to the pleas of the poor.

SOURCE B

'Mr Chadwick and Dr Southwood Smith have been deposed and we prefer to take our chance with the cholera than be bullied into health. There is nothing a man hates so much as being cleansed against his will or having his floor swept, his halls whitewashed, his dungheaps cleared away and his thatch forced to give way to slate. It is a fact that many people have died from a good washing. The truth is that Mr Chadwick has a great many powers, but it is not so easy to say what they can be applied to. Perhaps a retirement pension with nothing to do will be a way of rewarding this gentleman.'

'The Times', 1854.

SOURCE C

A painting by George Scharf showing the laying of the first water main in the Tottenham Court Road.

made matters worse. He was a stubborn and rather tactless man who offended many people. Those who opposed reform became known as the 'dirty party'. Their anger became hysterical at times (see Source B).

No further major reform came until the **Public Health Act of 1875**. By this time working people in the towns had been given the vote, so the government had to listen to their needs. This Act, sponsored by the Home Secretary, **Richard Cross**, made local councils take responsibility for public health. The government insisted that they should keep pavements lit, paved and cleaned, sewers efficient and clean, and refuse clear from the streets. They also insisted that slaughterhouses and markets should be inspected. All local authorities had to appoint sanitary inspectors and medical officers of health to enforce these laws. Outbreaks of dangerous diseases had to be notified to the government.

Another reform passed in the same year was the **Artisans' Dwellings Act**. This gave local authorities power to clear slums and build better housing for working people. It had an effect upon a few keen councils, like the one in Birmingham where Joseph Chamberlain was the mayor. In London it led to 30,000 people being rehoused. But it only *enabled* councils to act; it didn't *make* them act. Most councils ignored it. Some people were fortunate enough to live in areas where the council was active. Others benefited from generous employers like Cadbury at Bourneville and Lever Brothers at Port Sunlight. But for most working-class town dwellers progress was slow. It wasn't until the **Town Planning Act of 1909** that building back-to-back housing was banned; and it was another ten years before the **Housing Act of 1919** set up government loans for local authorities to help them provide cheap, sound **council housing** for working people.

9.6 SOCIAL REFORM, 1900–39

Despite efforts in the nineteenth century to come to terms with the **social problems** of an industrial society, much remained to be done by 1900.

Between 1886 and 1903 **Charles Booth** made a survey of the lives of the poor in London. He judged any family living on £1 per week to be 'poor' and those who had less as 'very poor'. He calculated that 8 per cent of people in London were very poor and another 22 per cent were poor. **Seebohm Rowntree** made a survey in York with similar results. He concluded: 'We are faced with the startling probability that from 25 to 30 per cent of the town populations of the UK are living in poverty.' Booth and Rowntree described a miserable way of life, with bad housing, poor diet and frequent illness. They also agreed on the causes of poverty, blaming low wages, unemployment, old age, sickness and bereavement. They did *not* blame the poor for being wasteful or lazy – but the Poor Law did.

The Poor Law

The **Poor Law** worked from the assumption that pauperism was the fault of the paupers and it had changed little since being set up in 1834 (see pages 142–5). Conditions in workhouses had improved a little, but many people still considered the treatment of the poor degrading (see Sources A and B). A **Royal Commission** was set up in 1905 to review the Poor Law. When it reported in 1909 its members were divided. The Minority Report wanted to scrap the Poor Law guardians and make local councils responsible for the poor. It wanted separate help for the old, orphans and the unemployed, so that everyone was treated according to their own needs. But the Majority Report recommended keeping workhouses and that help provided to all paupers should continue to be less favourable than the conditions of other workers. They didn't want the poor to become lazy and rely upon other people to support them. As a result the government made no changes to the Poor Law. It was not until 1929 that the **Local Government Act** abolished the Poor Law guardians and put the care of the poor into the hands of the local councils.

But the surveys of Booth and Rowntree were not wasted. Many reforms were passed between 1900 and 1939 to tackle the **causes of poverty** and thus keep people safe from the Poor Law.

The sick

Medicine had improved by 1900, but it was not free. Doctors and hospitals charged for their services. Friendly societies offered insurance schemes, but the poorest could not afford the subscriptions. They had to rely upon workhouse wards. **Sickness** meant loss of earnings which could send whole families into the depths of poverty.

In 1911 the **National Insurance Act** was passed. Part I of this Act concerned sickness insurance. It was a compulsory scheme for all workers between 17 and 65 years old who earned less than about £3 per week. This involved 14 million people. They had 4d

SOURCE A

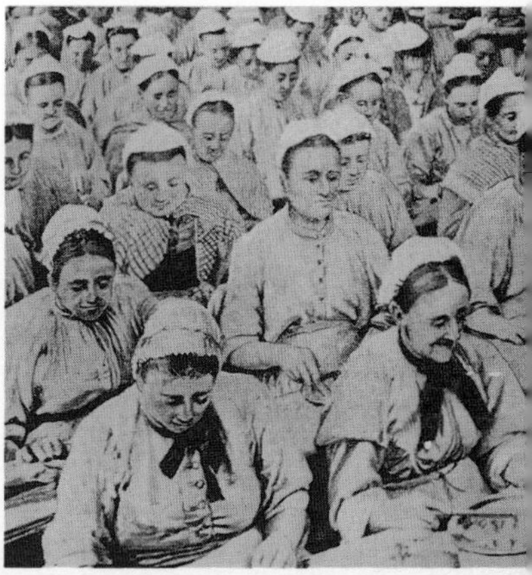

Mealtime at the St Pancras workhouse in 1901. Note the pauper uniforms and the strict organization. No one is talking.

SOURCE B

'On one visit I inspected the supper of oatmeal porridge served up with pieces of black stuff floating around. On examination we found it to be rat and mice manure. I called for the chief officer, who immediately argued against me, saying the porridge was good and wholesome. "Very good, madam," says I. "Here you are, eat one mouthful and I will acknowledge I am wrong." "Oh dear no," said the fine lady. "The food is not for me, and is good and wholesome enough for those who want it."'

Recalled by George Lansbury, a Poor Law guardian of the Poplar workhouse in 1892.

per week deducted from their wages to create a fund to pay their medical expenses. Employers added 3d and the government 2d for every worker. Lloyd George, the minister behind this reform, told the workers they were getting 'ninepence for fourpence'. In exchange, the workers could claim **free medical attention** from a doctor as well as free medicine. If the illness led to time off work, they could claim 10s (50p) per week sickness benefit for 26 weeks (7s 6d or about 38p for women). If the worker was then still not fit, he could have 5s (25p) per week disablement benefit.

Taxpayers resented the cost, and friendly societies complained about unfair competition. But this was a tremendous improvement for the poor, even though it did not cover hospital treatment or any cover for the worker's family. In 1918 the **Ministry of Health** was set up to supervise the scheme.

The unemployed

Loss of earning from **unemployment**, even if it was only temporary, was another cause of poverty. The **Workmen's Compensation Act** was passed in 1906. It covered all workers earning less than £250 per year and allowed them to claim 50 per cent of their wages if they were unable to work because of an illness or injury caused by their job. Another Act, passed in 1909, set up the first **labour exchanges**. They helped people find new work more quickly, and by 1914 there were 430 of them filling over one million job vacancies per year (see Sources C and D).

More important was Part II of the **National Insurance Act of 1911**, which introduced **unemployment insurance**. This scheme was compulsory for all manual labourers in industries with unemployment problems – for example, building, shipbuilding and saw-milling. It involved 2¼ million people. Workers, employers and the government all paid 2½d per week into a government fund, and if workers became unemployed they could claim a payment of 7s (35p) per week for 15 weeks. After this they had to fall back upon the Poor Law.

SOURCE C

'My wife obtained a job as a house-to-house saleswoman, and was able to earn a few shillings to supplement our dole income. It was from this time that the feeling of strain in our home life became more marked. I felt a burden upon her. Life became more and more strained. The final blow came when the Means Test was put into operation. I realized that if I told the Exchange that my wife was earning a little they might reduce my benefit. If that happened home life would become impossible. When I was sent a form on which to give details of our total income I neglected to fill it up. For this I was suspended benefit for six weeks. Quarrels broke out anew and bitter things were said. Eventually both my wife and son, who had just started to earn a few shillings, told me to get out as I was living on them and taking the food they needed.'

Recollections of an unemployed man, quoted by H. L. Beales and R. S. Lambert in 'Memoirs of the Unemployed', 1934.

SOURCE D

The new labour exchange opens at Camberwell Green, February 1910.

The scheme expanded in 1920 to cover 12 million workers. But government thinking was based on the assumption that unemployment would average only 4 per cent of the population. During the world depression of the 1920s and 1930s it averaged over 14 per cent. Also, long-term unemployment became so common that it was decided to pay the benefits for longer than 15 weeks. The Insurance Fund couldn't cope; by 1932 it was £115 million in debt. As a result, the **Unemployment Insurance Act of 1934** was passed, setting up the **Unemployment Insurance Committee** to pay benefits for the first 15 weeks, drawing on the Insurance Fund. An **Unemployment Assistance Board** was also set up to deal with the long-term unemployed.

The Board used funds from the Treasury. But there was no automatic *right* to this help. People could receive money only after a **means test** – after their finances had been investigated so that they could prove that they needed the money. Means tests were unpopular because they were degrading.

These reforms enabled people to survive unemployment but didn't reduce it. Only the build-up to war and its outbreak in 1939 achieved a return to full employment.

Workers

There were also attempts to improve the lives of those who were in work. The **Trade Boards Act of 1909** was passed to safeguard workers in 'sweated trades'. These were people who worked in small workplaces, often in the textile trade, in groups too small to be protected by the Factory Acts. They were often forced to work long hours under poor conditions for low wages. The new trade boards were able to fix minimum wage levels.

The **Coal Mines Act of 1911** improved conditions for miners. Boys under 14 were banned from underground work, and levels of dust were to be kept down. Training was set up for pit managers and deputies, and more mines inspectors were appointed.

The **Shops Act of 1912** guaranteed workers in the retail trade a proper lunch hour and a half-day holiday to compensate them for working on Saturday afternoons.

The aged

The **Old Age Pensions Act of 1908** gave a pension ranging from 1s to 5s (5p to 25p) per week to those people over 70 years old with an income of less than 12s (60p) per week. It was not a great deal even by the standards of the day, but it was to be given as a *right*, not as charity only if people asked, and there were no contributions which had to be made in advance. The spirit of the help was very different from the Poor Law, and some people were surprised by such generosity from the government (see Sources F and G). Others disapproved; they didn't see why taxpayers should support people in their old age.

SOURCE E

'Nothing wearies more than walking about hunting for employment which is not to be had. It is far harder than real work. The uncertainty, the despair, when you reach a place only to discover that the journey is fruitless. I've known a man to say: "Which way shall I go today?" Having no earthly idea which way to take, he tosses up a button. If the button comes down on one side, he treks east; if on the other, he treks west.'

Will Crooks, a cooper, who later became a Labour MP.

SOURCE F

'When the Old Age Pensions began, life was transformed for such aged cottagers. They were relieved of anxiety. They were suddenly rich. Independent for life! At first when they went to the Post Office to draw it tears of gratitude would run down the cheeks of some . . . and there were flowers from their gardens and apples from their trees for the girl who merely handed them the money.'

From the novel 'Lark Rise to Candleford', by Flora Thompson, who had once been a Post Office worker handing out the benefits.

SOURCE G

'What society requires is not that each man when he comes to the age of 60 shall find that his fairy godmother, the State, has put a balance at his bankers, but rather that, during his life, he shall have followed the prudent course of limiting his responsibilities to his income so that at 60 he finds himself in possession, by his own exertion, of adequate provision for his old age.'

An opinion opposing the idea of old-age pensions, written in 1892.

SOURCE H

A 'Punch' cartoon of 1908 showing Lloyd-George, the minister responsible for old-age pensions. Some people resented the extra taxes needed to pay for old-age pensions. This cartoonist is suggesting that they were highway robbery.

By 1925, with the economy and government income suffering from the post-war slump, ministers could not afford to be as generous. The **Widows', Orphans' and Old Age Contributory Pensions Act** extended the pensions scheme to include widows (10s or 50p per week plus extra for their children) and orphans (7s 6d or about 38p). It also extended old-age pensions to *all* old people and *lowered* the age of pensioners to 65 for men and 60 for women. But it insisted that all workers should help with the cost of these payments by a weekly deduction from wages of 9d for men (about 4p) and 4½d (2p) for women.

Children

There were also efforts to improve the lives of **children**. Children from very poor families were able to claim **free school meals**, paid for out of the rates, from 1906. The **school medical inspection service** started in 1907, in an attempt to find certain illnesses like rickets early enough to prevent deformity. In the same year special **juvenile courts** and young people's prisons (called **Borstals**) were set up so that young offenders were dealt with separately and did not mix with hardened criminals. An Act was also passed in 1908 to forbid shopkeepers from selling tobacco, alcohol or fireworks to children under 16. In 1934 cheap milk (free for the poorest) was introduced to provide extra nourishment for children at school.

Housing

Housing conditions were also improved. **Addison's Housing and Town Planning Act of 1919** made local councils conduct a survey of the housing in their area and submit plans to the government to solve the worst problems. The government offered grants to councils to cover part of the cost, so that rents could be kept low. Over 210,000 homes were built before the scheme ended in 1923. Further schemes followed. **Chamberlain's Housing Act of 1923** gave grants to private builders for building new housing of approved design. This produced 440,000 homes by 1929. **Wheatley's Housing Act** renewed grants to councils in 1924 and created over 500,000 new council homes by 1933.

All of these Acts produced more houses, but they didn't tackle the problem of the existing slums. **Greenwood's Act of 1930** gave grants to councils that cleared slums and rehoused the tenants. By 1939, 250,000 slum homes had been cleared. This spate of housing reform had not solved the problems, since 500,000 slum homes remained, but many families benefited.

These social reforms did not abolish hardship by 1939. But a further survey in York by Seebohm Rowntree in 1936 indicated that poverty had been halved there. Government spending on welfare services had risen from £63 million in 1910 to over £500 million by 1939.

9.7 SOCIAL REFORM SINCE 1945

During the Second World War a government committee led by a civil servant, William Beveridge, was set up to review the whole system of **welfare services**. Great progress had been made since 1900, but provision was still patchy; some people were covered while others were not, and a large number of different agencies were involved (see pages 154–7). The **Beveridge Report** was published in December 1942 and it proposed a unified welfare system to cover every single person in the country. As a result, three major reforms were introduced: the National Insurance Act of 1946, the National Health Act of 1946 and the National Assistance Act of 1948. These three Acts formed the basis of our **Welfare State**.

The **National Insurance Act** set up a compulsory insurance scheme for every citizen in the country. It provided a right to unemployment pay, sickness benefit, maternity grant, widow's pension, old-age pension, death grant and (under an associated Bill, the Industrial Injuries Act of 1946) accident insurance for all workers. The Act also obliged local councils to provide special housing for the aged. A family allowance payment of 5s (25p) per week to all parents for every child after the first had already been introduced in 1945. In exchange, all adults, except married women, had to pay national insurance contributions, which were deducted from wages. These payments financed about 20 per cent of the cost of benefits, employers paid 30 per cent, and the government provided the other 50 per cent. The Ministry of National Insurance ran the whole scheme. Since every citizen was covered, and benefits were a right, the stigma (sense of shame) of falling back upon welfare benefits was reduced.

The Beveridge Plan suggested a much higher level of payments than has ever been paid. There have, however, been some modifications to the system. National insurance contributions and benefits have been linked to people's income since the start of **graduated pensions** (1961) and **graduated benefits** (1966). This has meant that the better-paid workers pay bigger contributions but get a bigger sickness benefit if they are ill, for example, so that there is not a large fall in their income due to the illness. There has also been a commitment by governments since the 1970s to increase benefits in line with the cost of living.

The **National Health Act** also covered every citizen, 'from the cradle to the grave'. It did not require special contributions. The entire cost was to be paid by the Treasury, drawing upon income from taxes. The new **National Health Service** entitled everyone, without any payments, to a range of free medical treatment (see Source A). Almost all doctors and 3,000 hospitals previously run by local councils, Poor Law bodies and voluntary groups came into this national scheme under the Ministry of Health (see Source C).

The reaction of doctors was suspicious at first, since they were losing their independence, but the public were extemely enthusiastic. In the first year 187 million National Health prescriptions were issued; 8½ million people had free dental treatment; and 5¼ million were issued with glasses (Source B).

SOURCE A

'(The old arrangements) cover only 22 million; the rest of the population have to pay whenever they desire the services of a doctor; the National Health Insurance scheme (of 1911) does not provide for the self-employed nor the families of dependants. It gives no backing to the doctor in the form of specialist services. Our hospital organization has grown up with no plan. This Bill provides a universal health service with no insurance qualifications of any sort. It is intended that there shall be no limitations on the kind of assistance given – by general practitioners, specialists, hospitals, eye treatment, dental treatment, hearing facilities.'

Aneurin Bevan, the Minister of Health, describing the National Health Bill in Parliament in 1945.

SOURCE B

SOURCE C

'The collective principle asserts that the resources of medical skill and the apparatus of healing shall be placed at the disposal of the patient, without charge, when he or she needs them; that medical treatment and care should be a communal responsibility; that they should be made available to rich and poor alike in accordance with medical need and no other criteria. It insists that no society can legitimately call itself civilized if a sick person is denied medical aid because of lack of means.

'The essence of a satisfactory health service is that the rich and the poor are treated alike, that poverty is not a disability, and wealth is not an advantage.'

Aneurin Bevan, recalling the thinking behind the National Health Service, 'In Place of Fear', 1952.

"Dentist says if there are any more of you thinking of fitting one another up with National Health teeth for Christmas presents you've had it." Many more people were able to have dental treatment after it became free under the NHS in 1946.

The cost of the NHS in 1950 was £400 million. It was to rise to £1,200 million by 1965 and to £5,200 million by 1975. Such costs soon led to demands for extra finance. Dental charges were introduced in 1951. They saved the government £13 million per year, but there was a noticeable decline in the amount of dental treatment. Prescription charges were started in 1957. They were briefly abolished again in 1965 but later reintroduced.

The **National Assistance Act** completely replaced the Poor Law. It was financed by central government out of taxes. It said that if national insurance benefits were not enough to prevent hardship for the really needy, they could claim extra cash, accommodation, clothes or food from national assistance. It is a measure of the inadequacy of the national insurance benefits that, by 1950, 23 per cent of old-aged pensioners and 13 per cent of those on sickness benefit were also claiming national assistance. So that these payments went only to the really needy, they were means-tested, and thus some stigma remained.

There have been no fundamental changes since these reforms, only changes of detail. In 1966 the **Social Security Act** combined national insurance and national assistance under the same government department, the Ministry of Social Security. **Supplementary benefits** replaced national assistance for those without work. In 1971 **family income supplements** were introduced for workers in jobs with very low wages. In 1975 family allowances and child tax allowances for parents were replaced by **child benefit** payments, paid at post offices, normally to mothers. In 1968 the Ministry of Social Security was merged with the Ministry of Health to form the Department of Health and Social Security, which administered all of the welfare services.

Housing reform has also continued. The post-war housing shortage was first tackled by the provision of 160,000 'pre-fabs'; but, by 1948, 280,000 council homes a year were being built. New housing reached 300,000 per year in the 1950s and 400,000 by 1967, about half council-built and half new private dwellings. Private home ownership has been encouraged since the 1970s – by 1988, 65 per cent of people lived in owner-occupied homes. Legislation such as the **Town and Country Planning Act of 1947** governed the location of this new building, protecting **'green belt'** areas. In addition, the **New Towns Act of 1946** paved the way for **new towns** to be built with housing, employment and leisure facilities. Stevenage was the first new town, and there were thirty planned by 1972.

However, as the 1990s approached, a growing question mark hung over the Welfare State. High levels of unemployment, an ageing population and rising medical costs have made benefits much more expensive than anyone ever envisaged. The steady growth of state provision of help for those such as the sick, the poor and the unemployed may have reached its peak.

9.8 TRADE UNIONS, 1850–1918

'New model' unions

The first trade unions which successfully came to terms with Britain's new industrial society were the **'new model' unions**. The first of these was the Amalgamated Society of Engineers, formed in 1851; others included the Amalgamated Society of Carpenters (1860) and the Amalgamated Society of Tailors (1866). These unions were national societies formed when local groups of skilled workers joined together. Their members could afford fairly high subscriptions. This gave the unions **sound finances** which were used to provide efficient administration, including full-time paid officials, and a host of benefits to members (see Source B). These unions were generally **moderate** in outlook. They accepted the capitalist structure of industry and negotiated for improvements for their members within it. There were some strikes, but these were rare (see Source C). They were very successful. The ASE started with 12,000 members and by 1868 had grown to 33,000.

SOURCE A

BE UNITED
AND
INDUSTRIOUS
AMALGAMATED SOCIETY OF ENGINEERS, MACHINISTS, MILLWRIGHTS, SMITHS, AND PATTERN MAKERS.
This is to Certify

◀ *A membership card for the ASE.*

SOURCE B

The weekly subscription to the ASE was 1s (5p). In return, the union paid sickness and unemployment pay, pensions and funeral and accident benefits. The amounts paid out by the union in 1865 were:

Employment pay	£14,076
Sickness pay	£13,788
Pensions for aged members	£5,184
Funeral benefits paid to members' wives	£4,887
Accident benefits to disabled members	£1,800

SOURCE C

'(The union) does all it possibly can to prevent any strike, and where they have time and opportunity, they cause a deputation of the workmen to wait on their employers to represent their grievances, and then give advice afterwards. We endeavor at all times to prevent strikes. We believe strikes to be a waste of money, not only in relation to the workers, but also to the employers.'

William Allen, general secretary of the ASE.

SOURCE D

'I do not belive in having sick pay, out-of-work pay and a number of other pays. We desire to prevent as much sickness and men being out of work as possible. The way to accomplish this is firstly to organize, then reduce your hours of labour, and that will prevent illness and members being out of employment.'

Will Thorne, leader of the Gas Workers' Union, 1889.

SOURCE E

'The time for starting work is 6.30 in summer and 8.00 in winter. Work finishes at 6 p.m. A typical match girl earns 4s (20p) per week. If the feet are dirty or the ground under the bench is left untidy, a fine of 3d is inflicted, and in some departments a fine of 3d is imposed for talking.'

Annie Besant on the 'match girls'.

SOURCE F

'Emma Harris had pain in her upper and lower jaws. Her throat glands were swollen and painful, her gums were inflamed. Her teeth became loose and started to fall out. She was operated on twice. Fear prevented her from going back to hospital to have a third operation to get a false jaw and teeth put in.'

Annie Besant on 'phossy jaw'.

Several of these unions had their headquarters in London, and their leaders began to meet together to discuss co-operation. This group of leaders became known as the **Junta** and included William Allen of the ASE, Robert Applegarth of the ASC and George Odger of the shoemakers' union. Later, representatives from unions from all over the country began meeting together. The first of these national gatherings was in 1868 in Manchester. It called itself the **Trades Union Congress**. Meetings became annual events which still take place.

The influence of the TUC was needed by 1870. During a strike in the Yorkshire iron and steel industry in 1866 there had been, among other acts of violence, a bomb attack by Sheffield sawmill workers on blackleg workers. The **'Sheffield outrages'** appalled public opinion. In the same year, the Bradford Boilermakers' Society sued its treasurer for stealing £24 of its funds in the **Hornby versus Close case**. The judge ruled that trade unions had no rights in law and dismissed the case. In this hostile environment, the government set up a Royal Commission to investigate trade unions.

The TUC was able to impress the commission with its moderate views. The report, in 1869, was in the unions' favour. Subsequently several pieces of legislature were passed which strengthened the position of unions. The **Trade Union Act of 1871** gave unions legal status and thus made union funds safe from embezzlement. Later, they were able to reverse the Criminal Law Amendment Act of 1871, which had made peaceful picketing illegal; union leaders persuaded Parliament to pass the **Conspiracy and Protection of Property Act of 1875**, which legalized picketing again.

'New unionism'

The next stage in the development of trade unions is called **'new unionism'**. This involved the growth of national unions for unskilled labourers such as the Dockers' Union (1889) and the National Union of Gas Workers and General Labourers (1889). They had very low subscriptions – the gas workers paid only 2d (less than 1p) per week – and their outlook was very different (see Source D). Many of their leaders were socialists. This phase of union growth was spurred on by two well-publicized successes: the **'match girls' strike of 1888**, and the **London dockers' strike of 1889**.

The young women who made matches at the Bryant & May factories worked long hours and risked illness; the phosphorus used in the match heads cause 'phossy jaw' (see Sources E and F). But they were paid very little. When 1,400 of the young women went on strike, a London journalist, Annie Besant, publicized their cause in an article headed 'White Slavery' and appealed to the public to boycott the company's matches. Bryant & May were eventually forced to provide better wages and conditions.

Soon after this, the London dockers went on strike. Not only were they badly paid, but the men had to compete against each other every day for the work available. Sometimes they could go for days without getting work. They demanded a wage increase from 5d to 6d per day, 8d for overtime and a guaranteed minimum of four hours' work per day. **Ben Tillet**, the fiery leader of the dockers, organized daily marches through London to get publicity and donations (Source G). The Lord Mayor of London and Cardinal Manning both became involved in mediating between the dockers and employers, and a gift of £30,000 arrived from workers in Australia. The unions picketed the dock gates and stopped the use of 'blackleg' labour. Eventually the owners conceded, and the 'dockers' tanner' (sixpence) was won.

Inspired by these successes, **other unions** were formed. The General Railway Workers' Union started in 1889, and the Miners' Federation in 1891. Total union membership had stood at 750,000 in 1888. By 1900 it was 2 million.

The unions and the Labour Party

Another feature of trade union development in the years before 1900 was its role in the birth of the **Labour Party**. Working people in the towns had been given the vote in 1867, and the rural working class was enfranchised in 1885. Working-class MPs thus started to be elected to Parliament. Among the first was Henry Broadhurst, secretary of the Parliamentary Committee of the TUC. These early working-class MPs tended to vote with the Liberal Party.

However, many people didn't think that either of the two large parties in Parliament, the Liberals and the Conservatives, reflected the interests of working people. Several attempts were made to start a new working-class party. H. M. Hyndham founded the Social Democratic Federation in 1884. Union leaders like Will Thorne and Ben Tillett were members. Kier Hardy, elected MP for West Ham in 1892, shunned the Liberals and started the Independent Labour Party. But none of these attempts were successful, and the 1899 TUC Congress passed a motion to set up a new political labour movement. As a result, representatives from the socialist societies, the ILP and the trade unions met in February 1900. The agreed to form the **Labour Representation Committee** to promote working-class candidates for election to Parliament. Success in the 1900 election was limited; only two candidates were elected. But in 1903 twenty-nine LRC candidates were elected, and when they arrived at Westminster they decided to call themselves the **Labour Party**. By 1910 there were forty-two Labour MPs in Parliament, and there was a Labour Prime Minister by 1923. The early Labour Party thus owed much to the unions. Before 1914 the unions were to need the Labour Party just as much.

Two legal rulings, the **Taff Vale verdict** and the **Osborne judgement**, again showed how hostile the courts were to the trade unions. In 1901 the railway workers employed by the Taff Vale Railway Company had gone on strike and had successfully

SOURCE G

A procession of London dockers through the streets of the capital.

SOURCE H

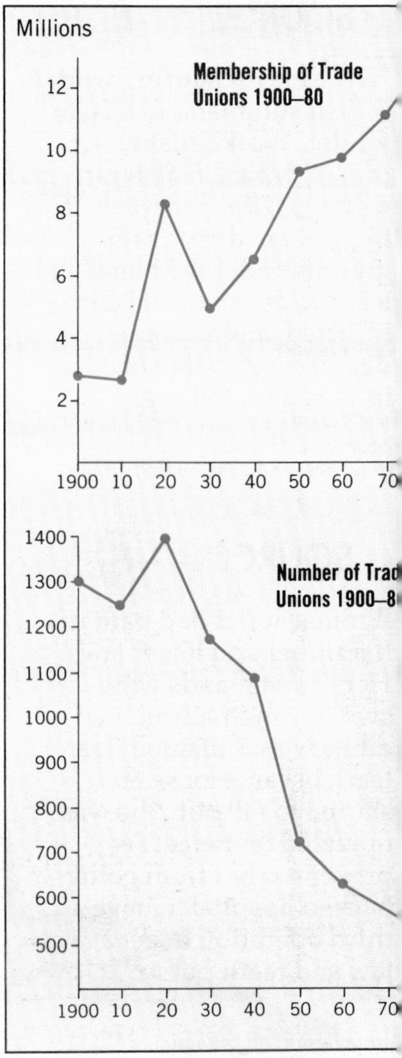

SOURCE I

'The three unions have much in common. But while we have achieved a great deal by our individual struggles, it must be admitted that a great deal of suffering has been caused. A strike on the railway system immediately affects the miners and transport workers. The idea of the alliance is that each of these three great organizations should work out a plan, submit it to the others, and that joint action should then be taken.'

Robert Smillie, president of the Miners' Federation.

SOURCE J

The threat of the 'triple alliance' as seen by a cartoonist in 1921.

prevented the company from continuing services with blackleg labour. The company sued the men's union for its losses during the strike. The judge upheld the claim and ordered the union to pay £23,000 damages. This was a shock to the whole trade union movement. If unions could be held responsible for the losses of companies during industrial action, then strikes would cripple the unions more than employers.

In a second case, W. V. Osborne, a trade union member, objected to his subscription being used by the union to support the Labour Party in Parliament. Osborne was a supporter of the Liberal Party. The courts ruled that the union was acting illegally in using his money politically. This was a blow to the Labour Party, which depended upon trade union financial support, but equally a blow for the unions, which relied upon the Labour Party to protect their interests in Parliament.

Both of these problems were eventually settled by new legislation as a result of pressure by Labour MPs on the Liberal government. In 1906 the **Trade Disputes Act** ruled that unions could not be held liable for the losses incurred by employers during a strike. And in 1913 the **Trade Union Act** stated that unions could use part of members' subscriptions for political purposes as long as members were given the opportunity to 'contract out' of paying that part of the subscription if they wanted to.

Further growth

Despite these temporary setbacks, union membership continued to rise (see Source H). Encouraged by their growing strength, the period 1910–14 saw the unions involved in a series of bitter disputes. This was particularly true of the miners. In 1910 the government used troops and police to clear the pit entrances so that the employers could use non-union labour to break a strike of 30,000 South Wales miners. After eight weeks the men gave up the struggle and returned to work. In 1912, however, the Miners' Federation organized a national strike involving one million men demanding a national minimum wage of 5s (25p) per week for miners. The pressure was enough. Six weeks into the strike, the government passed the Miners' Minimum Wage Act conceding the 5s per week.

In 1914 the three largest unions – the National Union of Railwaymen, the National Federation of Transport Workers and the Miners' Federation – formed the **'triple alliance'**. They realized that they had many common needs and that they could achieve more if they co-operated (see Source I). Together they were a frightening prospect for the government (see Source J). The idea of combining the smaller unions into more powerful federations was the key tactic of the **syndicalists**. There was even talk of co-operation with unions abroad so that the trade union movement could bring international pressure upon governments. However, the outbreak of war in 1914 concentrated the minds of workers, employers and government alike on foreign enemies, and further confrontation at home was avoided.

9.9 THE GENERAL STRIKE OF 1926

1921 and 1925

Trade union unrest returned after the war. The 1920s were years of **depression** for Britain's older basic industries such as **coal mining**. Foreign competition from the United States, Germany and Poland, domestic competition from electricity and the decline of traditional customers such as the railways all hit the profits of mine owners. Many of Britain's pits were becoming uneconomic as deeper and narrower seams were mined. In **1921** miners' wages were cut. The miners were outraged and proposed a joint strike to the other members of the 'triple alliance' to start on **15 April**. However, when the day came, the transport workers and the railway workers withdrew their support. The miners struck alone for three months, but eventually had to go back to work on lower wages. Lower pay followed for dockers, railway workers, building workers and others. 15 April became known as 'Black Friday'.

In contrast, in **1925**, when employers proposed further wage cuts, the miners did get firm support from the railway and transport workers, who promised not to move any stocks of coal while the miners were on strike. With no time to prepare, this threat of joint action so worried the Prime Minister, Stanley Baldwin, that on 31 July he suggested a Royal Commission led by a judge, Sir Herbert Samuel, to investigate the problems of the coal industry. In the meantime he gave a subsidy to the coal industry of £24 million to protect miners' wages for nine months. This was seen as a great triumph for the unions, which called 31 July **'Red Friday'**. However, the subsidy could not be a permanent arrangement (see Source A). Once it ended, there was bound to be renewed conflict; and in the meantime the government had time to prepare itself (see Source C).

SOURCE C

'We decided to postpone the crisis in the hope of averting it; or if not averting it, of coping effectively with it when the time came.'

Winston Churchill, Chancellor of the Exchequer in Baldwin's government in 1925. His comments reflect the way the Cabinet felt about the subsidy.

SOURCE D

'A general strike is not an industrial dispute. It is a revolutionary movement intended to inflict suffering upon the great mass of innocent people and put constraint upon the government. It is a movement which can only succeed by destroying the government and subverting the rights and liberties of the people.'

From an article written for the 'Daily Mail.' The paper's print workers refused to print it.

SOURCE A

A 'Punch' cartoon, 1925. Stanley Baldwin using taxpayers' money for the miners.

SOURCE B

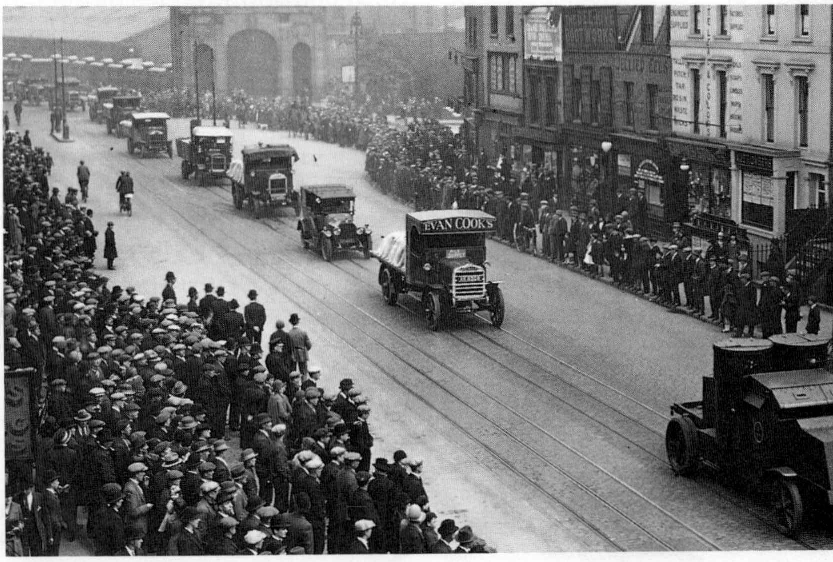

A convoy of lorries driven by volunteers and protected by an armoured vehicle and soldiers from the Grenadier Guards leaves the London docks on 7 May.

SOURCE E

'12 May. Thomas (leader of the railway workers) and I went to Downing Street. On the road we passed Wellington Barracks and saw troops drawn up on the parade ground. Arrived at Downing Street. Pugh (chairman of the TUC negotiating committee) said to me: "I wonder how much longer the unions will have to grovel to the miners." . . . Pugh announced the calling off of the strike and said that it had not been dictated by weakness but by a genuine desire for peace.'

The secretary of the TUC, Walter Citrine, remembers his feelings about the final stages of the General Strike.

QUESTIONS

1. People's *motives*, or the reasons for their actions, are sometimes not obvious.
   - **a** What were the *apparent* motives for Stanley Baldwin's actions in the coal crisis of 1925?
   - **b** With the benefit of hindsight, what do you think were his *real* motives?
2. What were the motives of the TUC leaders who called the General Strike on 3 May?
3. What were the motives of the same TUC leaders who on 12 May called off the strike?
4. 'In history, events don't always work out the way people hope.' How do the events of the General Strike throw light upon this statement?

1926

A year later that conflict occurred. This was the **General Strike of 1926**. The Samuel Commission reporting in March 1926 supported the mine owners' demands for a cut in wages. The mine owners also wanted men to work longer hours. The Miners' Federation was incensed; its leader, A. J. Cooke, declared: 'Not a penny off the pay, not a minute on the day.' But mine owners declared their intention to cut pay anyway. On 1 May they locked out all workers who would not agree. The miners appealed for help from other unions. TUC leaders, misled by 'Red Friday', were convinced that the government would again give way and promised a national strike if the miners' needs were ignored. But the government refused to protect the miners, and negotiations broke down in the early hours of 2 May. Britain's half a million mine workers came out on strike, and at midnight on 3 May the TUC started the General Strike. Although the TUC refused to disrupt hospitals or food supplies, it called out 1½ million workers from the transport, printing, power, textiles, chemicals and iron-and-steel industries. On the first day of the strike, 4 May, there were few trains, buses or trams; power stations came to a standstill; and there were no newspapers. The united strength of the country's union members were drawn up in confrontation with the government for the first time.

The government was well prepared and determined (see Source B). Ever since the crisis averted by the subsidy in 1925, it had been drawing up plans to deal with a general strike. An Organization for the Maintenance of Supplies had been set up and had enlisted 100,000 volunteers who were prepared to help. Soon white-collar workers and students were driving buses and lorries or working in the docks. Troops and the police operated other essential services. The government even published its own newspaper, the *British Gazette*, to keep the public informed. The unions printed a rival paper, the *British Worker*, with its own view of the situation. Both papers first appeared on 5 May and cost 1d. Lorries transporting goods and buses driven by volunteers frequently had to be guarded by police or troops; there was some vandalism to disable vehicles or factories. But there was surprisingly little violence.

As the strike entered its second week, support among the strikers seemed solid, and their morale was high. A second wave of workers joined the strike on 11 May. But the end came suddenly. Leaders of the TUC were basically moderate people. They wanted the best for the miners, but they were not out to seize control of the country. They didn't want to be used by some extreme union leaders who wanted to use the strike to challenge the authority of the government. So on 12 May the TUC leaders agreed to call off the strike if Sir Herbert Samuel would try to find a compromise settlement between the miners and mine owners. The miners were devastated. They had lost the support of other strikers without any guarantee of improvement. They continued their strike for a further six months but finally could hold out no longer and had to return to work defeated.

9.10 TRADE UNIONS SINCE 1926

Years of decline

The General Strike was a shattering setback for the **trade unions**. Public support for the unions fell. In 1927 the **Trade Disputes Act** made it illegal for workers to strike in sympathy with others. It also said that unions could use a member's subscription for political purposes only if that member *contracted in* to a political levy. Union membership fell by half a million as members resigned or lost their jobs. The **Labour Party** also suffered; its income fell as a result of the Trade Disputes Act and as union membership declined. The **coal industry** suffered too. Export markets lost during the strike were never fully recovered. Many smaller pits didn't reopen; 200,000 miners lost their jobs.

The period after 1927 was thus a difficult one for trade unions. **Unemployment** remained high well into the 1930s, and morale among union members was low. There were few strikes. Moderate leaders emerged, such as **Ernest Bevin**, who tried to improve relations with the government and the public. Bevin's ideas were spread by the Labour newspaper the *Daily Herald*. Slowly unions came to recover their influence. During the Second World War, Bevin was made the Minister of Labour with the task of matching Britain's labour force to its wartime needs.

Post-war recovery

After the Second World War the status of trade unions continued to recover. The Labour government passed the **Trade Disputes Act of 1946**, which amended the 1927 act. Unions could again use subscriptions for political funds unless members contracted out.

Union membership also flourished after the war, rising from about 9 million in 1950 to about 12.5 million in 1980, by which time about half of the workforce belonged to a trade union (see the graphs on page 162, Source H). The growth in numbers was mainly among women, white-collar workers like local government workers and public service workers such as hospital staff. The number of unions, however, fell from about 700 in 1950 to about 500 in 1980 as smaller groups amalgamated to form more powerful unions. Union membership and large unions seemed to offer the best way of ensuring pay increases which kept pace with price rises.

Relations with the government

These developments also brought increased tensions. The growth of the economy slowed down in the 1960s and 1970s, and there were periods of serious **inflation**. This was bound to cause conflict. Governments wanted to keep wage rises down to stop prices rising any faster; the unions demanded big pay increases to match the rises in prices. Unofficial 'wildcat' strikes became common as members became impatient and union officials seemed unable to control their members. There were over 4,000 strikes in 1970. How to handle the trade unions became a key issue in British politics.

In 1966 Harold Wilson's Labour government passed the **Prices and Incomes Act**, which insisted that all proposed rises in prices

SOURCE **A**

Car workers demonstrating against the 'social contract' in 1977. Wages were not keeping up with prices. One placard reads: 'Food Up! Rents Up! Fares Up! What about Wages?' Another says: 'Social Contract, Social Con-Trick.'

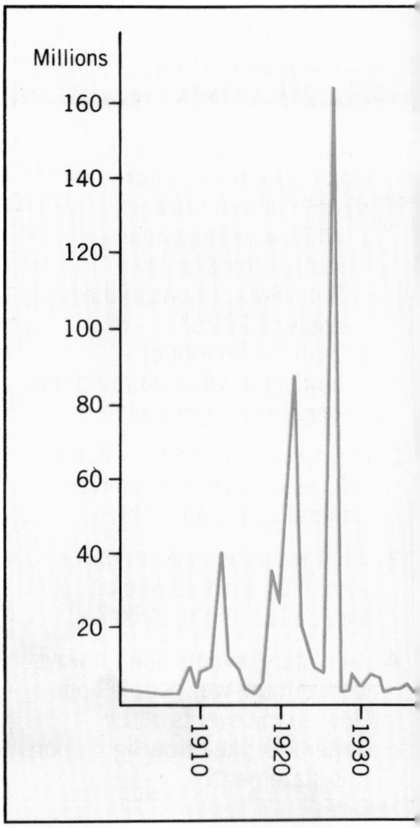

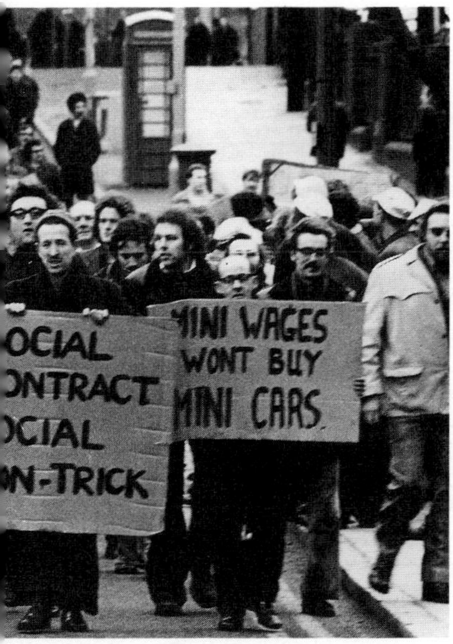

or wages had to be referred to a National Board for Prices and Incomes which decided whether the increase was fair. It proved an unworkable arrangement. Wilson's Secretary for Employment, Barbara Castle, produced a plan called *In Place of Strife*, which would have made secret ballots and 28-day 'cooling-off' periods compulsory before all strikes. But the TUC complained bitterly that the plan interfered in relations between unions and employers, and it was dropped.

Edward Heath's Conservative government's **Industrial Relations Act** (1971) made ballots compulsory before all strikes, banned 'closed shops' (arrangements where only union members could be employed at some workplaces) and set up a new court, the National Industrial Relations Court, to settle disputes between unions and employers. But the majority of the unions refused to co-operate and challenged the rulings of the court. The Act caused more confrontation than it solved. In 1972 and 1974 the miners voted overwhelmingly for national coal strikes. At one point there was such a shortage of coal that the government ordered rationing of electricity and put most of industry on a compulsory three-day working week. In the 1974 election the central issue again was how to manage the unions. Heath was defeated, and a new Labour government came to power.

Labour abolished the Industrial Relations Act. The Prime Minister, James Callaghan, wanted a *voluntary* working relationship with the unions called the **'social contract'**. Under this arrangement, the government and unions negotiated an average for fair pay increases every year. In 1975 they agreed upon a £6 per week increase; in 1976 it was 4.5 per cent. However, the government was not successful in keeping prices down (inflation averaged 16 per cent in 1977), and by the winter of 1978–9 many union members had lost patience. A series of strikes took place, notably among the lorry drivers, who eventually forced a 20 per cent pay rise. The 'social contract' had broken down. In the election of 1979 a Conservative government was returned with a clear mandate from the electorate to bring the unions under control.

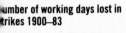

umber of working days lost in trikes 1900–83

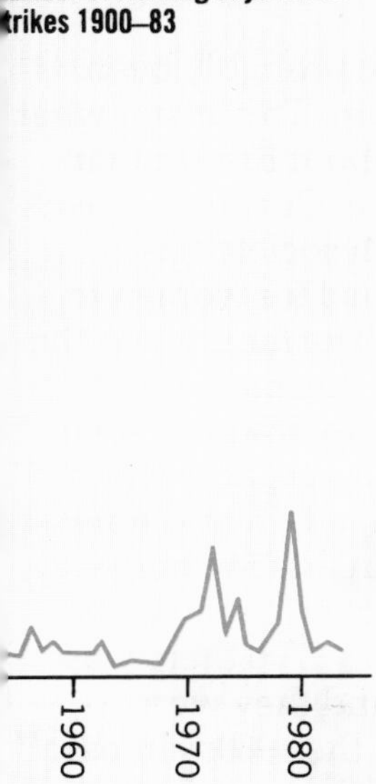

Margaret Thatcher's government's **Employment Acts** (1980 and 1982) and a **Trade Union Act** in 1984 made a vote of 80 per cent of members necessary to call a strike. 'Closed shops' became illegal unless 85 per cent of the workers involved voted in favour; and 'secondary picketing' (where pickets in a dispute are joined by workers from other areas or industries) were outlawed. These laws didn't end the confrontations. A run of disputes occurred in the printing industry; there was a long teachers' dispute; and, most serious of all, there was a year-long miners' strike in 1984–5. None of these strikes were completely successful. The government and employers seemed to have gained the upper hand, but industrial relations had become even more bitter.

Despite their difficulties in the 1980s, trade unions are now well established and powerful. Even though their progress seems to have often depended upon confrontation, millions of members now look to them for a range of benefits.

10.1 INTRODUCTION

ACTIVITIES

These questions might be better answered in small groups.

1 Using a copy of the chart below, work through the index of this book. Count the number of men and women listed, in the time zone most appropriate for them. You can miss out crowd scenes like the opening of railways.

	Women	Men
1700–99 1800–99 1900 – present day		

2 Using two copies of the chart work through the book looking at the pictures. On one chart count the number of men and women who seem to be the most important people in a picture: a leader or someone telling others what to do. On the other chart just count all the men and women. You can miss out crowd scenes like the opening of railways.

3 Read pages 22, 50, 82, 139. What can you say about the use of the words 'he' and 'she' and 'men' and 'women' rather than 'they' and 'person' or 'people' which tell us nothing about the sex of the people described?

4 Having compared the answers to questions 1, 2 and 3, what conclusions do you come to about:
a the relative position of men and women in the society this book describes?
b the way this position has changed between 1700 and now?

SOURCE A

A typical textile factory scene, c1840. What do you notice about the jobs done by men and women in the picture?

At any time between 1700 and now there have probably been slightly more women than men living in Britain. This is not what someone would think if they knew no more about Britain than they could find out by doing the activity above. During the years covered by this book the position of women in society has changed dramatically. It has never been unusual for women to work other than as housewives and mothers. The family was the basic unit of the pre-industrial economy, and this meant that most working-class women worked at the family trade and ran the home. Women of the upper and middle classes, however, usually did not work. Their position has changed, in that now women of all classes are likely to have a job outside the home. The change is more important than that, however, because the types of work open to women have changed. In 1700 there was little serious education available for women and they were limited to working in fairly mundane jobs. In the 1980s almost all jobs are in theory open to women and so is higher and further education.

There is not a section in this book called 'Men'. This is not because the position of men has not changed in society. Many men, especially working- and middle-class men, have many more opportunities than their ancestors in 1700 would have dreamed of. There has, however, been a change in the relative positions of men and women, and women have been the leaders in this change.

Nineteenth-century changes

The Industrial Revolution changed life for many women. Factory jobs took them out of the home and often paid better money than they had been able to earn under the domestic system. However there were no factories in large areas of the country, and the changes only really applied to working-class women. Among the middle classes of the time the view that women should stay at home as wives and mothers was very strong. Early changes in the law, like limiting the hours women worked or stopping them working underground in mines, were an attempt to extend these middle-class ideas. Changes in the later nineteenth century gave women more rather than fewer opportunities. In 1860, largely as a response to Florence Nightingale's work in the Crimean War, St Thomas' Hospital in London began to train nurses. The modern career of nursing dates from this. The **Married Women's Property Act(s)** of 1870 and 1822 allowed women to control their own property and income after marriage. Before these Acts it had all automatically become the property of their husbands. Education began to open up to women as well. In 1870 the first women students began to study at Cambridge University, although with many restrictions on what they could do and how they could behave. A very few women began to train as doctors in Edinburgh and London. The Education Act of 1870 made available many more jobs as schoolteachers, and these were often filled by women.

New jobs opened up for the less well-educated too. It became much more common for shop assistants to be women rather than men, especially in the big stores. The invention of the typewriter created jobs for typists, who were usually women although most other office jobs were still done by men. Early telephone exchanges needed a lot of labour, and nearly all telephonists were women.

Despite these changes, women had certainly not achieved equality. Even if they did the same jobs as men they were usually paid less. In many jobs, such as schoolteaching, a woman had no choice but to give up her job if she got married. Social changes still had some way to go. After 1857 it became slightly easier to get a divorce. However, a man only had to prove his wife's adultery to be given a divorce – women had to prove cruelty and desertion as well before the law recognized that they had a case. Most irksome of all to many women, they did not have a vote in parliamentary elections.

10.2 SUFFRAGISTS AND SUFFRAGETTES

SOURCE A

Emiline Pankhurst (second from left) leading a demonstration in Hyde Park, 21 June 1908. 200,000 were said to have attended.

The idea of giving British women votes in parliamentary elections was first discussed in the House of Commons in 1867. It was rejected. Women had been able to vote in elections for Poor Law guardians since 1834, in 1870 they were allowed to vote in School Board elections and from 1888 they could vote in local Council elections. In 1897 various local societies joined together to form the **National Union of Women's Suffrage Societies** to campaign for the vote. These women were called **suffragists**, they campaigned peacefully within the law, and had little effect.

In 1903 the **Women's Social and Political Union (WSPU)** was formed, also to fight for the right to vote. Its members were called **suffragettes** and, led by Mrs Pankhurst and her daughters, they ran an increasingly radical campaign. They started by heckling government ministers and organizing increasingly large demonstrations (see Source A). On 10 October 1908 they tried to 'rush' the House of Commons, during which Mrs Pankhurst and one of her daughters, Christabel, were arrested. One demonstrator, Miss Symonds, got inside the chamber.

By 1909 unlawful protest was becoming more common. The Prime Minister's windows were broken and a woman tried to attack Winston Churchill (who was Home Secretary) with a dog-whip. A number of suffragettes were now in prison and one of them, Miss Wallace-Dunlop, went on hunger strike. She was released from prison, but as the tactic became more common the government changed its mind and had suffragettes force-fed. This gave the suffragettes a useful propaganda weapon, and much of the sympathy they might have lost by their more violent demonstrations was won back by their bravery.

In 1910 the House of Commons voted on whether women should be given the vote. This was a so-called **free vote** in that the parties did not tell their MPs which way to vote. The vote was lost. At this time many men who did not own property did not

SOURCE B

24 October, 1908. Christabel Pankhurst and her mother in the dock in Bow Street Magistrates' Court after the attempt to 'rush' the House of Commons.

SOURCE C

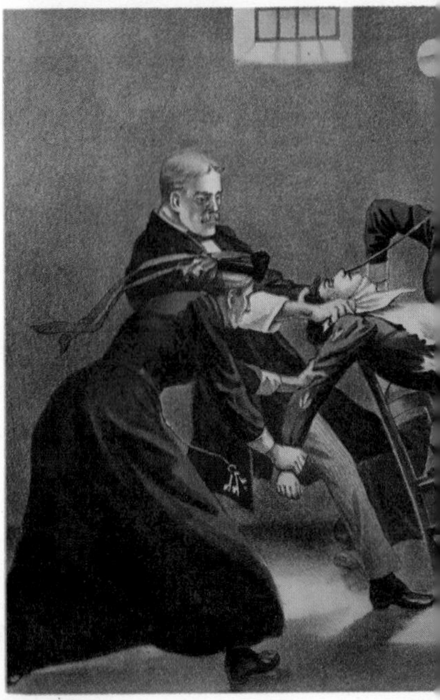

Poster, 1909.

SOURCE D

WSPU postcard, 1913.

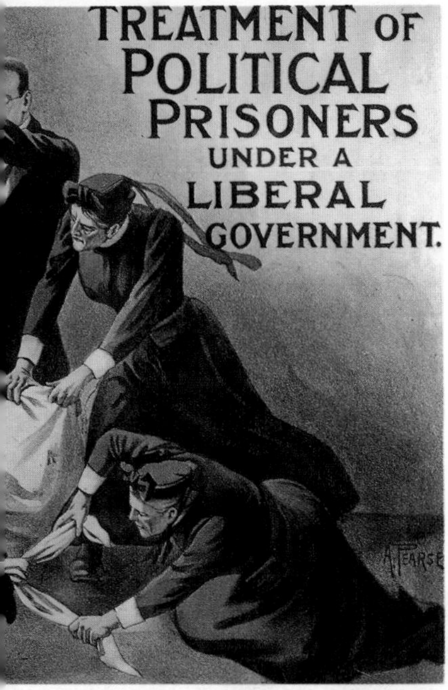

have the vote. The proposal was to give women who met the same property qualification the vote. As it was assumed that men owned the property of married couples only a few women from rich families could have qualified to vote. This was thought to give the Conservative Party an unfair advantage by most MPs, so they opposed it.

Following this defeat the WSPU was relatively quiet for two years. In 1912 the campaign gathered momentum again. Force-feeding of hunger strikers continued to lose the government support and in March 1913 force-feeding was replaced by the so-called **Cat and Mouse Act**. This let women out of gaol when their health began to suffer, and re-arrested them when they had recovered. In one of the most famous incidents of the campaign a well-known suffragette, Emily Davison, was knocked down and killed by the king's horse in the Derby. Anti-suffragette newspapers at the time claimed this was an accident, but the WSPU treated her as a martyr and her funeral was a great demonstration. A number of photographs of the incident have survived, and a newsreel, but it is impossible to be sure what she intended to do. Photographs do not show us what was going on in somebody's mind. In 1988 historians examined the contents of her handbag, and discovered she had bought a return ticket to Epsom that day, and that her diary included a number of appointments in the days immediately after the Derby. This is not conclusive, but it suggests she was planning a dangerous demonstration rather than a public act of suicide.

The campaign of the suffragettes continued until the start of the First World War. Suffragette leaders then called off the campaign and said they would show that women deserved citizenship by the role they played in the war. In 1918 the right to vote was given to all men over the age of 21, and to all women over the age of 30. The reason given for the difference was that so many men had been killed in the war, and the government did not want women to immediately become a majority of the electors. Women over the age of 21 were finally given the vote in 1928.

QUESTIONS

1 Why might some newspapers at the time have suggested Emily Davison was not taking part in a suffragette demonstration?

2 a How does the 'new evidence' described in the text help us to decide what Emily Davison intended?
  b What evidence would we need to be sure about what Emily Davison intended?

3 Who do you think produced Source C and what did they hope to gain by it?

4 Sources A and B show very dramatic moments. Are they, however, of any real use to a historian?

5 Source D is a fantasy picture. Does this mean historians of the suffragette movement will not find it useful?

10.3 ONE WOMAN'S WAR

EMPATHY

The First World War is usually said to have been a decisive time in changing women's position in society. With so many men away from their usual jobs in the services, there were not enough left to keep the economy running. Women did many jobs which had previously been thought suitable only for men. Many women had their first taste of a job that was not working as a domestic servant. While many women gladly gave up their new jobs after the war finished, others were not willing to lose their new freedom.

This unit concentrates on the experience of one woman, Ellen Harbard, who was recorded on tape in 1984 talking about what happened to her during the First World War. The memories of old people are an unusual type of historical source. They can be difficult to use, because people's memories often get confused. They can also offer special advantages. If you had been the interviewer you could have asked extra questions to find out more about something you didn't quite understand. This is called **oral history**. The exercise asks you to think whether it is a good or bad way for a historian to work out exactly how people felt about things at the time.

SOURCE A

'I was only 13 at the start of the First World War. We lived in Greenwich then. The headmistress of the school I went to told me I was 14, so I left to do a sewing job. I thought my mum had made a mistake, but when I told her, she said, "No, you're only 13, but go if you want to." I said, "Well, I shall earn some money, shan't I?" Anyway the lady next door knew I was only 13, and she gave me away. I had to go back to school for another year, 'till I was 14.

'When I was 15 I had a friend, Ivy. We both lived in Roan Street at the time, and we were going to work at a dressmaking place, only making half a crown a week (12½p), learning. It wasn't much money, from nine in the morning 'till six at night. One day, before we went in there, she said, "Here, I've heard, there's some women down at Abbey Wood, on munitions." I said, "My mother would never let me go there." "You got any money?" she said. I had 6d, and that was the fare, there and back, to the place we worked. So she said, "You've got 6d, I've got a shilling, and it's only 2d to Abbey Wood on the bus. Shall we go? I've heard it's good money." So I said yes. I was very easily led.

continued ▷

SOURCE B

Women munitions workers, May 1918.

EXERCISE

1. Study Source A carefully. Are there any places where Ellen's ideas and reactions seem unusual to you? In each case describe what it is that you think is unusual.
2. How do you think Ellen's father felt about women having greater freedom? Explain your answer.

'We went down there, and we saw the man on the gate. He said, "Yes, we do want some girls. How old are you?" We said that we were 15. He sent us along to another office, and they asked if we could start straight away. I said to Ivy, "Whatever will my mother think? I won't get home 'till seven o'clock tonight. She'll go mad." Well, when I told my parents, my father said, "I'll kill you. Now go inside before I do." I said, "Oh, dad, let me go. Look at what I'm going to earn. Nearly £4 a week!" It was a lot of money in those days. Mum said, "Let her go, let her go, if she thinks it's going to be all right." She was thinking of the money. "All right," he said, "but if anything happens to her I'm going to lay it at your shoulders."

'After a good few weeks we became lady loaders. They called us lady loaders because we had uniforms. They were a deep yellow, and they did right up to the chin, with a pale blue collar and long sleeves. The shoes were fawn leather.

'We had to leave our top things down in the cloakroom, with a woman called Queenie, our supervisor. Everything was left with her, our coats and hats and shoes, and hatpins or hairpins. We had our hair tied back with a big bow.

'I was working filling the bullets. You sat there with boxes of empty bullets, and you filled them with powder from a big thing like a dispenser. Then we put them into trays, and a couple of men came and took them away. There were people there working with lyddite and cordite. Their faces went all yellow from the yellow stuff. You wouldn't sit near them, because if your clothes touched them, all the yellow stuff would come out. They had to have a place apart from us.

'One day, it was on the 16 April, some flames started coming along the line towards us, and two men in the shop got hold of us and threw us outside on to the grass. It was raining like the dickens. They knew something was going to happen. The alarm was going, and Queenie, our supervisor, had to go back for her watch. She was blown to pieces. They found her corsets on the line. She was a lovely person, with ginger hair. I'd lost a coat, and I'd lost my tammy hat, and my boots. It was a new coat, a mauve coloured one that my mother had just bought me. They didn't give us anything, though. We never got a penny. Another friend of mine lived up near Abbey Wood, in the huts, and her mother took us in and gave us tea and something to eat. We were only a bit shaky, but we weren't frightened. We didn't see the worst part of it. We had to go back next day to see what was happening. They laid all the stuff out on the grass, and we were to pick all the good bullets out from the bad bullets. We were only there a fortnight, and then we were put off. I was late home, and my father went to the police station, but nothing was heard. They were waiting for me on the doorstep, and my father said, "Here she is. Take her in and give her a good hiding."'

Ellen Harbard, interviewed in 1984.

3 Do you think Ellen felt she was taking advantage of new attitudes towards women?

4 Is oral history a useful source for empathetic work?

10.4 WOMEN IN THE TWENTIETH CENTURY

The twentieth century has seen dramatic changes in women's lives. This unit does not try to describe these changes. Rather, it considers the importance of **four factors** in bringing about those changes.

- The first is the **action of women** themselves, such as the suffragettes described in pages 170 and 171. Such campaigning by women, which did not stop when women won the right to vote, has been important in making society consider issues which might otherwise have been forgotten, and in encouraging women to examine their own lives and ambitions.
- Second is the **influence of war**. In both the First and Second World Wars many women found they were encouraged to do things which had previously been denied them. Middle- and upper-class women had a chance to work, and many of them liked it. **Stereotypes** of what women were capable of, held by both men and women, were shown to be far from the truth.
- Thirdly, **technology** has affected women's lives. Running a house, unless there were servants, was hard physical work at the start of the century. If there were servants in a household it was hard physical work for them. Now far fewer households have servants, but most households have labour-saving devices like gas or electric cookers, washing machines, fridges and freezers, and a variety of ready-prepared foods.
- Finally, **attitudes** have changed, particularly over **contraception**. In 1871 Annie Besant and Charles Bradlaugh were prosecuted for publishing pamphlets about contraception. From the publication of her book *Married Love*, through to the end of the 1920s, Marie Stopes was involved in much public controversy over her books about contraception and setting up clinics to offer contraceptive advice to all women, particularly working-class women.

SOURCE C

Washing clothes, 1910.

SOURCE D

Washing clothes, 1988.

SOURCE A

'War work, with good wages, has not only taught women the comfort and luxury of earned money, and raised their standard of the necessities of life – it has not only proved their power as workers for the community, but it has given them hunger for work as well.'

Grace Curnock, in an article called 'Demobilising the Women' in 'The War Illustrated', 18 January 1919.

SOURCE B

'How could we have carried on the war without women? Short of actually bearing arms in the field, there is hardly a service which has contributed, or is contributing, to the maintenance of our cause in which women have not been at least as active and efficient as men, and wherever we turn we see them doing work which three years ago would have been regarded as falling exclusively within the province of men. But what I confess moves me still more in this matter is the problem of reconstruction when the war is over. The questions which will then necessarily arise with regard to women's labour and women's functions in the new order of things are questions in which I find it impossible to withhold from women the power and the right of making their voices directly heard.'

Asquith, who as Prime Minister before the war had opposed giving women the vote, speaking on a bill to give women the vote in Parliament in 1917.

SOURCE E

Birth control clinic, 1920s.

SOURCE F

From a letter written to Marie Stopes in 1923:
'I have seen the article you have written for the *People Sunday* paper on the subject of Birth Control and I am taking the liberty of writing to you to ask you if you will send me some information about it, for I so dread having any more, I have five children. Three of them I had in just over three years, and it seemed no sooner did I give in to my husband than I was in a certain condition. Our wages are not sufficient to have and keep a lot of children. Farm labourers' wages today are about twenty-six shillings a week, and there is three shillings to take out for rent and two shillings and fourpence to take out for coal. What is left is to feed and clothe man wife and children and pay club and insurance. If you would kindly send me some knowledge I shall be so glad. I could not come to your office as we have no money. Hoping to hear from you soon. I remain yours truly.'

SOURCE G

'It seemed clear that emancipation had failed; the number of women in Parliament had settled at a low level; the number of professional women had stabilised as a tiny minority; the pattern of female employment had emerged as underpaid, menial, and supportive. The cage door had been opened and the canary had refused to fly out. The conclusion was that the cage door ought never to have been opened because canaries are made for captivity; the suggestion of an alternative had only confused and saddened them.'

Germaine Greer, a modern feminist, writing about the progress made in women's liberation up to 1970.

SOURCE H

ELIZABETH II

Sex Discrimination Act 1975

1975 CHAPTER 65

An Act to render unlawful certain kinds of sex discrimination and discrimination on the ground of marriage, and establish a Commission with the function of working towards the elimination of such discrimination and promoting equality of opportunity between men and women generally; and for related purposes. [12th November 1975]

BE IT ENACTED by the Queen's most Excellent Majesty, by and with the advice and consent of the Lords Spiritual and Temporal, and Commons, in this present Parliament assembled, and by the authority of the same, as follows:—

PART I

DISCRIMINATION TO WHICH ACT APPLIES

1.—(1) A person discriminates against a woman in any circumstances relevant for the purposes of any provision of this Act if— *Sex discrimination against women.*

(a) on the ground of her sex he treats her less favourably than he treats or would treat a man, or

(b) he applies to her a requirement or condition which he applies or would apply equally to a man but—

(i) which is such that the proportion of women who can comply with it is considerably smaller than the proportion of men who can comply with it, and

(ii) which he cannot show to be justifiable irrespective of the sex of the person to whom it is applied, and

(iii) which is to her detriment because she cannot comply with it.

The Sex Discrimination Act, 1975, which made discrimination against women illegal. A triumph for women's rights campaigners.

QUESTIONS

1 Which of the four factors do you think has had most effect on women's lives?

2 Can you suggest factors other than the four given here which have significantly changed women's lives in this century?

3 Is it sensible, or is it sexist, to suggest that inventions like washing machines have mainly influenced the lives of women?

11.1 SCHOOLS BEFORE 1830

There were no schools provided by the government or local councils in the eighteenth century. They were all privately run.

The most wealthy families employed private tutors or sent their sons to **public schools** like Eton, Winchester, Rugby and Harrow. These were usually boarding schools, few in number, which charged high fees and aimed to prepare boys for public service in the church, the army or government. Lessons consisted of little more than Latin and Greek. Older boys sometimes made the lives of younger ones a misery; discipline was harsh; and school life was generally brutal. At Winchester in 1818 a riot among the boys had to be quelled by two companies of soldiers.

Grammar schools were also at a fairly low ebb at this time. There were only about 100 of these by 1800, catering for about 3,000 boys, mostly day pupils. They usually charged fees and tended to copy the style of public schools, although some grammar schools taught more useful skills like book-keeping or navigation. In parts of the country there were **academies** for boys and for girls. These charged lower fees and claimed to give a more general education including household management for girls, but standards varied.

For poor children there were the **dame schools**. These were run, in their own homes, by old ladies and provided little more than a place for children to be left while their parents went out to work (see Source A). For older children there were similar places called common day schools. Dame schools were usually held in crowded rooms and often gave little real education at all. There were fees, but they were very small. A parliamentary inquiry in 1818 reported 3,000 such schools.

A better option for the poor were the **charity schools**. These were schools run by religious charities like the Society for the Propagation of Christian Knowledge. Formed in 1699, and funded by public donations, the SPCK had 1,500 schools by 1730 providing for almost 25,000 pupils. However, its income was irregular and unreliable; it often had to limit each child's attendance to two years; and since the SPCK was a Christian movement the lessons consisted mainly of reading, writing or memorizing from the Bible.

Similar in this respect were the **Sunday schools**. These began to flourish after 1780 when Robert Raikes, a newspaper owner in Gloucester, set up a Sunday school to improve the behaviour of the local children, most of whom worked during the rest of the week (see Source B). Others, like Sarah Trimmer and Hannah More, founded similar schools, and by 1830 about 1½ million children attended Sunday schools. However, attendance was only for one day each week, and lessons again consisted mainly of Bible studies.

One other type of school for poor children was the **factory school**. Some factory owners cared enough about their workers to provide housing, churches and other facilities for them, and occasionally these included a school for workers' children and for young workers. Robert Owen provided some schooling in his factory at New Lanark. The Factory Act of 1833 said that all

SOURCE A

A dame school. How much learning is going on?

SOURCE B

'I was struck with concern at seeing a group of children, wretchedly ragged, at play in the street. "Ah sir," said the woman to whom I was speaking, "if you could see this part of the town on a Sunday, you would be shocked indeed; for then the street is filled with multitudes of these wretches, who, released on that day from employment, spend their time in noise and riot, playing at chuck, and cursing and swearing." I applied and made agreement with them (local teachers) to receive as many children as I should send upon the Sunday, whom they were to instruct in reading and church catechism (a chant which teaches the beliefs of the Church of England).'

Letter from Robert Raikes to the 'Gentleman's Magazine', 1783.

SOURCE D

'Present 170 boys; the room will hold 400. The average time during which the scholars stay is about 1 year. The only book in use for the upper classes was the Bible, nor were Bibles or Testaments enough to afford one to each of the boys who were reading them. There were no maps in the school. The children were taught nothing either of History or Geography. Indeed the master, occupied with the superintendance of 170 little boys, could hardly find time to give any direct instruction to the school, but was obliged to depend on his little monitors, not one of whom was 12 years old. Three out of the six classes into which the schools is divided, were sitting, when I entered, without books in their hands, and doing nothing, and so continued for above half an hour.'

Report by the Privy Council Committee for Education on a church society school using the monitorial system.

SOURCE C

'A ragged school is a Sunday school, established by private charity in a city district of the meanest kind, where every house is worn-out and crazy, and almost every tenant is a beggar or perhaps something worse. A school, moreover, in which no children are to be found who would be admitted into any other school; for ragged, diseased and crime-worn, their very appearance would scare away the children of well-conducted parents; and hence, if they were not educated there, they would receive no education at all.'

'Chambers' Journal', 1845.

children between 9 and 13 working in factories should have two hours' schooling a day, but this was never properly enforced.

Ragged schools were set up by kindly individuals as acts of charity for the very poorest of children who were often barred from other voluntary schools (see Source C). In 1844 the Earl of Shaftesbury founded the Ragged Schools' Union to help with fund-raising for these schools.

The largest expansion in schools for the poor before 1830 involved the **church society schools**. These were run by the National Society, founded in 1811 for Anglican children, and the British and Foreign Schools Society, founded in 1814 for Nonconformists (Christians who disagreed with the teaching of the Church of England). These societies used money raised by charity and by charging small fees to build schools and employ teachers. By 1830 the National Society alone had over 3,500 schools.

Teaching in church society schools was shaped by the ideas of Dr Andrew Bell and Joseph Lancaster, who both spread the **monitorial system**. This involved the teacher in teaching a few 'monitors' (usually older children) and then supervising them while they taught the rest of the children. This enabled one teacher to 'teach' several hundred children and reduced the cost of teaching each pupil to about 7s 6d (less than 40p) per year. But it meant that the only kind of study was rote (memory) learning, and it wasn't always well done (see Source D).

The Parliamentary Committee on the Education of the Labouring Classes estimated in 1818 that England and Wales had 18,000 day schools with about 500,000 children on roll.

11.2 THE GROWTH OF ELEMENTARY EDUCATION

During the nineteenth century, a system of **elementary education** for *all* children developed. This growth of schools depended upon government involvement. But not everyone in the nineteenth century wanted education for every child, or government involvement in schools.

Those *against* elementary education for all and government involvement said that:

- Schools would **undermine society**, giving poor children ideas above their station (if they were destined to be poor labourers, what was the point of filling their heads with ideas?); it could even make them frustrated and **politically dangerous** (see Sources A, B and C).
- Governments should not interfere in education; at the start of the nineteenth century governments were expected to keep a strong enough army and navy to protect the country, to keep law and order and to look after their funds carefully; many people were opposed to the government **interfering** in the lives of the public.

Those *for* elementary education for all and government involvement said that:

- Proper schooling was necessary for *all* the children of the poor in order to create a better **workforce**.
- The decline of the church meant that more schools were needed for **religious education**.
- Proper schooling was essential to ensure **social stability** in the rapidly growing towns; as the working class became more politically powerful, so the need to make it more responsible grew; working-class men were given the vote in the towns in 1867 and in country areas in 1884; Robert Lowe MP spoke in favour of the 1870 Act (see page 179), telling Parliament: 'We must educate our masters.'
- In **country** districts, the population was often too scattered to allow any schools; equally, in the rapidly growing **towns**, the growth of schools could not keep up; government help was needed.

Gradually those in favour of more education, supported by the government, gained the upper hand in the public debate.

In **1833** the government agreed to give an **annual grant** of £20,000 to be divided equally between the two church societies. They could use this grant to match, pound for pound, any funds they could themselves raise from charity. It was only a small start; in the very same year Parliament voted £50,000 for the upkeep of the King's stables! However, in 1839 the grant was increased to £30,000, and increases then became regular. By 1858 the sum had reached £600,000 per year.

The government was also doing more than just giving money. In 1839 a committee of the Privy Council was set up to supervise the use of the grant. **Government inspectors** were appointed to visit the society schools with grants, to make sure the public money was well spent. The government was becoming involved

SOURCE A

'To make society happy, and people easy, under the meanest of circumstances, it is requisite that great numbers of them shall be ignorant as well as poor. Knowledge both enlarges and multiplies our desires; the fewer things a man wishes for, the more easily they are supplied.'

The Rev. Dr Mandeville, 'Essay on Charity Schools', about 1805.

SOURCE B

'I am not one to sneer at education, but I would not give 6d in hiring an engineman because of his knowing how to read or write. I believe that of the two, the non-reading man is best. I require a species of machine, an intelligent man, a sober man, a steady man, but I would rather not having a thinking man.'

Isambard Kingdom Brunel, the leading engineer of the Victorian period, 1844.

SOURCE C

'It would teach them to despise their lot in life, instead of making them good servants in agriculture and other employment. It would enable them to read seditious pamphlets, vicious books and publications against Christianity; it would render them insolent to their superiors.'

Davies Giddy MP, speaking against education for the poor in a debate in Parliament in 1807.

in ensuring the **quality** as well as the quantity of schools. By 1857 the government grant was so large that a **Department of Education** was set up to monitor it.

The government was soon also involved in **teacher training**. The first secretary of the Privy Council Education Committee, James Kay-Shuttleworth, encouraged the pupil-teacher system. This involved selected children staying at school from the age of 13 to 18 to get extra tuition from the teachers and to help them teach. Then they could apply for a scholarship to go to a teacher training college. Kay-Shuttleworth opened the first of these at Battersea in 1840. It was passed on to the National Society to run in 1843. By 1861 there were 35 such colleges, 28 Anglican and 7 Nonconformist, training 2,000 teachers.

By the 1850s the public money involved in schools was so great that a Royal Commission chaired by the Duke of Newcastle was formed to investigate the state of schools. The **Newcastle Commission** reported in 1861 that great progress had been made in the number of schools and that most children now received some kind of formal education. But the commission was dissatisfied with the quality of schooling and it argued for closer supervision. Thus the **Revised Code** was established in 1862, introducing a system of **payment by results**. Government inspectors would test pupils in schools on the 'three Rs' – reading, writing and arithmetic – and base the school's grant, up to a maximum of 12s (60p) per pupil, on their performance and on the attendance registers. Robert Lowe, the vice-president of the Department of Education, claimed: 'If it is not cheap, it will be efficient, and if it is not efficient, it shall be cheap.'

The new system was certainly cheaper. The government grant fell from £813,000 in 1861 to £637,000 in 1865. It also had harmful effects on teaching as pupils were drilled over and over again on the tests. They learned but they didn't understand (see Source D). Some inspectors reported that pupils read the test passages while holding the books upside-down! Payment by results lasted until 1900.

There still weren't enough schools for *all* children. Some people believed that the government should make sure that the gaps were filled. **Forster's Education Act of 1870** did this. It said that, where the voluntary schools were insufficient to meet all local needs, a **school board** should be elected by ratepayers to provide extra schools and teachers for children no younger than 5 and no older than 13. The school board could raise money by increasing the rates or charging fees from parents. **Religious teaching** in these board schools would be Christian but non-denominational; under the Cowper-Temple clause, parents were given the right to withdraw children from religious instruction if they wanted. These extra schools enabled the government to make elementary education compulsory up to the age of 10 in 1880 and free in 1891.

SOURCE D

'It is found possible to get children through the Revised Code examination in reading, writing and ciphering (arithmetic) without their really knowing how to read, write and cipher. A book is selected at the beginning of the year for the children of a certain standard; all the year the children read this book over and over again, and no other. When the inspector comes they are presented to read this book; they can read their sentence or two fluently enough, but cannot read any other book fluently. Yet the letter of the law is satisfied.'

From the general report of Matthew Arnold, a government inspector, 1869.

SOURCE E

National Schoolmaster (going round with Government Inspector), "Wilkins, how do you bring shillings into pence?"
Pupil, "I takes it round to the Public House, sir!"

This 'Punch' cartoon shows little respect for testing in school.

11.3 THE GROWTH OF SECONDARY EDUCATION

The school-leaving age was raised to 11 in 1891 and 12 in 1899, but by 1900 there was a feeling that elementary education was not enough. Britain needed more children to stay on into **secondary education** (see Source A).

Public schools and **grammar schools** provided secondary education, and the quality of education in those schools had improved greatly during the nineteenth century. Thomas Arnold, headmaster at Rugby in the 1830s, based his school on Christian virtues and character-building activities. Dr Thring of Uppingham introduced music and organized games. The Taunton Commission of 1868 criticized the dominance of the classics (Latin and Greek), and by the end of the century science, history and geography were generally taught in public and grammar schools. But these schools still catered only for the wealthy minority.

Some **school boards** in large towns like London and Manchester had built higher grade schools for children who wanted secondary education. Yet technically this was illegal, since the 1870 Act enabled them to provide only for children up to 13 years old. In any case, most of the school boards couldn't afford to do this. The **Bryce Commission** was set up in 1894 to investigate this problem, and its recommendations were put into effect by **Balfour's Education Act of 1902**.

This Act abolished the school boards. It made the County Councils and County Borough Councils responsible for setting up **Local Education Authorities**. These LEAs took over control of all board schools. They also became responsible for supporting the voluntary church society schools, which were struggling more and more for funds. LEAs were given the powers to create a system of secondary schools and to charge fees if necessary.

From 1907 **grammar schools** could get grants from the LEA as long as they left 25 per cent of their secondary places open to children with scholarships from the LEA. In theory, this opened up secondary education to even the poorest of able children, though in practice things were sometimes different (see Source B). The brightest children took a scholarship examination at the age of 11. If they passed, they could go to the grammar school; if they failed, they stayed in the senior section of the **elementary schools** with other children until the legal leaving age.

Broadly, this was the situation until the end of the Second World War. There were slight changes – the school-leaving age was raised to 14 by **Fisher's Education Act of 1918**, meaning that elementary schools had to expand their senior departments. The **Hadow Report of 1926** recommended turning the senior sections of elementary schools into separate secondary schools and raising the leaving age to 15, but shortages of government funds meant that no action was taken.

Significant change had to wait until **Butler's Education Act of 1944**. This Act made education compulsory and free for all children up to the age of 15. It recommended a leaving age of 16, though this wasn't put into effect until 1972. Elementary schools were to teach children until the age of 11, when secondary

SOURCE A

'The need for higher education is every day becoming more apparent to the public. Our commercial success is under threat from foreign competition all over the world. It will be impossible for us to keep our markets unless our workmen are on a level with the best workmen in Paris, Berlin or Philadelphia.'

'The Times', 6 June 1890.

SOURCE B

'I was eleven years old in 1920, and due to change schools. I won a scholarship to Cambridge County School, but my mother knew we could not cope with uniform, books, satchel and hockey stick. She was realistic and right. It would have been painful.'

J. Burnet, 'Destiny Obscure', 1984.

Comprehensive schools in the 1980s.

SOURCE C

'The majority of children learn most easily by dealing with concrete things and following a course rooted in their own day-to-day experience. It is for this majority that the secondary *modern* school will cater.

'Some children, on the other hand, will have decided at quite an early stage to make their careers in branches of industry or agriculture requiring a special kind of aptitude in science or mathematics. Others may need a course, longer, more exacting and more specialized than that provided in the modern school, with particular emphasis on commercial subjects, music or art. All these boys and girls will find their best outlet in the secondary *technical* school.

'Finally, there will be a proportion whose ability and aptitude require the kind of course with the emphasis on books and ideas that is provided at the secondary *grammar* school.'

Ministry of Eduction pamphlet No. 12, 1947.

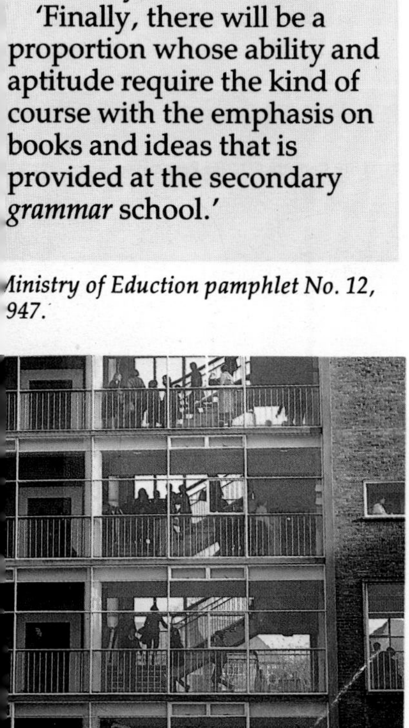

schools would take over. There would be three types of secondary school: the **grammar schools** for those who passed a test, the 11-plus, and **secondary modern** and **technical** schools for the rest. All the schools were supposed to be of equal status, differing only in the education they gave, which would be suited to the talents of the children they received (see Source C). The **voluntary church schools** could become either 'voluntary aided', with some help from the LEA, but funded and run mainly by the church, or 'voluntary controlled', funded by the LEA with the church only controlling religious education. In the rest of state schools, the vast majority, there was to be compulsory non-denominational religious education and an 'act of worship' at the start of each day.

However, few technical schools were ever built, and secondary moderns were often regarded as second best to the grammar schools. Pressure began to grow for equal opportunities for all. **Comprehensive schools**, which take all pupils of secondary age, were pioneered by Local Education Authorities in Anglesey and London and then by other LEAs in the 1950s and 1960s. In 1965 the Labour government invited all LEAs to publish plans for comprehensive schools in their area. Labour-controlled councils introduced these plans; and when a Labour government returned to office in 1974, many other LEAs were forced to follow suit. By the late 1980s, 90 per cent of children were educated in comprehensive schools.

From the middle of the 1970s a **'great debate'** took place about the quality of education in secondary schools. One result was the introduction in 1986 of a new examination course, the **GCSE** (General Certificate of Secondary Education). Another result was the **Education Act of 1988**, which reduced the control of LEAs over schools. It introduced a **National Curriculum**, giving the government powers to decide what subjects are taught in schools. Programmes of study were planned in English, mathematics, science and seven foundation subjects, with tests for all children at the ages of 7, 11, 14 and 16. School governors were given more control of school spending and more freedom from LEAs. Schools could even 'opt out' from LEA control completely and become grant-maintained, funded directly by the government. Parents were given greater freedom in choosing a local school for their children.

The success of secondary education can be seen in the numbers of pupils going on to universities or colleges. In 1902 only 2 per cent of 17-year-olds were at school, and just 20,000 students attended a handful of universities. But by 1983 almost 20 per cent of 17-year-olds were still at school, and there were almost 600,000 students at universities or colleges.

11.4 RELIGIOUS ISSUES

Christianity in Britain up to the Industiral Revolution

During the Reformation in the sixteenth century many people rejected the practices of the **Roman Catholic Church**, and several new Christian churches were formed in Europe. These are known as **Protestant** churches. In Britain the main new churches were the **Church of England** and, in Scotland, the Presbyterian Church. Others included the Baptists, Congregationalists, Unitarians and Quakers. In England the Church of England was the **established** or official church. Members of the other Protestant churches, who didn't *conform* to the ideas of the Church of England, were known as **Nonconformists** or **Dissenters** (see Source A).

SOURCE A

A contemporary view of the Church of England in the eighteenth century.

SOURCE B

'The men professing to be Methodists are the spokesmen on these occasions, and the most difficult to deal with. These men may be the superior men to the rest in intelligence and generally show great skill and cunning and circumvention.'

A coal owner giving evidence to a Royal Commission in 1840.

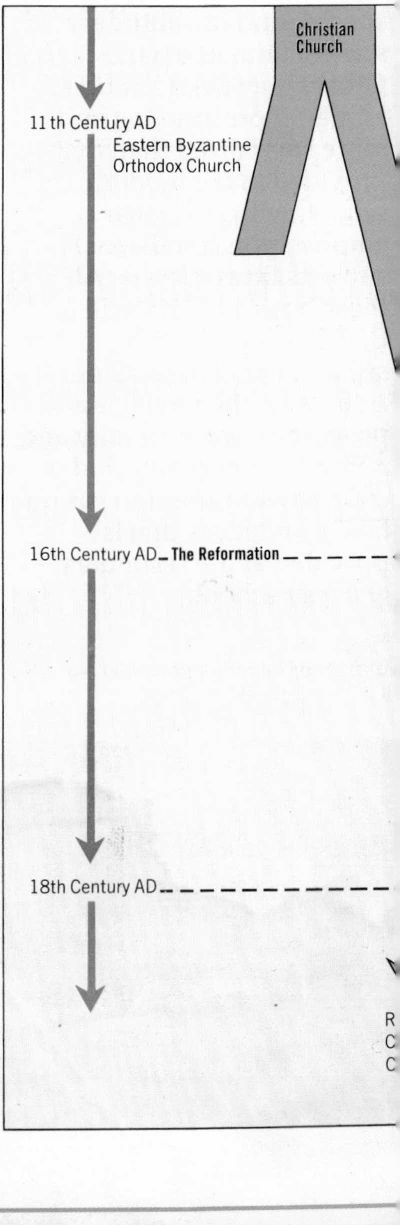

By the eighteenth century the Church of England was an essential part of the fabric of society. The monarch was, and still is, always a member of the Church of England and the figurehead of the Church. The monarch also, in theory, appointed the two Anglican **archbishops** and twenty-six **bishops** who ran the church, although in practice this was usually done by the Prime Minister. The whole country was divided into Church of England **sees**, the areas run by bishops, and **parishes**, with their own **vicars** and **curates**. The government also used the parishes, appointing magistrates in each one to look after local government.

There were still a minority of people, about 60,000 in 1800, who were **Roman Catholics**. They were allowed to follow their own beliefs, but were barred from all professional and official posts and could not become MPs. These restrictions lasted until 1829. There were also a minority who were **Nonconformists**. They worshipped freely in their own chapels, and restrictions about what public offices they could hold were usually waived. But the majority of people were baptised, married and buried by the Church of England.

In Western Europe before the sixteenth century Reformation there was one united christian church, the Roman Catholic Church. Several Protestant churches split away from the Catholic Church during the Reformation. In Britain, the biggest is the Church of England. Others include the Presbyterians, Baptists, Congregationalists, Unitarians and Quakers. These are called the Nonconformist churches or Dissenting churches. In the eighteenth century, the Methodists split from the Church of England.

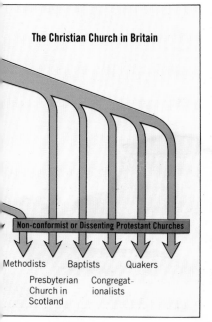

The Christian Church in Britain

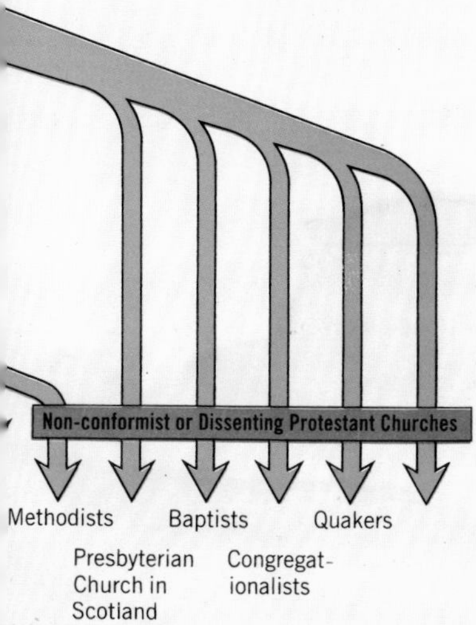

However, the Church of England was at a low ebb in the eighteenth century. There were about 12,000 of the lower clergy, and only 1,500 of these were appointed by the bishops. The rest were appointed by landowners or bodies like the universities and public schools. The positions were often filled for political or family reasons by men who enjoyed the benefit of the salary but were not suited to spiritual tasks. About 6,000 posts were filled with **non-residents** who didn't even live in their parish. Many people held several posts, so that they couldn't possibly do all the work properly; this was called **pluralism**. There was very little religious zeal about many of the clergy. In fact, religion for most Anglicans had become reduced to a code of respectable behaviour, including prayer and visits to church; but any form of religious enthusiasm was frowned upon.

These would have been serious problems at the best of times. But during the Industrial Revolution they were even more unfortunate. As the population increased, particularly in the urban and mining areas, even energetic clergymen found that they could not cope with the growing size of their parishes. The church became even more divorced from the lives of ordinary people. Out of this situation, two new movements emerged from the Church of England: the **Methodists** and the **Evangelicals**.

Christianity since the eighteenth century

Methodism was the work of **John Wesley**. Wesley was born in 1703, the son of an Anglican rector. He was ordained in the Church of England in 1725 and went to study at Oxford University in 1729. It was there that he joined a religious group founded by his brother Charles, called the Holy Club. John produced a *methodical* set of religious rules by which the group were to live their lives, and this gained them the mocking name of 'methodists'.

Wesley left university to embark upon a lifetime of spreading his beliefs to ordinary people. He preached the simple virtues of purity, honesty and abstinence to the poor in the industrial areas with such feeling that people were sometimes roused to wailing with religious fervour.

The Church of England began to disapprove of what it saw as Wesley's fanaticism. Since churches were closed to him, Wesley took to preaching to huge numbers in the open. He declared: 'The world is my parish.' During the next fifty years he travelled over 200,000 miles and preached about 50,000 sermons. He had no desire to break away from the Church of England; he saw himself as revitalizing it. But the Anglican bishops refused to appoint Wesley's followers to church posts, leaving the growing number of his converts without sympathetic ministers. This is what led Wesley to break with the Church of England in 1783, setting up his own Methodist church with its own chapels and appointing his own ministers. There were about 250,000 Methodists in Britain by 1815.

Ordinary **working people** could play a much bigger role in the Methodist Church than in the Church of England, and this was a wonderful training for future working-class leaders. The strict rules of Methodism encouraged moderates like William Lovett, who wrote the People's charter in 1838 (see page 138), rather than revolutionaries. The stress upon self-discipline and acceptance of hardships in this world in preparation for the next made employers think that Methodists made good workers too.

A second revival of religious fervour arose in the form of the **Evangelicals**. These were Christians who, from about 1780, decided to put their religious convictions to work by attacking un-Christian features of society. They campaigned against cruel sports, child labour, prison conditions, bad living and working conditions and slavery. Most notable among the early Evangelicals was **William Wilberforce**, one of the 'Clapham sect', whose campaigns led to the abolition of the slave trade using British ships in 1807 and the end of slavery in the British Empire in 1833. The most famous Evangelical campaigner was Lord Ashley, later **Earl of Shaftesbury**. He was an MP in 1826–45 and 1847–51 and then a member of the House of Lords. He entered politics to apply his Christian principles to the great social issues of the age. He campaigned on behalf of the mentally ill in the late 1920s, helped the 'ten-hour movement' in the 1830s (see page 146), piloted the Mines Act of 1842 through Parliament, served on the Public Health Board from 1848 to 1852, was president of the Ragged Schools' Union for poor children and helped bring about legal protection for apprentice chimney-sweeps in 1864. Society benefited enormously from the work of Evangelical Christians like Michael Sadler in factory reform, Hannah More's Sunday schools and Elizabeth Fry's prison reforms.

The Evangelicals also campaigned for **reform of the Church of England**. In 1831 critics of the church published the *Extraordinary Black Book* listing its faults. Demands for action increased, and Sir Robert Peel established an **Ecclesiastical Commission** in 1835 to

SOURCE C

'The people in agricultural districts are generally indifferent about the Church – lukewarmness is their sin; the upper and middle classes uphold her. But in the manufacturing districts she is the object of detestation to the working classes. They consider themselves to be an oppressed people. They consider the Church belongs to the party of the oppressors; hence they hate it. Paupers and persons in need may go to church on the principle of living on the enemy, but woe to the young man in health and strength who proclaims himself a Churchman.'

From a letter written by Dr Hook, vicar of Leeds, 1843.

SOURCE D

A contemporary cartoon of Charles Darwin.

recommend changes. As a result, the boundaries of the sees and parishes were redrawn to take account of population changes, and the lower clergy were paid more. Pluralism was tackled; in future, clergy could hold more than one post only if there were two very small parishes close together. This removed the worst abuses, and soon the improvements could be seen.

However, this interference in the affairs of the church was not welcomed by the **Oxford Movement**. John Keble, John Henry Newman and Edward Pusey, all Anglicans from Oriel College, Oxford, saw the church and its clergy as the focus of religious belief. In a series of *Tracts for the Times* in the 1840s, they urged the clergy to promote the glory of the church by reviving traditional styles of worship. They argued for more music, vestments and ceremony in church services, which had become plain and uninteresting. This **'High Church'** approch of the Tractarians was in stark contrast to the emphasis on the simple direct appeal to ordinary people by the Methodists and Evangelicals. In fact, their outlook was very similar to that of the Roman Catholic Church. Many supporters of the Oxford Movement, Newman for example, eventually joined the Roman Catholic Church. But their ideas did leave a mark on Anglican church services.

Despite all of this, the **Religious Census of 1851** still provided a shock. Only about a third of the population were attending church on Sundays, and these were mostly from the middle and upper classes. Attendance among religious minorities, such as the Catholics and Methodists, was high, but was very poor among those baptised into the Church of England. People, particularly working people, were becoming apathetic, even hostile, to religion. Scientific challenges to the Bible may have contributed. In1830 Charles Lyell's book, *Principles of Geology*, had made it quite clear that the Earth had not been created in six days in the way the Bible described. In 1859 Charles Darwin's *The Origin of Species* argued that the human race was not the special creation of God, but had evolved from simpler forms of life.

Attempts to reverse this decline in religious enthusiasm later in the nineteenth century met only limited success. Charles Booth's **Salvation Army**, for example, was formed in 1878 with its bright uniforms, brass bands and a direct approach to working people. It has flourished and done good works all over the world. However, nothing reversed the overall trend. Although Britain remained a country whose culture and beliefs are totally based on Christian ideals, the number of practising Christians continued to be a minority. In the course of the twentieth century several **non-Christian religions** – notably Judaism, Hinduism and Islam – have become a small but significant part of British religious life through the process of immigration.

12.1 LAW AND ORDER PROBLEMS

The responsibility for keeping **law and order** in the eighteenth century rested upon the local **justices of the peace** or **magistrates** in each parish. But their time was spent largely in resolving legal disputes brought to them; they did little to *prevent* crime or to *catch* criminals. The magistrates were assisted by **parish constables**. These were part-time, unpaid officials elected annually who had to be on call to break up fights, deal with beggars or arrest a suspect on the orders of the magistrate. This was a system which had been devised in medieval times and it had worked satisfactorily in the villages. However, in the towns magistrates needed more help. In prosperous areas **watchmen** were employed to watch over people's property, especially at night. They would be posted in sentry boxes at key spots or patrol the streets. London had 4,500 watchmen by 1822.

As towns grew, magistrates found that they needed even more help. In 1750 Henry Fielding, a magistrate at Bow Street courts in London, employed a group of men to help him track down criminals and recover the property they had stolen. They became known as the **Bow Street Runners**. Later, his brother, John Fielding, also a magistrate, set up the **Foot and Horse Patrols** – men armed with swords and pistols and dressed in crimson uniforms – to reduce crime on London's streets and highways. However, Londoners feared that semi-military groups like these were a threat to their personal freedom, and they never became very large or popular. Magistrates usually had to rely upon criminals being caught in the act by passers-by or informed upon by accomplices for rewards. In emergencies, magistrates could call upon **troops** to keep order; soldiers were used to quell the Chartist uprising in Newport in 1839 (see pages 138–9).

Since the likelihood that criminals would be caught was so small, the only way to deter crime was to increase **punishments**. The general rule at the beginning of the eighteenth century was for minor crimes to be punished by **fines** or **flogging**. There were **'houses of correction'** where beggars or prostitutes might be sent, and there were a few **prisons**. These were very badly kept. In 1777 John Howard published a survey called *The State of Prisons* which told of overcrowding and disease. Gaol keepers and their assistants ('turnkeys') made their money by charging prisoners for their food and bedding. Higher payments could buy a prisoner a better cell on the 'master's side'. On the 'common side' the other prisoners – young and old, the convicted and those awaiting trial, debtors and their families – were all crowded together. 'Gaol fever', an infectious disease caused by the unsanitary conditions, was common. Over half of all prisoners were debtors, held until they could pay the money they owed.

More serious crimes could be punished by **transportation**, compulsory exile to one of Britain's colonies, usually in North America or Australia. In 1776 when the American colonies declared their independence, the government was suddenly short of places to send convicts. It collected together old warships, beached or anchored them around the coast and used these **'hulks'** as floating gaols. They remained in use until 1858.

SOURCE A

The TOWNS-END.
Mr. Townsend, Police-Officer, Bow-Street.

John Townsend, a Bow Street Runner.

SOURCE B

'Two prisoners in one bed to pay 1s 6d (7p) a week; for a single bed 2s 6d (12p) a week chamber rent.

Those who provide their own bedding to pay 1s (5p).

The keeper to sell beer in sealed pots.

No felon to share a bed with a debtor, unless the debtor agrees.

No dogs or pigeons to be kept in the gaol.

1s (5p) to be paid to the gaoler on delivery of declaration against any prisoner.

Every debtor and felon to pay on his discharge 13s 4d (67p) to the keeper and 2s 6d (12p) to the turnkey.'

Rules of Reading Gaol, 1731.

SOURCE C

'Nearly three hundred women, some untried and some under sentence of death, were crowded together in two wards and two cells. Here they kept their multitudes of children; and they had no other place for cooking, washing, eating and sleeping. They all slept on the floor; at times, 120 in one ward, without so much as a mat for bedding; and many of them were nearly naked. Everything was filthy to excess, and the smell was quite disgusting.'

escription of the women's prison at ewgate in London, by T. F. Buxton in 318.

The ultimate punishment was the **death penalty**. Hangings were held in public until 1868 in order to deter crime, but it is doubtful whether this did. Hangings became popular spectator spectacles at Tyburn and Newgate; owners of houses overlooking the Newgate gallows charged £10 a seat at their windows, and in 1802 twenty-eight people were killed in the crush at a Newgate hanging. As towns expanded rapidly in the eighteenth century, crime also increased. In desperation, the government made more and more crimes punishable by death, until by 1800 over 200 crimes carried capital punishment. Most of these were to protect property, but many were for trivial offences like shoplifting goods worth more than 5s (25p), stealing a sheep or forging money.

However, this attempt to reduce crime didn't work. Witnesses, judges and juries were unwilling to condemn criminals to death for such minor offences. Many sentences of death were never carried out; over half of those sentenced to death in the years 1761–5 had their sentences reduced to transportation. Worse still, some thieves, faced with the prospect of hanging for theft, murdered their victims to reduce the chance of being caught – the punishment was the same. A campaign to abolish the death penalty for many of these trivial crimes was started in Parliament by James Mackintosh and Sir Samuel Romilly, but it had little success before the 1820s.

SOURCE D

n execution scene by Hogarth.

12.2 LAW AND ORDER REFORMS

The growing problem of law and order led to **reforms** in three areas: the penal code, the police and the prisons.

Penal reform

The **penal code** is the list of crimes and their punishments. We have seen before how the number of capital offences grew in the eighteenth century, and that the death penalty was not working as a deterrent. When he was Home Secretary in the 1820s **Sir Robert Peel** removed over 100 trivial crimes from the capital list. Others followed up his work, and by 1837 in practice the death penalty was used only for murder, attempted murder and treason. Public hangings ended in 1868.

The police

Peel also tackled the problem of a **police force**. By 1822 London had a population of over one million, but only 450 runners and patrolmen. Therefore in 1829 Peel put through Parliament the **Metropolitan Police Act**. This set up a force of 3,000 men, responsible to the Home Secretary and led by two commissioners based at Scotland Yard, with a duty to police an area within a twelve-mile radius of Charing Cross. To reduce the impression that this was a military group, the men wore blue uniforms with long-tailed coats and tall hats, and were armed only with truncheons. Despite this, there was a great deal of opposition from people who thought that the police would be either wicked or useless. Fortunately, fears were short-lived, and the **'Bobbies'** or **'Peelers'** soon won support and drove many criminals out of the capital.

In 1835 one of the clauses of the **Municipal Corporations Act** allowed town councils across the country to follow London's example. Liverpool, with a population of 250,000 was policed by only fifty watchmen. In 1839 the **County Police Act** allowed county councils to follow suit in country areas. However, councils were slow to act, and the 1856 **County and Borough Police Act** forced all these councils to create their own police forces. It also employed government inspectors to make reports to the Home Secretary on all of these forces; if its report was favourable, a council could claim a grant from the government to help pay for its police.

Prison reform

Both the reform of the penal code and of the police meant that more criminals went to **prison**. Conditions had not improved since the survey made by John Howard in the 1770s. Demands for reform were taken up in 1817 by **Elizabeth Fry**. She was a wealthy Quaker who had visited Newgate women's prison in 1813 and had been horrified by what she found. She persuaded the governor to clothe the women in clean, plain uniforms and to appoint a female warder. Classes were started for the children in the gaol and sewing projects for the women.

Elizabeth Fry's work at Newgate became well known; and when the government came under pressure to encourage her

SOURCE A

Cartoon of a London 'Bobby', 1830.

SOURCE B

Cartoon of 1829 showing Peel announcing his new police force.

SOURCE C

A painting showing Elizabeth Fry at Newgate prison. Her visitors (left) look impressed, but the prisoners (right) don't all look as happy.

methods elsewhere, Sir Robert Peel got Parliament to pass a **Gaols Act** in 1823. This said that women warders should be employed for women prisoners; that warders should be paid salaries; that charging prisoners fees should be abolished; that different types of prisoners – for example, those convicted and those awaiting trial – should be kept separate; that all prisons should have chaplains and doctors; and that prisoners should have work to keep them occupied as well as education and religious instruction. Government inspectors were appointed to supervise conditions in prisons in 1835, and there were fifty new gaols by 1850 with over 12,000 new cells.

Although the goals became less crowded and more sanitary, **conditions** were deliberately kept harsh. Elizabeth Fry had argued for prisoners to be allowed to mix during the day, but the prison authorities began to insist on keeping them all isolated. Work remained boring and pointless, like picking oakum (untwisting the strands of old ropes to make new ones); flogging and bread-and-water diets remained as punishments. When transportation ended in 1853, it was replaced by the equally harsh punishment of **hard labour** in domestic prisons, involving work in places like the Dartmoor stone quarries. When all prisons were finally brought under the direct control of the government in 1878, Edmund du Cane, the chairman of the Prison Commission, said he wanted a prisoner's life to be 'hard labour, hard bed and hard fare'.

INDEX

adulterated foods 137
Agricultural Marketing Acts 42
Agricultural Research Council 43
agriculture 18, 20, 22, 24, 26, 28, 30, 32, 34, 36, 38, 40, 42, 45
Agriculture Act (1947) 44
air travel 104
aircraft industry 81
airships 104
Albert, Prince 34
Allen, William 161
Amalgamated Society of Carpenters 160
Amalgamated Society of Engineers 160
Amalgamated Society of Tailors 160
anaesthetics 148
Anti-Corn Law League 34
antiseptics 148
Applegarth, Robert 161
Arkwright, Richard 51, 55
Arnold, Thomas 180
Artisans Dwellings Act (1875) 116, 153
Asquith, Herbert 174
Attwood, Thomas 138

Baird, Logie 107
Bakewell, Robert 23, 26
Baldwin, Stanley 164
Barrow-in-Furness 72
Bedford, Duke of 26
Behring 151
Belfast 72
Bell, Dr Andrew 177
Bell, Dr Patrick 36
Bessemer 72
Bevan, Aneurin 158
Beveridge, William 158
Bevin, Ernest 76, 166
Birmingham Political Union 138
birth rate 108, 111, 114, 116, 117
Black Friday 164
blood transfusion 149
blue books 124
Booth, Charles 154
borstals 157
Boulton, Matthew 46, 47, 50, 59, 62
Bow Street Runners 186
Bridgewater, Duke of 51, 87, 123
Bridgewater Canal 51, 87, 89, 94
Bright, John 34
Brindley, James 87, 88
British and Foreign Schools Society 177
British Gazette 165
British Leyland 80
British Shipping (Assistance) Act (1935) 73
British Worker 165
Broadhurst, Henry 162
Brunel, Isambard Kingdom 98, 178
Bryce Commission 180

Caird, James 36
Callaghan, James 167
canals 51, 62, 67, 87, 88, 96, 103
Canterbury 96
Canterbury and Whitstable Railway 91, 94
capital 50, 51
capitalism 122, 123
carbolic acid 148
cars 100
Cartwright 55
Cat and Mouse Act (1913) 171
catholics 109
Central Electricity Generating Board (CEGB) 78
Chadwick, Edwin 143, 144, 152
Chamberlain's Housing Act 1923 157
Chamberlain, Joseph 153
charter 184
chartism 113, 138, 140
chemical industry 79
child benefit 159
child labour 16, 111, 126
children 66, 126, 157
chloroform 148
cholera 125
Church of England 109, 108, 182
Churchill, Winston 164, 170
class 14, 93, 121, 125
clippers 99
Clyde 72
Co-operative Society 121
Co-operative Wholesale Society (CWS) 137
Co-operatives 137
coaches 84
coal 17, 128, 164, 166
Coal Mines Act (1911) 156
coal mining 64, 76
Coalbrookdale 58, 59, 90
Coalbrookdale Iron Company 68
Cobden, Richard 34
coke 58
Coke, Thomas 26
Colling, Robert and Charles 23, 26
Combination Acts 134
Common Agricultural Policy (CAP) 44
common day schools 176
common land 19, 20, 22, 25
communication 97
Complete Suffrage Association 141
comprehensive schools 181
Concorde 105
Conspiracy and Protection of Property Act (1875) 162
Cooke, A.J. 165
Cooper, Sir Anthony Ashley (later Earl of Shaftesbury) 146, 184
Corn Laws 30, 45
Corn Production Act 40
Cort, Henry 60
cotton 55, 72
cotton gin 55
council housing 153, 159
County and Borough Police Act (1856) 188
County Councils 85
County Police Act (1839) 188
Crawshay, Richard 60
Crewe 97
Criminal Law Amendment Act (1871) 162
Crompton, Samuel 55
Cross, Richard 153
Crystal Palace 70, 71
Cyfarthfa Ironworks 60

dame schools 176
Darby III, Abraham 59
Darby, Abiah 59
Darby I, Abraham 58, 59
Darwin, Charles 185
Davison, Emily 171
Davy, Sir Humphrey 65
death rate 108, 110, 116
Defoe, Daniel 15, 17, 53
dental charges 159
Department of Education 179
Department of Health and Social Security 159
depression 1929–34 73
diesel engine 76
discrimination 119
dissenters 182
Dockers' Union 1889 162
Document, The 135
domestic system 16, 52
Dover 103
Dowlais Ironworks 60
drainage 36
drop box 55

Ecclesiastical Commission 1835 184
education 176, 178, 180
Education Act
  1870 169, 179
  1902 180
  1918 181
  1944 181
  1988 181
Ehrlich, Paul 151
electricity 76, 78
emigration 118
Employment Act
  1980 167
  1982 167
enclosure 20, 22, 24, 28
Engels, Friedrich 53, 127
entrepreneurs 50, 51, 78
ether 148
Etruria 63
European Economic Community (EEC) 44, 81
evangelicals 184

Fabian Society 123
Factories and Workshops Act
  1867 147, 148
  1874 148
Factory Act
  1819 146, 148
  1833 146, 148, 176
  1844 146
  1874 146
  1878 147, 148
factory reform 146
factory schools 176
factory system 56, 69, 126
family allowance 158
family income supplements 159
fertilizers 36
Fielden, John 146
Fielding, Henry 186
flying shuttle 54
Friendly Societies 136
Frost, John 138
Fry, Elizabeth 184, 188

Game Laws 32
Gaols Act (1823) 189
gas 76
General Certificate of Secondary Education (GCSE) 181

ieneral Medical Council 149
ieneral Railway Workers' Union 162
ieneral Strike 76
ilchrist-Thomas, basic process 72
raduated benefits 158
rammar schools 176, 180
rand National Consolidated Trades
Union (GNCTU) 135
rand Trunk Canal 88
reat Britain, SS 98
reat Exhibition of 1851 70, 71, 97
reat Western, SS 98
reat Western Railway 96
reenwood's Act 1930 157
rey's Factory Act 1850 148
uest, John 60
uildford 17
uilds 134

adow Report, 1926 181
ardy, Kier 162
argreaves, James 55
armsworth, Lord 105
ealth and Morals of Apprentices Act
(1802) 146, 148
eath, Edward 167
gh church 185
gh farming 35, 36
ill Farming Act (1946) 44
orse-drawn hoe 23
orse-drawn seed drill 20
ospitals 110
ot blast furnace 61
ousing 116, 157, 159
ousing Act (1919) 153, 157
oward, John 186, 188
ume, Joseph MP 134
yndham, H.M. 162

mmigration 118
dependent Labour Party 162
dustrial Injuries Act (1946) 158
dustrial Relations Act (1971) 167
dustrialization 68
fant mortality 110, 111, 116, 125
fection 148
frastructure 82
oculation 110, 150
terest 50
ventions 51
sh potato famine 35
on and steel industries 58, 60, 72, 73, 75,
76
onbridge 59

rrow 74
nner, Edward 12, 150
engine 104
nt Stock Companies 50, 89
nta 161
venile Courts 157

y, John 54
y, Robert 54
y-Shuttleworth, James 179
ble, John 185
nnet & Avon Canal 50
ng, Gregory 14, 15, 108, 121
ch, Robert 151

labour exchanges 155
Labour Party 40, 162, 166, 181
Labour Representation Committee 162
Laissez-faire 120, 143, 146, 152
Lancaster, Joseph 177
Law Commission 144
Leeds 15, 17, 68, 120
life expectancy 116, 125
Lister, Joseph 148
Liverpool 96
Liverpool and Manchester Railway 91, 92,
94
living conditions 124
Lloyd George, David 155
Local Education Authorities 180
Local Government Act 42
Local Government Act 1929 154
locomotives 90
London and Birmingham Railway 92, 93
London and North-West Railway
Company 70
London Working Men's Association 138
Loveless, George 136
Lovett, William 138, 184
Lowe, Robert 178, 179
luddites 132

MacGregor, Ian 75
machine breaking 132, 133
Mackintosh, James 187
Maidstone 17
Mallard 102
Manchester 48
Manning, Cardinal 162
Marconi 107
marriage, age at 111, 117
Married Women's Property Act (1870) 169
Marx, Karl 121
McAdam, John 83
means test 156
medical progress 148
mercantilism 120
Merchant Shipping Act
1859 99
1876 99
Mersey 72
Metcalfe, Blind Jack 83
methodists 182
Metropolitan Police Act 188
Midwives Act (1902) 149
migration 113
Milk Marketing Board 42
Miners' Federation 162, 163
mines 128
Mines and Collieries Act (1842) 146, 148
Ministry of Food 43
Ministry of Health 155, 159
Ministry of Social Security 159
monitorial system 177
moral force 138
More, Hannah 176, 184
motor industry 80
Municipal Corporations Act (1835) 188
Murdoch, William 47

Nasmyth, James 61
National Assistance Act (1948) 158
National Association for the Protection of
Labour 134
National Coal Board 77

national curriculum 181
National Federation of Transport
Workers 163
national grid 78
National Health Act (1946) 158
National Health Service 123, 158
National Insurance Act
1911 155
1946 158
National Land Company 139
national newspapers 97
National Society 177
National Union of Gas Workers and
General Labourers 162
National Union of Railwaymen 163
National Union of Women's Suffrage
Societies 170
nationalization 75, 77, 81, 123
navvies 92
Neilson, James 61
Nestlé 39
New Commonwealth 118
New Towns Act (1946) 159
new unionism 162
Newcastle 17
Newcastle Commission 179
Newcastle, Duke of 179
Newcomen, Thomas 49, 59, 64
Newman, John Henry 185
newspapers 105
Nightingale, Florence 149, 169
nitrous oxide 148
nonconformists 109, 177, 182
North Atlantic Shipping Act (1934) 73
northern star 139
northrop loom 72
nuclear power 79
nursing 149
nylon 75

O'Conner, Feargus 138, 140
Oastler, Richard 146
Odger, George 162
oil 76
oil refining 79
Old Age Pensions Act (1908) 156
open field system 19, 20
Osborne judgement 162
outdoor relief 144
Owen, Robert 127, 135, 137, 176
Oxford 81
Oxford Movement 185

Pankhurst, Christabel 170
Pankhurst, Mrs Emily 170
Parish Register Abstracts 109, 108
parliamentary trains 96
Pasteur, Louis 148, 151
patents 50
pauperism 142
Peel, Sir Robert 34, 127, 146, 188
penicillin 79
pensions 134, 158
Place, Francis 134
plimsoll line 99
plug plot 139
police 188
Poor Law 111, 142, 154, 159
Poor Law Amendment Act (1834) 33, 144
Poor Law Commission 152

population 20, 28, 45, 108, 110, 112, 114
population, age structure of 114
Post Office 105
pottery industry 62
poverty 8, 142, 154
power loom 55
prescription charges 159
Prices and Incomes Act (1966) 166
prisons 186, 188
privatization 123
Public Health 148
Public Health Act
  1848 152
  1875 153
public schools 176, 180
punishments 186
Pusey, Edward 185

racial tensions 119
radar 104
radio 107
ragged schools 177
Raikes, Robert 176
Railways Act
  1844 96
  1921 102
Railways 36, 38, 51, 70, 82, 92, 94, 96, 102
Rainhill trial, 1829 91
rationing 40, 44
Red Friday 164
Reform Act (1832) 138
refrigeration 38
Religious Census, 1851 185
Repeal of Combination Acts 134
reverberatory furnace 60
revised code 179
Reynolds, Richard 59
river transport 86
Road Traffic Act
  1933 101
  1986 100
roads 17, 82
Rochdale Canal 96
Rochdale Pioneers 137
Roebuck, John 47
Roman Catholic Church 182
Romilly, Sir Samuel 187
rotation of crops 19, 23
roundsman system 142
Rowntree, Seebohm 154, 157
Royal Agricultural Society 36
Royal Commission of Inquiry into Children's employment, 1840 128
Royal Commission on Conditions in the Mines, 1840 68
Royal Commission on Health of Towns, 1846 124
Royal Commission on Roads, 1839 85
rubbish disposal 124
Rural Sanitary Authorities 85

Sadler, Michael 146, 184
Salvation Army 185
Samuel, Sir Herbert 164
Savery, Thomas 46
school boards 179, 180
secondary modern schools 181
secondary picketing 167
seed drill 23
Senior, Nassau 143
service industry 81
sewage disposal 124
Sex Discrimination Act (1975) 175
shares 123
Sheffield outrages 162
shipbuilding 72, 73, 75
Shops Act (1912) 156
short-time committees 146
Siemens' open-hearth process 72
Simpson, Dr James 148
Sinclair, Sir Clive 79
sliding scale 31
smallpox 12, 110, 150
Smith, Adam 120
social contract 167
Social Democratic Federation 162
Social Security Act (1966) 159
socialism 123
Society for the Propagation of Christian Knowledge (SPCK) 176
Southwood, Dr 152
speenhamland system 111, 142
spinning jenny 55
spinning mule 55
St Thomas's Hospital 149
stage-coaches 17
steam engine 47, 48, 50, 59, 62
steam engines 46, 64, 90
steam hammer 61
steam power 36
steamships 38, 98
steel industry 61
Stephenson, George 90, 95
stock exchange 123
Stockton 96
Stockton and Darlington Railway 90
Stopes, Marie 175
Strutt, Jedediah 51, 54
Sturge, Joseph 141
Suez Canal 99
suffragettes 170
suffragists 170
Sugar, Alan 79
sun-and-planet gear 47
Sunday schools 176
supplementary benefits 159
swing riots 32, 132, 133
Swing, Captain 32, 133
syndicalists 163
synthetic fibres 75

Taff Vale verdict 162
tarmacadam 83
technical schools 181
telegraph 107
telephone 107
television 107
Telford, Thomas 83
ten-hour movement 146
terylene 75
textile 54
textile industry 15, 51, 52, 54, 56, 72, 73, 75
Thatcher, Margaret 75, 123, 167
Thring, Dr 180
Tillet, Ben 162
Titanic, SS 99, 107
Tithe Commutation Act (1836) 33
Tolpuddle Martyrs 136
tommy shops 92
Town and Country Planning Act (1947) 159
Town Planning Act (1909) 116, 153
Townsend, Lord 23, 26
Trade Boards Act (1909) 156
trade clubs, 134
Trade Disputes Act
  1871 162
  1906 163
  1913 163
  1927 166
  1946 166
  1984 167
Trade Unions 75, 113, 134, 160, 164, 166
Trades Union Congress 162
trams 100
transport 17
Transport Act (1947) 102
transportation 136
trappers 128
Trent-Mersey Canal 62, 63
Trevithick, Richard 90
Trimmer, Sarah 176
Tull, Jethro 23, 27
Turnpike Trusts 50, 82
turnpikes 16, 51, 63, 83, 85
Tyne 72

unemployment 155, 156
Unemployment Assistance Board 156
Unemployment Insurance Act (1934) 15
urbanization 112, 115
utilitarians 143

vaccination 12, 110, 150
Victoria, Queen 70, 140, 148

wagonways 90
Walker brothers' iron foundry 51
War Agricultural Committee 43
water frame 55
water supply 124
water-mills 46
Watt, James 46, 49, 50, 59, 62
Wedgwood 62, 63
welfare state 158, 159
Wellington, Duke of 34, 140
Wesley, John 183
Weston, Sir Richard 26
Wheat Quota Act (1932) 42
Wheatley's Housing Act 157
Wilberforce, William 184
Wilson, Harold 166
windmills 46
Witney 55
women 16, 66, 168
Women's Land Army 43
Women's Social and Political Union 170
workhouse 142, 144
working conditions 126, 128
working class 130
working class identity 131
Workmen's Compensation Act (1906) 15
world depression 74
World Health Organization 12

X-rays 149

Yarranton, Andrew 26
yeomen farmers 18, 24, 30
Young, Arthur 20, 27